scarlet ribbons

a priest with aids

Rosemary Bailey

Library of Congress Catalog Card Number: 97–067370

A complete catalogue record for this book can
be obtained from the British Library on request

The right of Rosemary Bailey to be identified as the author
of this work has been asserted by her in accordance with the
Copyright, Designs and Patents Act 1988

First published in 1997 by Serpent's Tail,
4 Blackstock Mews, London N4, and
180 Varick Street, 10th floor, New York, NY 10014

Set in 10pt Jansen by Intype London Ltd
Printed in Great Britain by
Mackays of Chatham plc, Chatham, Kent

Rosemary Bailey was born in Yorkshire in 1953, and studied English and Philosophy at Bristol University. She has worked as a journalist for twenty years, writing about sexual politics, culture and travel for many publications including the *Sunday Times*, *Guardian* and *Vogue*. She now lives in London and France with her husband, biographer Barry Miles, and their son.

contents

To my mother and in memory of my father

acknowledgements

I began this book while my brother was still alive, and he always encouraged and supported the project. I owe him an an enormous debt for his trust in me. His own book of stories, *The Well Within*, about AIDS and its metaphors, was published six months after he died, and an excerpt is included at the end of this book. It seems right he should have the last say. I have drawn freely on his papers, quoting from private journals and letters, as well as sermons, published articles and books and the conversations we taped in the last year of his life. I hope his trust has been justified.

I am profoundly grateful to my mother for her willingness to share the process of writing with me, and to my sisters and brother for their encouragement and understanding.

My thanks are due to all those I interviewed, both in Dinnington and beyond, many of whom appear in this book. Andrew Abbs, Jenny Adlam, Caroline Bailey, Jenny Bott, Dr Carol Bradbury (special thanks for her patient translation of the medical notes), Charles Bruce, Mike Cameron, Sue Cameron, David Clarke, Jim Cotter, Sylvia Fairhurst, Geoff Gillard, Kath Graham, Margaret Hawley, Walter Hawley, Malcolm Johnson, Nancy Johnson, Margery Keeton, Dr George Kinghorn, Richard Kirker, Steven Kohut, Archdeacon Stephen Lowe, Bishop of Sheffield David Lunn, Janet Makin, Phyllis Marriott, Derek Norbury, Janette Moon, Jackie O'Carroll, Sue Peters, Sue Proctor, Sue Rafferty, David Randall, Joyce Robinson, Sam Robinson, Abigail Saxon, Alma Servant, Margaret Selby, John Spencer, Suzanne Tate-Russell. Though often sad, the interviews offered insights and consolations for which I am profoundly grateful. Of course this is only my version of events and any mistakes are my own.

Thanks to those who read and commented on the manuscript at different stages, often, I know, a painful process. Thanks to all those friends and colleagues who helped in so many ways, especially Martha Stevns, Dierdre Hardwick, Philip Hardwick, Sara Davies, Peter Boyden, Felix Dennis, Kathy John, Frances Bentley, Pierce O'Carroll, Suzie Mackenzie, Liz Jobey, Guy Martin, Ilona Medved-Lost, Dom Basil Matthews OSB, Abbot of Elmore, and Simon Caulkin.

Thanks to Robert Creeley for permission to reprint 'Love Comes Quietly', to Macmillan to quote from R. S. Thomas and to Darton, Longman and Todd for permission to reprint 'All Shall Be Well' from *The Well Within*.

Thanks to my agents, Andrew Wylie and Georgia Garrett, for their support and to my publisher for his original belief in the project. A special thanks to my esteemed editor, Ann Scott, for her rigorous, creative and sensitive editing.

To my husband Barry Miles for his unswerving support and cool editorial eye, and to my son Theo, who will, one day I hope, feel glad he was part of the story.

'Unlimited, unconditional, unquestioning love, freely given with no expectation of return: with comradeship and equality for all.'

Dinnington parish church motto

prologue

At 5.30 on a bitterly cold Easter morning in April 1995 I rouse myself to go to church. It is the highlight of the year for my brother, the Reverend Simon Bailey, Rector of St Leonard's parish church, Dinnington – the early morning service to greet the sunrise and celebrate the risen Christ. Dawn is just breaking as I scuttle round the corner from the Rectory, the first fingers of light are creeping above the horizon, and the birds are beginning a tentative morning chorus. Despite the bone chilling cold there is beauty in it.

In the church porch a loyal band is clustered around Simon and his curate, both resplendent in the celebratory white and gold vestments of Easter. Standing beside them is the crucifer, grasping the processional cross in readiness. A little band of pilgrims has just returned from a long walk through the night, setting off as usual after the service the evening before. The walk symbolises the bleak darkness after the crucifixion, though as one parishioner put it, there is usually a bottle or two floating around to cheer things up. Now they blow on their fingers and stamp feeling back into numbed feet. My sixty-seven-year-old mother, Irene Bailey, is leaning on her stick, wincing from arthritis, but as this year's confirmation candidate, feeling a distinct obligation to attend.

The parish stalwarts are here, all devoted to their church, occupied daily with funerals, flowers, christenings and church repairs, and most recently with the care of their beloved Rector. Two years previously he told them he had AIDS and since then they have supported him with stubborn devotion. And then there is me, latterly agnostic, drawn into this new world of pain and beauty and love, of coffee mornings and roof appeals.

There is, it must be said, something inescapably pagan about the whole business, as we circle the church in the pearly dawn light. Eroded stone crosses and pitted grey stone slabs flank the little path through the churchyard. The grass is hillocky with subsidence from the coal mine below which once extended way beyond the confines of the village itself. Close to the church wall lies the grave of an earlier rector of St Leonard's. He too died young and still in office, and I find myself wondering who he was and how he died.

There is a strong wind whipping the robes and the flames of the brazier, making it difficult to light the great beeswax candle the curate is holding. Eventually the wick catches and we all take lights for our little candles from it and process solemnly into the dark womb of the church, following Simon as he raises the candle high and intones the litany for Easter, 'The light of Christ. The light of Christ,' in the strange sing-song priestly voice which makes him sound so utterly other. Since Good Friday the little church has been left cold and bare, the altar stripped and the golden doors of the triptych fastened shut.

Now the dawn light illuminates the rich reds and golds of the stained glass window, revealing the bowls and vases of fresh flowers arranged the night before, the triptych open once again, the crisply ironed white linen on the holy table and the silver eucharistic vessels. The Easter mass is the central moment of the Christian year and Simon, presiding at the holy table, is in his favourite place doing what he loves best.

Increasingly, this moment, celebrating the Eucharist in his beloved parish, has accrued critical significance for Simon; if he can still celebrate the eucharist he will live, it seems to me. Returning from frequent sojourns in hospital for blood trans-fusions and other treatment, he describes his pleasure in returning to the church, 'There is a tremendous sense of coming home – to our altar, where I offer my prayers, putting com-munion into those familiar hands...there they all were kneeling, waiting for the host, "our dearest and our best".'[1]

His heavy brocade robes provide a perfect disguise for his emaciated body. They hang stiff, wide to the ground, with a white amice wrapped round the neck. No other profession has more concealment of the body. Underneath the heavy garments his upper arms and thighs are so thin he can encircle them with his own hand; the tube for the Hickman line, which delivers drip feed and drugs direct to the bloodstream, dangles permanently from his chest.

The sacramental elements are waiting on the altar table, the wafers of bread, the chalice of wine. To be blessed by Simon in his mysterious capacity as priest and shared with those who believe. A thanksgiving for the breaking of a body on a cross, administered by one whose own body is slowly being consumed by AIDS. This association of wine, blood and bodily fluids seems inescapable; yet still very few have refused the communal chalice. Simon had preached about it in a sermon a few months ago, 'It comes to me vividly as I place a fragment of broken bread into your outstretched hands and say "the body of Christ." These are infected hands, fingers, doing the distributing – not contagious and yet infected with a life-threatening, a body-threatening virus. And what I place in your hands is, I say also, a broken, crumbling, fragmented body for you to share in. As you share in the wide open brokenness of Christ's body, his blood, his heart, you share in my destruction too – and in my reconstruction, in my healing, because my body is healed, eased, soothed by knowing that you share my pain. The body is infected so the church – one body, one fragmented soul – has cancer, has heart-disease, has AIDS.'[2]

As Simon breaks the bread and consecrates the wine I weep, warm tears overflowing easily, a welcome catharsis. I am sad of course, my brother is dying. But so much good seems to have come out if it too, the love and support he has received, triggered both by his illness and his controversial situation, as a priest in a church agonising over sexual ethics. And not least, the relationship with him I feel developing which might otherwise never have happened. We would have rubbed along, affectionate but distant, me cracking jokes about him becoming my brother the Bishop one day, he wearing more and more flamboyant bow ties, writing poetry and perfecting his calligraphy.

Simon by this stage has lived almost two years longer than was expected when he developed full-blown AIDS in 1993. Since October 1993 when he was started on TPN* he has been spending five nights a week hooked up to an intravenous feed

---

* (Total parenteral nutrition)

which supplies all his food requirements as well as a complex cocktail of drugs. Apart from the TPN he eats almost nothing save tinned fruit, ovaltine and jelly babies.

Instead of being discreetly hidden away, he is supported by a group of his parishioners; carers who stay at the rectory overnight when he is hooked up to his feed line. Although initially the hospital did not believe it was possible for Simon to administer the TPN and drugs himself at home they eventually agreed so long as he always has someone staying with him. Until now Simon has nearly always lived alone. When he asked for volunteers he was overwhelmed with offers from friends and parishioners – there is even a waiting list – and for almost two years a faithful rota of regular carers has helped care for him. A parish retreat held not long before had decided a parish motto, 'Unlimited, unconditional, unquestioning love, freely given with no expectation of return: with comradeship and equality for all.' Now this has been put to the test, as a community of people who in most cases have not even had to consider their feelings about homosexuality have suddenly been confronted with the fact that their own rector has AIDS.

I wanted to discover who this person was; who this somewhat priggish little brother of mine had become. Someone described to me as a holy man, someone who inspired such love and devotion, and who appeared to be coping with the experience of illness with such reserves of strength, and with the prospect of death with such grace. I had rejected Christianity and all its works in my early teens without a backward glance, but I wanted to try and understand the faith that sustained him and explore the philosophy and the poetry, the 'journey inward' that underpinned it.

By early 1995 Simon had become the Vicar with AIDS. His natural inclination had been to avoid the spotlight but eventually he had grasped the media nettle and agreed to make a television programme for the BBC Everyman series[3] about his illness and the remarkable support he had received from the parish. The programme, which was broadcast in January 1995, produced a phenomenal response – hundreds and hundreds of letters, sympathetic, supportive but many also pouring out their own problems; gay and straight, bereaved, grieving, carers and people with AIDS themselves. An avalanche of suffering detonated by Simon's own pain; he had become the wounded healer, able to articulate and understand the pain of others.

When I declared myself a journalist to the TV producer I knew I had made a decision to engage, that it was going to be impossible to sit on the sidelines and let someone else tell the story. The journalist and the bossy elder sister combined inexorably. I wrote an article for the *Independent on Sunday*[4] to complement the TV programme and we talked about the possibility of a book. Simon and I began recording conversations, and I started to interview his parishioners and his friends. It seemed very important to put on record what had happened here, the symbiosis between Simon and his parish which had produced such a surprising response to a situation which most would have expected to end in bitter and scandalous tragedy. When I told my pagan friends what was happening they were always astonished. It didn't sound at all like the church they had rejected either.

I began to realise that in choosing to get to know Simon better I would suffer more grief. But I knew this was better than an unresolved relationship. And I wanted to try and find this brother of mine; I wanted to know who he was and where he found his strength and power to live. That Easter morning I went up to the altar rail and knelt to take communion. At one time I had sworn I would never kneel to my own brother, but now this fragment of wafer and sip of wine from the silver chalice had a different meaning for me. I didn't believe in the sacrament, but I found myself believing passionately in this community, this particular place, these ordinary folk.

from whom no secrets are hidden

Neither contemplative prayer nor priestly ritual were major features of the religion our family grew up with. We were raised as Baptists, worshipping in stark chapels, dominated by a simple wooden cross and devoid of religious iconography or statues. There was little room for beauty in the churches we knew then. The minister was always the centre of the drama, certainly for us; the most honoured and powerful role for a man to have in our lives as children.

Our father, Walter Bailey, was a traditional Baptist minister, preaching hell fire or heaven, and his fierce evangelical Christianity dominated our lives, both at home and in church. One of my strong images of him from childhood is of an impassioned figure preaching from a pulpit high above us, shaking his fist and addressing his words accusingly at us children. On of his favourite pieces was a speech from the play, *Brand* by Henrik Ibsen. He would declaim,

> 'My God is of another mind.
> A storm, where yours is but a wind . . .
> He stayed the sun in Gideon's vale
> And other wonders, passing tale
> He did, and even yet would do
> Had not the age grown slack, like you.'

At which point he would lean over the pulpit stabbing the air with his finger to emphasise the last words, 'like you' as everyone wriggled uncomfortably in their pews.

Walter fancied himself a latter day John Wesley and was a constant embarrassment to us all, with flamboyant campaigning and open air preaching; every opportunity was taken to declare

Jesus and win converts. We were first and foremost children of the manse, as the minister's house was called, first in Halifax in Yorkshire, when the family consisted of me and two younger brothers, Simon and Martin. My sister Jacqueline was born in 1959 and Caroline much later, in 1969. Walter was involved in the mid-1950s with the beginnings of CND (Campaign for Nuclear Disarmament). The historians, Dorothy and Edward Thompson also lived in Halifax, and occasionally came to visit with their children, who according to my well organised mother, never had matching socks on. J.B. Priestley came to tea after speaking at one of the CND meetings. It must have been an atmosphere of great zeal and optimism for young children to grow up in.

Family holidays were usually spent in the Lake District, attending an evangelical Christian convention in Keswick – two weeks each July, going to meetings in huge marquee tents smelling of wet grass, singing rousing hymns and choruses and giving our hearts to Jesus on a regular basis. We stayed in a camp overlooking Derwentwater, surrounded by craggy mountain peaks. Accommodation was mainly in ex-military bell tents, or wooden chalets with iron bunk beds. Washing facilities were in rudimentary huts with cold water in enamel basins; chilly early mornings accompanied by persistent Lakeland rain drumming on the corrugated iron roof. Men and women were carefully divided with women's tents and chalets to one side and the men's at the bottom of the field. Surrounding lanes were the location for late night trysts. Almost always at some point during the holiday the camp leaders held meetings to instruct everyone in the proper Christian way of conducting their liaisons. No sex for a start. We gleaned what we could with great fascination.

Witness and testimony were the watchwords and the Bailey children made perfect little missionaries. I think my father would have liked to produce four little missionaries, or at least, a doctor, a priest, a missionary and a nurse – some sort of crack team to Save the World. Every five or six years we were uprooted as Father moved churches on a regular basis. In 1959 we moved from Halifax to Birkenhead, across the Mersey from Liverpool, and then to the Potteries, where Father finally resigned in disgust at the reluctance of his congregation to put his dramatic ideas for converting the heathen into practice.

Throughout it all my mother struggled to provide for us, making our clothes by hand, reading us stories and often singing to us. Her grandparents were Welsh and Irish and she had a great fund of sentimental old songs and lullabies like 'Danny Boy' and 'Scarlet Ribbons'.

She fulfilled the role of minister's wife competently, but balked at Father's more extreme ideas, and now admits that she·was never very comfortable with the constant evangelical imperative to proclaim Jesus to everyone. Sundays meant church, usually twice a day with Sunday School, of which we were naturally the leading lights, in the afternoon, and very little else. We were not allowed to read anything other than biblical books on the Lord's day, and we had no television. We usually went for walks on Sunday afternoons though we were forbidden to run, which merely led us to devise various means of escape. Indeed our heads were full of fantasy and adventure, and we particularly loved the Narnia tales of C.S. Lewis, relishing knowingly the heavy Christian symbolism with which they are saturated. We would hide in wardrobes and wish ourselves in Narnia, clamber about ruined houses seeking treasure, and spend hours in games and adventures of our own devising.

We seemed to be constantly shuffling bedrooms, with all the children crammed into one room so the other bedroom could accommodate visiting missionaries from the Congo or the Amazon, or friendless young men Dad had adopted. It was often a case of the shoemaker's children going without shoes. I remember with the unalloyed bitterness of childhood the Shrove Tuesday when a tramp and his son turned up on our doorstep. Mother invited them in and we had to sit and watch while they ate all our pancakes. Only now do I fully begin to appreciate how my long-suffering mother coped with four children, a full-time job much of the time and a husband anxious to give away what little they had. 'God will provide,' he would say, and berate her for her lack of faith. He had cherished an early ambition to be a missionary himself, in Tibet. He sometimes blamed my mother for distracting him from his true purpose.

He made up for all this with his huge enthusiasms. He had a profoundly sentimental attachment to the English landscape, manifested in an abiding love for the Yorkshire moors and dales, in enormous reverence for the Lake District and Wordsworth's poetry, and in the terrible reproductions of Constable paintings on the walls. He was very emotional and wept easily. Television was regarded as the devil's work until Walter finally weakened for the funeral of Winston Churchill, one of his great heroes, whereupon he sat and wept throughout. Walter combined his strict fundamentalism with a socialist view of the world, and it was entirely characteristic that he should die whilst distributing leaflets for the Labour party.

Family prayers were always said every day after the evening meal and Father often included prayers from the Anglican liturgy. Simon later observed that it was probably these prayers that started him off on his long journey to the Anglican church. A perennial favourite was the Collect for Purity:

'Almighty God,
to whom all hearts are open,
all desires known,
and from whom no secrets are hidden:
cleanse the thoughts of our hearts . . .'

From whom no secrets are hidden, for me, though, is most of all a reminder of terrible prying into my personal life. Walter tried to rule his children's lives completely and never had any compunction about opening letters, and reading private diaries. I suppose such a personality could have cowed us all, but instead his children inherited his capacity for rebellion. Of five children only two remained within the faith, and they often had the fiercest arguments of all with my father. He once complained sadly that he had failed to break my spirit. He never saw that the spirit we inherited was his own.

Of course as soon as we began to think for ourselves, we all in different ways negotiated ourselves rapidly out of his world. While Simon went inward I went outward, grasping the world greedily with both hands. We all became adept at pursuing parallel lives. Mine being a predictable combination of sex, drugs and rock 'n' roll, pursuing worldy pleasures as fast as I could. For Simon actually going to church became a form of rebellion, since by the time we reached our teens Dad had fallen out with everyone and set up his own church at home, conscripting his unwilling family to participate.

My brothers were polar opposites, due probably to their

close proximity, sharing a double bed, and later bunk beds in a tiny room until the first of them left home. Martin read Tolkien and listened to Radio Luxembourg. Simon read C.S. Lewis and played classical music records, conducting with a knitting needle.

Simon was a quiet academic boy, who seemed to me an embarrassing old fogey, with his old-fashioned haircut, tweed jackets and ties, and his friends, pompous as only twelve and thirteen year-old boys can be. He and his friends were always in the school play, and took a perverse pride in coming last on cross country runs. They were keen contributors of poems to the school magazine; agonised, adolescent verses about death and the plague. Simon later acknowledged that there were others of his friends who were probably gay, though none of them had any idea at the time. He realised that there were teachers who tried to help, suggesting books he might read, Christopher Isherwood for example, but their attempts were so oblique he didn't understand. Even then Simon had acolytes, younger boys for whom he was clearly a mentor, exchanging long letters with them when he went to Oxford.

What must it have been like for Simon as an adolescent coming to the realisation that he was gay I can only begin to imagine. Certainly I had no idea at the time. It is hardly surprising he internalised it all. According to my mother I was a domineering child, and Simon, the next sibling, was the one I bossed about, insisting he played with my dolls and prams. If there was a choice he would always play with girls rather than boys. He was always keen on ritual, his soldiers always marched in formation, he loved heraldry and pageantry of all kinds. We all loved dressing up from a huge tea chest full of old clothes and I still remember Simon parading in the backyard in a long purple taffeta dress and high heels. Mum says now that she always had a suspicion that he might be gay, 'But in those days it was entirely negative, they were queers, pansies . . .'

Mother supported Father in his opinions, but as we grew older it became clear that she was always ready to listen to us, and even more important, to adapt to our changes and sometimes change herself. It meant that despite the great gulfs that appeared between her and our various lifestyles we never ceased to communicate. Even if she did not agree she was always prepared to try and understand our new lives as we grew older, and to appreciate new ideas. Perhaps without the fear of father's disapproval Simon would have found her a sympathetic confidante even then.

By the time Simon was ten he had begun to realise he was 'different'. In an article in 1995 called 'The Transforming of Wounds',[1] he wrote, 'I grew up within a conservative, evangelical religious culture that reflected and only slightly exaggerated the prevailing attitudes of a wider social setting – everything told me I was flawed, misshapen, wounded.' But as he wrote later in 'My Story'[2] an account of his homosexuality written for his parishioners in 1993, he was also feeling a strong religious vocation, 'I was always a very religious youth, inward, intense. It fascinates me that my sense of vocation, the desire to be ordained, also begins at about the age of ten. . . .what could be the connection?'

In early adolescence he wouldn't even have put a name to what it was that made him different. 'I don't really remember how I learnt about it,' he laughed in a later conversation with me. We recalled our struggles to extract forbidden fruit from father's unpromising library. It was an eclectic collection, from dusty theological tomes to turquoise spined Penguins on the decay of society, forcefully annotated with pencil exclamation marks. Our sexual education was sadly by no means as thorough as our religious education, and we had to comb through books on Christian attitudes to sexuality in order to find out what sex actually was. 'I probably looked it up in some of those books Dad had.' Simon recalled. 'He gave me one that was supposed to tell me the facts of life, but it was all too vague, and there was nothing about homosexuality. But he had a lot of Penguin books on psychology – there was probably one called Sexual Deviancy. Those were the only books with sex in the title in the house!'

During his teens Simon did have girlfriends and indeed there has always been an irony in his appeal to women, but in the end he said it was the physical contact he found impossible to cope with. I have sometimes wondered how he felt embracing his women friends or indeed his sisters.

Both my parents, having left school young themselves, were anxious that we should get a good education. Father never had

any desire to keep us in ignorance as a way of keeping control.
Indeed his great mistake was to educate us all. It was a matter
of enormous pride when Simon was offered a place at Oxford
where he read English at Regents Park College, Oxford, still
planning to enter the Baptist ministry. Although hardly of the
Brideshead contingent Simon thoroughly relished the dreaming
spires, and all the traditional pleasures of Oxford. His letters at
the time (I was by then living in a hippie commune in Somerset)
enthusiastically encouraged me to visit with promises to take
me punting, which indeed he did.

He loved studying, happy in the small world of the college,
attending lectures and tutorials, writing and reading in his little
room overlooking the tranquil, tree-shaded quad, drinking tea
with other students and earnestly discussing the ills of the world.
Studying literature, especially Shakespeare, helped widen his
thinking and his approach to religion. He particularly cherished
what he described as, 'Shakespeare's ability to stand back and
let another human being come alive.' As Simon explained it to
me later, 'It helped me discover and grow in reverence for the
integrity of other people.'

Another great influence was the Christian mystic poet
Charles Williams, one of a group of High Church Oxford
scholars and writers which included J.R.R. Tolkien, C.S. Lewis,
T.S. Eliot and Dorothy Sayers. They called themselves, endear-
ingly, the Inklings, writers who had caught a glimpse of the
divine. Simon particularly delighted in Williams' concept of
'co-inherence'; the idea that all experience is indivisible, suffering included, and that all human beings could bear one
another's burdens and ease one another's pain by offering their
own pain in a mystical exchange. For Simon it was a prescient
concept for his subsequent experience of AIDS, and one that I
struggled to understand when he tried to explain it to me much
later, 'Charles Williams saw the potential for relationships of
every kind to have a mutually affirming capacity; a relationship
in a way that affirms you and them and everybody else as
persons with integrity.'

Even in those days he was addressing the question of death.
In an early notebook from Oxford, he wrote, 'Death is the great
Unknown – they say people won't talk about it, but it wouldn't
matter if they did, they wouldn't understand . . . it is beyond

human thought. If only people could see that then they might begin to see that there can be things beyond us . . . that there are a great many things beyond.' Already it seemed he perceived that facing the idea of death could be a way to enrich the spirit. And he began to move away from the evangelicalism with which he was brought up, 'I began to see that it is possible to achieve the same depth of spirituality without that crude first stage of evangelical conversion. I wanted to try and work in a parish without promoting that.'

In retrospect I now see that his longing for integrity, for wholeness, mirrored in many ways the aspirations of the Sixties generation that I had embraced so fervently. There were so many parallels, which at that time of our lives we would have found hard to explore and very difficult to articulate. We seemed entirely opposite then. He was responding to the aesthetic and sensual appeal of the Anglican church; his love of drama and poetry made it a more natural environment for him, as he told me later, 'It felt like I'd come home. It was very important that physical movement, gesture, colour and so on could also express a life of prayer.' Perhaps too it was a more comfortable place for a homosexual Christian, with its long, if tacit tradition of homosexual clergy. In particular he cherished a deeper reali-sation of the sacrament of communion, and his journal records the deep fulfillment he felt, and how disappointing it had been before when 'nothing happened' ; the non-conformist tradition of communion as a simple act of remembrance. He wrote passionately, 'Something does happen, I know he comes to me in bread and wine. Like food he's becoming part of my life.' He was confirmed into the Anglican church at twenty-one, a moment of great joy. He later described it as the most existen-tial moment of his life; the most significant choice he ever made.

I remember feeling great dread at my father's reaction to Simon's decision to leave the Baptists and be confirmed an Anglican, but in the event Walter was clement, even under-standing. His own father had been an Anglican and despite his own evangelical conversion to the Baptists as a teenager, Walter had always retained an affection for the Church of England and the familiar rhythms of the liturgy.

Simon graduated with a first in 1977 and he was encouraged to continue his studies, but was not tempted. Had he ever had any doubts about wanting to be a priest, I asked him. He was adamant that he did not. Nevertheless his journal expresses his doubts about his own fitness for the task, and he records R.S. Thomas's words:

> 'Priests have a long way to go. The people wait for them
>   to come
> To them over the broken glass
> of their vows . . .'

Already it seemed he was aware of the tension between his own flawed humanity and the expectation that a priest would inevitably be somehow holier than everyone else.

His great struggle remained trying to reconcile his homo-sexuality and his vocation. His last attempt at a 'normal' relationship with a girlfriend was abandoned in Oxford at twenty-one. He decided he would have to be celibate, as he wrote in 'My Story', 'I still had no homosexual experience – but I was quite certain inside. My strict background also meant guilt about it – it was wrong to be this way, the Bible said so, wrong to have the feelings and fantasies I had. I tortured myself over this. I'd moved from trying to be "straight" to accepting that I was "made this way" but it was still a problem, a wound, a flaw in me, a sin.'

One of his letters to me at the time poignantly describes the break-up, 'My little romance is over – I think we discovered, quite simply, that we were completely unsuited for each other – I'm not particularly "sad" I think I realised it long before she did. I know it didn't last very long but you don't need long to go below the superficial attraction and discover the fundamental differences.' Did he think I should be able to read between the lines? I didn't.

He still believed however that celibacy was his only recourse, that his homosexuality was a flaw he somehow had to bury. In his journal he wrote, 'Dare I, need I take a vow of celibacy? or is that pure sensationalism? I can tell no one of even the possi-bility.' He did record a solemn vow of chastity, but through all the agonising he is still trying to understand why he is homo-sexual, what is its purpose, how he can use it creatively – perhaps, he wonders doubtfully, God had made him the way he

was so that he could serve him as a celibate priest... Then
he noted a quotation from Martin Luther, 'God gives only one
person out of several thousand the gift to live chastely in a state
of virginity.'

What he sought was friendship, 'that sharing and communion
with a friend "surpassing the love of women" but I don't know
if it's ever been fulfilled – Ashok perhaps comes nearest (the
trouble is of course that these days anything more than acquaint-
ance is deemed homosexual)' he added ruefully. Ashok was one
of his closest school-friends, a sensitive and intelligent boy from
an Indian family. He went to Cambridge, where he became an
Anglican, perhaps influenced by Simon; they shared a love of
poetry, music and the liturgy. They always corresponded, and
were great confidantes, but neither homosexuality nor relationships with women were ever mentioned. Such matters remained
a taboo area for them both.

After Oxford, Simon spent 1977–78 working in a children's
home in Huddersfield before taking a further degree at Cambridge. The period at the children's home was tough – it was
an experience that must have given Simon significant insight
into the demands of parenthood. He recalled the intense anger
he once felt with a child, sympathising with my struggles as a
mother, and especially the moments of total anger and frustration.

He was pleased to return to the academic world again, and he
studied for a further degree in theology at Emmanuel College,
Cambridge, followed by training for ordination at Westcott
House. Westcott is one of the leading theological colleges in
Britain; it has been criticised as a forcing house for priests, and
Simon remembered the college photographs liberally embell-
ished with purple rings to signify those who had become
bishops. Others have commented that there was not enough
practical training, but I suspect that in Simon's case his experience of my father's style of ministry gave him all the hands-on
experience he ever needed.

It was at Westcott that Simon embarked on transmuting his
academic studies into a spiritual life, and really began to formu-
late his own philosophy with the emphasis on the importance
of relating the spiritual life to the real world. He took his
spiritual journey very seriously, and has left more than two

dozen notebooks of poems, prayers, devotions, and personal journals which trace his spiritual development; hundreds of pages of neatly written analysis of his feelings, his spiritual doubts and joys, his understanding of his role as a priest. He records the small epiphanies of beauty he found in landscape, the sea, a waterfall, a light shining through the fog; anything it seemed could give him a new metaphor and be transmuted into poetry or sermons.

He was greatly influenced by radical theologians like Don Cupitt, John Macquarrie and Dietrich Bonhoeffer, the German writer who was killed by the Nazis. Another influence was John Robinson, whose controversial book, *Honest to God*, a best-seller in the 1960s, challenged the basic tenets of the faith in a way that my father found totally shocking. Other Christian writers like Alan Ecclestone and the French humanist poet, Charles Péguy, also had a lasting impact. In his well-worn copy of Ecclestone's classic, *A Staircase for Silence*, Simon copied out the following quote, 'To learn to be silent in the presence of words, to be courteous and chaste in relation to them, is a task which only silence can enable a man to undertake.'

It seems that the changes in Simon's religious life were reflected on a personal level, and he began to come out, very cautiously, encouraged perhaps by the freer spirit of the times. There was a substantial minority of gay ordinands at Westcott, and Simon embarked on one or two tentative relationships. His notebook speculations were neglected in favour of reality, though he occasionally found time to note his pleasure in simple gestures of love like holding hands, little things that in the heterosexual world are so taken for granted. He also started to go out to gay clubs, and discovered how much he loved dancing. Typically that too became something sacred.

He wrote later in 'My Story', 'As my religious life developed and changed at Cambridge, as I became less conservative and evangelical, as I became increasingly liberal and found myself examining everything I believed and discovering an approach much more suited to me, so inevitably it raised questions about the rest of my life too, my sense of identity, my sense of integrity, at precisely the same time as I was learning to be a priest I was also learning to be more honest with me, to trust myself, my feelings, my desires. If I "fell in love" – and it was a man – why was it wrong to act on those feelings? Did I really believe God disapproved? No, I didn't. That's what happened of course – someone came along, I fell in love, we became partners, lovers . . .it wasn't anything spectacular – it was quite ordinary, it didn't last all that long, we did what all human beings do. We just happened to be of the same gender. It ended in fact when I was ordained – I told him I felt I had to go alone (and I know I hurt him).'

Then in 1979 Ashok committed suicide. It was a terrible blow to Simon. Ashok had left Cambridge, and then returned again a year later, abandoning his philosophy studies for French and Persian. He wrote to Simon about the possibility of becoming a monk, or working in an Indian Mission, but was clearly deeply disturbed about his future. At the end he had been working as an English teaching assistant in Paris, and all Simon ever heard was that he had thrown himself from a cliff and had left a cryptic note which implied it was because of a love affair. Simon marked his death with poetry, trawling Tennyson, Milton, and Christina Rossetti, 'Remember me when I am gone away . . .' He continued to dream and write of Ashok for many years, the relationship unresolved, the death a continuing mystery. The loss somehow became symbolic of Simon's own conflicts.

Father remained a burden, 'I have always been independent but I've also always been following and rebelling against him,' Simon observed to me. While Simon was at Cambridge my father found a pile of gay magazines he had put in the dustbin after a visit home. 'From whom no secrets are hid, and all desires known . . .' Walter immediately charged off to Cambridge to confront his son. The thought makes me tremble even now. For Walter homosexuality was another work of the devil, and homosexuals were to be condemned and if at all possible saved. Simon said he couldn't remember what happened with Father, and no doubt was not inclined to. (We were taping this conversation in the car, and there was a very long silence indeed after that. 'But I certainly didn't take the opportunity to say anything more about myself, partly because I didn't know, I certainly wasn't confident enough.' It cannot have been a comfortable encounter.)

Unless Simon dissembled very effectively, it seems obvious

now that Father must have known the truth. He chose for himself a very difficult course, one quite contrary to his natural desire to plunge into any situation and act. He left it alone, and for once in his life remained passive. He certainly couldn't deal with it, but fortunately therefore did not attempt to deal with Simon, except for occasionally suggesting he got himself a wife. My mother recalls much later making a reference to Dad about Simon's friends at a party; Dad cut her short, replying that he didn't want to talk about it. It would have been impossible, then, for Dad to come to terms with Simon being gay – he too would have found it much easier to accept him being ill, and perhaps might have come to terms with it through AIDS. Perhaps it was one of the best things he did, since his inter-ference would have caused great pain and bitterness and achieved the exact opposite of his intentions. He may indeed have understood that. I wish I could ask him.

Simon made his first trip abroad to visit monasteries in Italy, invited by an Italian monk he had met on the bus to Oxford. He went to Verona, Venice, Florence, revelled in Rome and said mass in St Peters. In the end though he felt uncomfortable with the Byzantine extravagance of it all. He liked Assisi best as he wrote in his journal, 'The cave of St Francis out in the woods with only the wind and the trees and the rough stones is probably the place I felt to be holiest of those I've visited in Italy.' Best of all though he liked coming back, he truly loved England and deeply cherished his Northern heritage.

He returned to Yorkshire, and in June 1981, at Petertide when ordinations traditionally take place, Simon was ordained a Deacon by the Bishop of Sheffield. He went as a curate to Norton, a parish on the outskirts of Sheffield. In the Church of England priests are first ordained deacons and usually serve a period as a curate, under a vicar. A year later, according to tradition, he was fully ordained as a priest. The crucial differ-ence is that priests can then preside over communion, that is to say, actually break and bless the communion bread and wine. There is a photograph of Simon in the church doorway, after celebrating his first eucharist. White robes billowing round him, his face is lifted to the sunlight with an expression of pure joy. It looks like the happiest moment of his life.

But it was a momentous commitment too. During the ordi-

nation service, one of the ordinands read from the Epistle to
the Romans, 'I appeal to you brethren, by the mercies of God,
to present your bodies as a living sacrifice, holy and acceptable to God, which is your spiritual worship.' As part of the
ordination process Simon committed himself to accept the 'doctrine of the Christian faith as the Church of England has
received it,' and 'to accept the discipline of this church and give
due respect to those in authority.' It was to become increasingly
difficult to keep those vows.

At that stage the doctrine of the Christian faith as the Church
of England had received it, was already open to review. It
was looking rather shaky over two highly controversial issues;
women's ordination and homosexuality. The fissures were to
widen rapidly in the next few years. But at that moment attitudes
were perhaps as liberal as they have ever been. In December
1979 the long awaited Gloucester Report on Homosexual
Relationships,[3] commissioned several years earlier by the
Church of England, concluded that, 'in the light of evidence
we have received we do not deny that there are circumstances
in which individuals may justifiably choose to enter into a homosexual relationship.' In 1980 the British Council of Churches
influential document, 'God's Yes to Sexuality'[4] concluded that
'in the light of the abiding central message of the Bible . . . we
find it impossible to reckon homosexual orientation as a vice or
a disorder of nature.'

However in 1981 the Archbishop of Canterbury stated in
a debate on homosexual relationships in General Synod, the
governing body of the Church of England, that he inclined to
the idea that homosexuality was a 'handicap.' The issue was
finally coming out into the open. The Gay and Lesbian
Christian Movement was formed – a direct result of the more
liberal ideas of sexuality which developed in the Sixties and
Seventies.

Simon was beginning to explore this whole issue, becoming
aware of the role of women in the church and the value of their
particular spirituality, and this led him to ask questions about
the connection between his sexuality and his spirituality. 'Is
there a gay love for Christ?' He began to see that his homosexuality was not necessarily a burden and wrote in his journal,
'I have a deep wound, a kind of flaw at the centre . . . it can in

itself be turned into a glory . . .' But, he asked himself, 'Can I really explore the shadows the way I do – and still carry the light for people? I think maybe there would be no light without the shadows. People assume that priests are pure and holy – most honest priests know more about shadows than anything else.' He nevertheless continued to keep his homosexuality secret. Later in 'My Story' he wrote, 'For the first years after I was ordained I lived in "fragments" – kept the job and my sexual identity quite separate, secret as far as possible. Still no one knew but me – I'm sure people guessed but I talked to no one.'

Apart from Norton's very beautiful 12th century Norman church, flanked by a wood of bluebells in the spring, Simon's new parish had little to recommend it, at least to me. If this was his chosen path I couldn't wait for him to become my brother the bishop and at least get a palace. But that was not his way. Instead Simon went to live on the council estate. 'Norton – I have to empty myself into this place, to sink down and in . . .' he reflects in his journal.

He wrote an account of his neighbours in an article published in 1986 in the *Guardian* while he was there. 'It had all started as an exercise in "living with the people" . . . fresh from Cambridge, dutiful, high principled (and naive), I agreed to live on the council estate at the bottom end of the parish. A "nice council estate" I was told – and so it is. But nobody pointed out I would be living on its worst block, the finest graffiti, the most frequently ignited staircase, and then there were the neighbours . . .'

He described his upstairs neighbour Pete; after drinking fourteen pints he would regularly threaten to kill someone. Pete became a frequent visitor, sometimes listening to music, bringing dubious gifts including two televisions neither of which worked. 'I think he thought I could use bits of one to repair the other,' notes Simon with incredulity. After a particularly spectacular row the night before Simon's ordination, Pete's wife sought sanctuary in Simon's flat, only to be pursued by her irate husband, fists flailing. Finally Simon called the police. The next day Pete came to apologise, but adding that he would kill whoever it was called the police. Simon writes, 'In the maddest moment of honesty in my entire life I said, "I phoned them." '

'If I ever find out I'll kill them,' Pete repeated, choosing not to hear him. One day soon after, Simon came home to the smell of freesias, left in a milk bottle in the kitchen. 'I forgot to wonder how he'd got into the house, or off the back of which lorry they had fallen, in sheer astonishment.'

None of his neighbours went to church, but they always took comfort in the knowledge that Simon went every day to say prayers for them. 'How much they expect of us, we're supposed to have all the answers, to know why people die, why they suffer, somehow we have to soak it up – to act as channels for the questions even if there are no answers,' he writes in his journal.

One day the Bishop came to tea and met the neighbours. He and Simon posed for a photograph on the scruffy verandah, Simon in his clerical grey vest and white collar, the Bishop in purple, looking distinctly out of place. David Lunn, the Bishop of Sheffield is a gentle, old-fashioned character who seems not quite of the 20th century. Simon took a wonderful photograph of him on the annual Bishop's Pilgrimage to Holy Island that same year, as he waited to board a train with a group of parishioners. He is wearing his long purple gown, his hand resting on his Bishop's crook, sporting an incongruous little green rucksack on his back.

He nevertheless appreciated Simon's efforts to involve himself in the wrong end of the parish. The Bishop recently described it to me, 'It was unspeakable, you picked over the lads demolishing their motorbikes in the corridor, the debris, the row going on outside, the unbelievable neighbours, the violence. Then Simon's flat was like going into a don's room at Cambridge, elegant, beautiful, with lots of books. Simon maintained his distinctiveness and yet had a readiness to share that without any pretence that he liked Top of the Pops or whatever, and they recognised in him his care for them. I don't know if the parish ever recognised the significance of that ministry.'

Everything became a sacrament, even the graffiti strewn subway tunnel to the estate, with 'light at the end but a steeply curving path, and, on the way, broken glass.' He made a book of photographs and quotations for the journey, a stations of the cross from the subway tunnel to the church door. Then that became a poem too.

He spent four years as a curate but he was impatient to get a parish of his own as soon as he could. He became involved in CND; his letters are full of reports of Greenham Common and other protests, and he began publishing articles and poems. He made some good friends in the parish, in particular Sue Proctor, her husband Richard and their two young sons. They were both librarians, and their house soon became a second home for Simon, and he would drop in for tea on a regular basis. Simon and Sue quickly became friends; he responded to her warm, extrovert manner, her sensitivity and intelligence, while for Sue, Simon touched depths of her life she was only just beginning to acknowledge.

'We met at the right time,' says Sue. 'I had just had two weeks in hospital after an emergency hysterectomy, and it had given me time to think. I had wanted all my life to be a priest, but women couldn't be, so I thought I must have got it wrong. I came out of hospital just as Simon arrived – somehow there was a match of needs.'

Simon loved his job, and wrote in his journal, 'It has so many of the critera I want – freedom of operation, no "factory-mentality", a wholly blurred distinction of work and leisure, a freedom from large scale property-owning, no career structure, equality of stipend, no overloaded hierarchy but accessible superiors – and all the elements of mystery that belong to life – one thing is missing, the big thing, the total engagement with a wounded world.' There is an almost unbearable poignancy about these journals just before he contracts the virus, almost as if he is waiting for this great trial, 'I feel on the threshold of something, I don't know what . . . it hurts but it's a good feeling – waiting.'

He went to Iona for the first time in 1983, as chaplain for a retreat. It felt like coming home, and he revelled in the sea and sky, hiking alone for hours over the island, scrambling over rocks and contemplating the waves, as he wrote, 'We are all streams, tributaries, heading one day for the endless sea, death is the estuary and as we flow on we sense at times the vast space to come . . . but death and beyond is a common sea.'

Then in 1984 he got hepatitis B. Later Simon noted, 'Nineteen-eighty-four was a watershed year for me, I see now . . . the space that followed, went with it, illness took me to face certain things, sharpened and tautened things . . .' I remember on one level being curious about how he got hepatitis. I was living in New York by then, close to Greenwich village and the Christopher Street gay scene, and beginning to hear about AIDS, hepatitis and other illnesses that threatened the homosexual population. And yet my journal notes innocently, 'S. has had a dose of hepatitis – inexplicable in origin, except that he does meet a lot of people.'

Now I understand that hepatitis is often the body's first reaction to infection with the HIV virus, and this was probably the case for Simon. He was ill for several months. But as he convalesced he took the opportunity to travel, go on retreats, read and ponder his life. His response to the hepatitis was as I now see highly characteristic, presaging his eventual response to AIDS itself. He tried to use it. The Chinese use the same character for crisis as for opportunity; it is almost as if the body's initial reaction to the infection is a warning, a time to prepare.

Simon described his response to me later, 'It was a moment of crisis. I felt there was no time to waste, when I discovered how serious it was . . . I remember sitting thinking, is priesthood what I want? And I immediately did three things; I joined the Movement for the Ordination of Women, the Gay and Lesbian Christian Movement, and CND.'

All three were statements. CND and Greenham Common were perhaps the first points of renewed connection between us; when we realised we actually shared some of the same concerns, and I began to appreciate that he was also a feminist. We began to have quiet intense conversations, sharing books – me recommending feminist writers; Sara Maitland, Simone de Beauvoir, Doris Lessing. I wrote to him a lot while he was ill, creating I now realise an atmosphere of understanding and empathy for him to talk to me about being gay, since there was clearly no way I was going to work it out for myself!

He wrote in his journal, 'I decided life was too short to waste, to hide from, to be secret about and in my own way I changed gear . . . I began to tell people – my sisters and brother (not my parents), my friends (a few). I ceased to be frightened of gay

pubs and clubs, the gay community. I began to have gay friends.'
He came to London and went dancing at Heaven, the big gay
nightclub in Charing Cross, relishing the irony of the name,
entering fully into the elation of coming out at last.

Among the friends he met at that time was Andrew Abbs,
whom he met dancing at the City Hall monthly gay night in
Sheffield. Andrew is half-Iranian and half-Scottish, a small, neat,
gentle man, with a little moustache and a strong Glasgow
accent, who worked for many years as a residential social worker
with maladjusted teenagers. Despite a difficult background of
adoption and abuse, he has not the slightest trace of bitterness.
I first met him when he was visiting Simon at the Rectory in
Dinnington, and he was dressed head to toe in black leather
and chains. I remember thinking he might not be a very suitable
lodger. But his companionship was refreshing for Simon – they
loved to talk about clothes and holidays – and Andrew for his
part, valued Simon's education and wider experience.

Early that summer Simon went on retreat to Bardsey, a tiny
rocky island off the coast of Wales. Bardsey is a bird sanctuary,
uninhabited apart from the wardens and a resident hermit. It
was one of the great centres of Celtic pilgrimage – in the Middle
Ages three pilgrimages to Bardsey were counted equal with one
to Rome, and it is said to be the resting place of twenty thousand
saints. The poet, R.S. Thomas who had his parish in Aberdaron,
the embarkation point for Bardsey, describes it thus, ' that green
island, ringed with the rain's bow, that we had found and would
spend the rest of our lives looking for.'

It is a favoured place for retreats, but it is accessible by boat
only once a week, winds and waves permitting. Accommodation
is very basic, without running water or electricity and visitors
have to bring their own food with them. Simon's journal records
boarding the boat for the first time with two nuns, 'without a
thought they strode straight into the water in their sandals – it
was like a baptism, an initation:'

Among the family photographs framed on my wall is one of
Simon celebrating mass at the altar of the bare medieval ruins
of the abbey church on Bardsey. He is dressed in a long white
robe, on top a scarlet embroidered chasuble. Behind him an
altar of granite and slate is covered in a white linen cloth

prevented from blowing away in the wind by pebbles carefully placed at each corner. Above it is a single candle and a small vase of red and yellow flowers. I asked for the photograph when Simon first told me he was gay and I always cherished the eccentric romanticism of it.

Simon's first visit played a major part in helping him to reconcile his vocation and his sexuality after his long struggle. He was to return many times to Bardsey, a place which became a precious place for contemplation, though I don't believe his ornithology advanced much in the process. He wrote a description of the island in an address on contemplative prayer in 1991,[5] which remains a good summary of the religious philosophy which sustained him,

'The Holy Island of Bardsey off the north coast of Wales, remote and difficult to reach, is also a bird sanctuary. On one corner of the island is a hide for bird watchers, low, stone with a slit to look out of across the sea as it breaks on the rocks ahead of you. If you sit in there your vision is filled hour after hour with the waves of the sea, with the clouds of the sky and the sun, with the birds, the rare ones and the flocks, the great and the beautiful – the tiny, the ugly and the curious. If you sit there for any length of time you join the rhythm of the place, the tides and the days, the times and the changing light: your hiding for observation becomes an invitation to participate in the rhythm that underlies the world ... It is about deeper engagement with the world, about more pain, not less, about exposure and vulnerability not seclusion and privacy.'

Bardsey was everything he loved. He climbed the mountain, searched out the holy well, spent hours watching sunlight glittering on the sea and contemplating the night stars. He made bread for the first time which he then consecrated at mass. Best of all he met two very special companions. He shared a house with two other members of the retreat group, Richard a gay ordinand, and Alma, a woman who wanted to be a priest but could not, both as marginalised in their way as Simon.

'It was a revelation to me,' Simon recalled, 'They were both riotously funny, both had a really anarchic sense of humour. But they were also open and frank and honest about the whole sexual side of things. And all the things that for Dad were opposite to religion – sex, smoking, drinking, all those things.

Alma and Richard spent the whole time smoking these dreadful cigarettes that they borrowed from somebody on the island because they'd run out, they had secret stores of booze, and told racy jokes the whole week. And yet they were so devout as well. I had this really intense week with them, intense for me anyway, of long deep conversations.'

Alma tells the same story of the apprehension of spending a week with a complete stranger, who was later to become one of her dearest friends. Alma, now, finally, an ordained priest herself, is also in the photograph, her dark head bent over a prayer book, white robes and sandals, looking very much the medieval pilgrim. But she is far from the humble, gentle figure the image might suggest; instead she is a pugnacious, outspoken Yorkshirewoman, who smokes assiduously, and can in her own words, 'talk the hind leg off a donkey'. It was her combination of devoutness and plain vulgarity that Simon found enormously attractive. Most of all when he tentatively mentioned he was gay, she passed no comment and expressed no surprise, which for Simon was a profound relief.

Like Sue Proctor, Alma did not know what to do with her desire to be a priest, 'It's hard to say you've always wanted to a priest because you weren't supposed to be. I imagined being a kind of Abbess, but it was really more like a priest dressed as a woman.' She went through several tortuous relationships before declaring herself celibate. She had graduated in philosophy and trained as a librarian, but by the time she met Simon she was in training at Westcott to become a deacon, the closest women could get at that time to the priesthood.

Simon and Alma became 'soul-friends' as Aelred of Rievaulx termed it, whose book *Spiritual Friendship*[6] was one that Simon treasured. Folded neatly into Simon's journal from that time is a note from Alma, with a quotation from Simone Weil which summed up their relationship, 'But the greatest blessing you have brought me is of another order. In gaining my friendship by your charity (which I have never met anything to equal) you have provided me with a source of the most compelling and pure inspiration that is to be found among human things for nothing among human things has such power to keep our gaze fixed ever more intensely upon God than friendship for the friends of God.'[7]

In July 1984 I returned from New York for a visit, and went to stay with Simon in his council flat, a haven of peace and calm. I was intrigued by the small white Buddha in the bedroom and I began to understand that Simon's religion had departed considerably from that of our childhood. He was so happy then. More talkative than I can ever remember (before or since). He told me about Bardsey and his new friends. 'A feminist who wants to be a priest, and is active in support of gay clergy, though not gay herself, and a gay priest,' I noted in my journal that night, earnestly, blindly. I was most intrigued by his talk of women priests and the effect they might have on the church. My journal goes on merrily, 'He has changed so much! this new person with a shorter but less old-fashioned haircut, a tan, more relaxed clothes, so happy and talkative and full of wonderful projects. He has written a play and been asked to write a book of prayers . . . He is even making his own bread.' I still didn't get it, though.

My journal continues the next night, 'Simon comes out of the closet. It's not every day your brother tells you he's gay – and happy. What a beautiful person he is, how I love him. I feel that I have made a new and precious friendship with a very special person. Oh, for more time to talk to him about religion, poetry, literature. He tried to tell me and I was so stupid, references to sex that he had never mentioned before.' We had talked about Bardsey and looked at his photographs and I was utterly beguiled by the beauty and spirituality of it, the light, the sea, the ancient Celtic crosses. Finally I asked, 'So you've given up on the idea of marriage?' And then he said bluntly, putting his hands firmly on his knees, 'I'm gay, and I'm not celibate either.' Then I was so happy – that he wasn't lonely, could have an emotional and sexual life, companionship. I noted, 'He is right to stay a parish priest as he wants to.' In a family talk about careers with my sister Jackie, no-one had been able to say like Simon, 'I know I'm doing the right thing and I feel happy doing it.'

He had several relationships during that period, but always withdrew, a pattern that was to repeat itself until Simon concluded that he actually preferred to live alone. I wondered at first how connected this was to discovering he was HIV-positive, to not wanting to be involved, but in a letter to me a year before his diagnosis, he is already expressing the sentiments that were to develop into his ideas of friendship. He described the end of what was an important relationship, 'I think we've settled into a rather looser relationship – it all got a bit too "intense" for me when he came up here to stay ... It's a bit too easy for gay people to try and mimic the straight romantic myth. All-consuming passionate intensity isn't really my sort of thing – maybe it works for some people – I enjoy quieter, steadier, more relaxed friendships really – and a lot of time on my own.' However sometimes this emphasis on freedom and independence back-fired. Another relationship foundered when his lover, also a young priest, took Simon at his word and opted for independence, leaving Simon devastated.

It was time for Simon to move to a parish of his own and he discussed various options with the Bishop throughout that year. Dinnington eventually emerged, although there were delays to the decision because the patron of the parish, who was responsible for approving any appointment, wanted to find a rector for himself.

The highlight of that last year in Norton was the performance of *St Chad – A Miracle Play*,[8] in the ancient, shady churchyard of St James. It took place over six nights in July 1985, a week of perfect sunny weather. It was Simon's swansong at Norton, and through it he succeeded in expressing the ideas about religion and the function of the church that he was trying to put into practice. Religion for Simon had become increasingly something to share, a way of uniting a community in a profound way, rather than something to be taught or preached to the unconverted: 'faith as fullness of life, as community, and as deepened spirituality' rather than as 'personal salvation'. It was his alternative to Billy Graham's mission to Sheffield.

The play had been in preparation for over a year, occupying much of Simon's spare time, and co-opting a vast cast and support team of local people and school children. Simon wrote the play in the style of the mystery plays of the Middle Ages, and cheerfully acknowledged his debt to playwright Christopher Fry. 'The play was conceived of, first and foremost, as the activity of a community – it is much less important as an attempted "work of art".' He wanted to explore the question, how did the faith come to this particular place? His researches led to the story of Chad bringing Christianity to Mercia, of which the parish of Norton was a part in the 7th century. Simon had searched the Venerable Bede for characters, and written a simple tale in powerful language, located just where the performance takes place, in what was once forest and is now the church of St James, Norton. The old Gods are ranged against the new and the Celtic cross is planted in the earth of Mercia. (The same cardboard cross for years continued to adorn the upstairs landing in Dinnington Rectory.)

Simon brought together all his ideas about using art to explore the religious experience, 'There is something holy about the theatre, about drama and acting . . . the links between theatre and religion are strong if they are not actually in the end the same thing. There is something sacred about this all-embracing, all-involving use of our imagination . . . So our human experience becomes our way to God – the road of our worship – not something to be escaped or abandoned.'

I missed the original production, and watched the video afterwards in a rather perfunctory way. But ten years later, a few months before Simon's death, I watched it again. The idyllic scene was exquisitely poignant. The performance began at 8 pm, long golden shafts of evening sunlight piercing through the trees of the churchyard, with birdsong as backdrop. The play opens with delicate music, dancing and cartwheels, and a chorus to describe the setting of woods and moors. Chad arrives, sent from Lindisfarne in Northumbria, with twelve monks to convert the heathen. One young monk, Trumbert, exhausted by travelling, elects to stay when Chad journeys on, 'I'll guard the cross, teach the folk, illuminate my books, clear a little way.'

An old woman, a dwarf and a child are the first to convert, and the priests of the old religion are enraged. When the child refuses to recant death is threatened. Despite pleas for mercy the deed is done. The child is killed. It is genuinely horrifying; somehow one waits for a miracle that does not come. Nor is the child miraculously brought back to life; it is a moment of reality somehow, which gives the play an impact beyond fairy tale. Trumbert cradles the child's head and looks up to the sky, 'The sun comes blazing back – but not his sun . . .'

This is the turning point of the play; Chad returns, and the pagans turn to Christ. The play ends, the cast return and disperse to be congratulated by parents and friends. There is more applause and calls for the author, 'Simon – where is he?' There is a brief tantalising glimpse of Simon as he takes a bow in white trousers and shirt sleeves; youthful, ambitious, idealistic, with, it seemed, all of life before him.

this is my body

It was Remembrance Day, November 11, 1985. Simon had been on a retreat to Holy Island off the coast of Northumberland to prepare for his new post as Rector of Dinnington. He had visited St Cuthbert's shrine in Durham Cathedral, one of his most cherished sacred places. His journal records, 'Sitting in Cuthbert's shrine today I was overwhelmed by a sense of "fear-lessness" – of whom then shall I be afraid?' There is nothing to fear . . . I don't know why I felt that there, but I did.'

Although Simon had already been ill with hepatitis he hadn't made a deliberate decision to take an HIV test. News of the 'gay plague' was only just beginning to get through to Britain. He had been to the dentist to have a tooth extracted, and they had initiated hospital tests because they were concerned his blood took so long to clot. The hospital then sent him a letter.

He wrote about the moment he received the letter in his book, *The Well Within*,[2] published not long after he died, 'I never unpack my bags before I've been through the post and so, sitting among the luggage, I found a letter from the hospital. The letter simply said I needed to contact the hospital urgently. It was as vague as that, but I knew. I hadn't really thought about it seriously until then, but somehow I knew. The dread – even then in 1985 – of every gay man. HTLV III, as they called it then, the HIV virus that leads to AIDS. Like everyone else I knew very little about it, but it hovered already, rightly or wrongly, as the great fear of the gay community. And now they were going to tell me it was there in my blood. The diagnosis was confirmed a week later at the hospital and I, fit and healthy and well, found myself from then on living in the face of dying.'

He wrote in his journal at the time, 'I'm terribly self-con-scious, self-aware, febrile, shaking . . . The lust to live is incredibly strong – an angry strength: I have just too much, too many people, to live for . . .' His immediate reaction was to dance; he put on a favourite record and danced on his own, amongst the luggage and the other unopened mail, 'I keep dancing' says the journal 'a kind of frenzy, the liveliest thing I can do . . .'

Recalling my happiness at his decision to come out of the closet, to be glad to be gay, I realise now the terrible irony that by that time he was already HIV-positive, though he was not to find out for another eighteen months. At least he had that short period of enjoying and celebrating his homosexuality before he knew, but it was so terribly brief.

He was of course used to thinking about death. Ashok's suicide had made an indelible impression, and he had often pondered philosophically about death in his journal. He was trained to think on these things, to wrestle with them on behalf of his flock. So he had the language and experience to try and explore the implications of his diagnosis for himself. The Sunday after the letter from the hospital he preached a sermon on the promise of redemption and liberation, and quoted the foreign minister of Nicaragua, on whether he was afraid of dying, 'I don't want to die, I want to live, and I fear that waking death of not getting involved, and keeping silent.'

The clergy often take two or three funerals a week so it must often seem that death is the main business of the Church of England these days. Only a week or so before his diagnosis, Simon had written a description of a traditional Sheffield funeral. He notes the gathering of the family, the mourners taking leave of the corpse, and most importantly the recounting of the details of the death. He was quite used to writing funeral orations – and quite naturally wondered about his own. His journal entry is a revealing piece of self-analysis, 'If I were writing my own funeral oration what would I say? Despite all appearances he was a deeply physical person – sexual, tactile, earthy inside, longing for the roots that went down deep into the earth . . . He learnt freedom slowly and steadily, inwardly determined to have it and so in many ways was powerfully content. He was not holy, but he did know it – it even distressed him that often other people thought he was holy; he was as afraid of death (but maybe even more afraid of "the known" of being found out?) as anyone else but he clung by his fingernails to some kind of meaning, "Lord where else can we go . . .?" '

What he did not claim, however, was the traditional comfort to the dying, of treasure in heaven. He wasn't sure he really believed any of that. Indeed it wasn't ultimately what interested him. He was trying to work out his own part in a vast tapestry, rather than preserve and exalt himself. It really seems not to have mattered to him what happened to his own ego 'afterwards', although he truly believed in some kind of continuation, some kind of blissful union with all creation.

Then there were the resolutions. What did he want to do with the time he had left. He frequently invokes G.K. Chesterton, 'One should leave nothing in the world of which one is afraid.' His fears were as much of revealing his homosexuality as of revealing he had AIDS, as he wrote in his journal, 'One thing I should like to achieve in whatever time I have, perhaps an ordinary lifetime, is to tell more people – everyone – that I'm gay: not merely so that the HTLV III is less of a shock, but so that I am ready to die if it comes to that – I want people I'm close to to know that I'm gay and normal – that bit of education, that fraying away of prejudice, I can contribute.'

Simon was given a basic health screening at the Royal Hallamshire Hospital, high up on one of Sheffield's seven hills. He would continue to go there for regular clinic checks and, later, treatment for the rest of his life. From then on he would have a minimum of three routine examinations a year. His consultant was Dr George Kinghorn, who for the first few years was Simon's only confidante. Simon told no-one else, confided in no-one, about the diagnosis. He wrote later in *The Well Within*, 'I had no idea what to do with this "information" about myself. I would look at it, hold it up, walk round it – "you might soon be dead" – but somehow it didn't sink in. At other times I could even forget about it completely. There were the times too, of course, when suddenly it would overwhelm me: "I do things," says the journal, "and suddenly something sinks away – the possibility, it yawns and gapes, an abyss." I felt of course as someone who tries to pray, that I ought to be able to face this. At least to begin, to try.'

The HIV-positive diagnosis was only two weeks before he

was due to be inducted as Rector of Dinnington, after four years in Norton. A few days before, he went to stay with Alma, by then curate of Retford, a few miles away. For the first time he and Alma celebrated mass together, with Alma assisting as Simon presided. It was to be another nine years before Alma herself was entitled to preside, as a fully priested woman. But it established a profound connection between them.

Becoming Dinnington's priest was still what Simon wanted to do. His HIV diagnosis only made him more sure that this was how he wanted to spend his life – or what remained of it. He had told the Bishop he didn't want another curacy, but preferred to go straight into a parish of his own. He wanted a community, a small town, with different community groups and plenty of opportunity for the church to get involved. His hope was to use the church to encourage people to express their spirituality in different ways. He wanted a two-way traffic between church and community, not what he called a 'holy huddle'. He was unfamiliar with the parish – Dinnington was then just a destination on the front of local buses. But it was exactly the kind of place he had in mind.

So he arrived in the Yorkshire pit village of Dinnington, his talents already highly regarded, fired by South American liberation theology, feminism and CND. 'Glad to be gay' – but also HIV-positive.

'great things in small parishes'

Simon was appointed Rector of St Leonard's parish church, Dinnington, in a traditional induction service in December 1985. The Bishop of Sheffield presided, formally attired in gold vestments and mitre. In a simple black cassock, white surplice and his Cambridge academic hood, Simon swore his oaths of allegiance, promising to observe only authorised forms of service and sacraments. He was instructed by the Archdeacon to care for the sick, the bereaved and the dying; those seeking marriage and baptism and for all children. 'Your care must extend to all who are hurt, whether within or beyond the church. You are to be a minister of healing and reconciliation wherever there is pain or conflict.' The Bishop stressed Simon's particular responsibility to the parish, 'to lead the people here in their pilgrimage. You are called to be available, to be humble, to be human. You are called to ensure that you also grow in grace, learning from the people whom you serve; making time for study, for quiet reflection and for prayer.' Archdeacon, church-warden and the new Rector walked solemnly in procession to the door of the church where the churchwardens formally presented him with the keys. Then the new Rector tolled the bell ten times to signify his taking possession.

It was one hell of a job description. No longer was the parish a cure of two hundred souls, but a sprawling jumble of ten thousand people spanning an area of roughly four square miles. Simon however was quite sure this was what he most wanted to do, 'I wanted to be rector of Dinnington then because it represented for me the sharp end: if all I had been taught about the faith could be put into practice here, then it really might work,' he said, adding in a sermon much later how arrogant that came to sound.

Dinnington may have a population of ten thousand, but people still insist on calling it a village, joking about the brand new signs to the Town Centre at the roundabout. Despite new commuter housing on the outskirts there are still many people who have lived here all their lives. Until the pit came this was farming country, twelve miles to the east of the massive industrial conurbation of Sheffield, where the Pennines flatten out into gentle rolling fields and fenland. Now, the area is scarred by pit workings and newly risen slagheaps, by memories of bitter strikes, rising unemployment, increased vandalism, the familiar litany of decline. The commuters travel to Sheffield and Rotherham to work, while the core of the town remains a picture of stubborn deprivation and decay. The M1 is only three miles away but it's not much use if you don't have a car. There used to be a railway station, introduced after the pit opened, but it has gone again now.

Still, Dinnington was here when the Domesday-book was written, and will no doubt weather the changes wrought by the 20th century along with many more. Evidence of the past is not hard to find. The oldest part of town, clustered around Dinnington Hall and St Leonard's church, is built of a creamy local limestone and a few little limestone cottages remain. Sadly there was none left for Dinnington high street, which is mostly Victorian redbrick, low-rise gabled shops. They were erected in a flurry of building activity when the pit first opened, and though well worn and shabby for the most part, they have an oddly temporary quality, like a newly built wild west town. Most of the town is 1920s pit housing, small terraced houses many of which are now in a serious state of neglect.

It has become a cliché of pit villages that they are renowned for their sense of community and support of each other, but its sheer survival is evidence that Dinnngton's sense of community is nothing new. It still feels like a village. People are brusque but friendly, greeting each other across the high street, pausing to discuss their ailments or their holidays, queueing at the one remaining post office for pensions and benefits. Harassed young mothers, high-heeled and bare-legged even in the most bitter weather, manouevre double buggies round the market, while determined old ladies on shopping scooters negotiate the morning traffic. There are a lot of men with children too, contemplating the newly familiar aisles of the supermarket or watching them play on the spanking new playground at the Miner's Welfare Institute.

Since 1902, when the first shaft was sunk until 1991 when it was closed, the pit has totally dominated peoples lives. Always towering over the horizon was the slagheap, so large it was a landmark for miles around, overshadowing the village, blocking the light at the end of the streets. A 1950s photograph shows children playing in the street with the great hulk of the tip, threatening behind them. Not until 1966, after the Aberfan disaster when a slagheap slid on to the school and killed 116 children, was the danger fully appreciated. After that the Dinnington tip was reduced in size. Now, it is discreetly grassed over though occasionally small fires still smoulder on the surface.

The acrimonious miners' strike of 1984–85 had only recently ended when Simon arrived in Dinnington, and a deep under-current of bitterness and cynicism remained. The village had stood firm in the strike, and there were marches reminiscent of the 1920s. After several months there was real deprivation, in the face of which the community rallied round as it had done before. As in other mining villages food parcels were distributed and some miners began growing their own food just as they did in the 1920s. Coal was scavenged from the pit, and delivering it to the old age pensioners, still dependent on their coal fires, became a major preoccupation in Dinnington. One young father with two children actually dug his own tunnel into the pit to get coal, attempting to secure it with pit props. It collapsed and killed him.

People still have very strong feelings about the strike. Parishioner Sam Robinson remembered, 'It really brought a lump to your throat, when they were marching down the street in middle of strike, the speeches and the banners.' He asserted, 'There was a very strong sense of community during the strike. If it's not the same people, it's the same community that supported Simon.'

Dinnington is not, it must be said, the most devout of places. Everyone can hear the church bell as they do their shopping in the high street, but the village is part of the borough of Rotherham, which not so long ago had a reputation for the lowest church-going population in Europe. Still, St Leonard's is regarded as Dinnington's church even by people who never go there; all feel they have a right to be baptised, married and buried there. The December 1985 issue of the parish magazine when Simon first arrived, reflected the typical concerns of a small parish; events varied from choir practice to scouts and brownies, the Mothers Union to the St Leonard's Players, a struggling amateur theatre group, begging for new members. Donations were requested for the new church carpet, and plans were afoot to make tapestry kneelers for the pews. There was plenty going on that Christmas; the Yorkshire Brass Ensemble was playing, the Dinnington Theatre Club presented Mother Goose, its annual traditional pantomime at the Lyric theatre, and the date for the switching on of the Dinnington Illuminations in the high street was announced.

Despite the fact that only about one per cent of the parish attend on any regular basis the church still seems an integral part of the village, highly visible at the top of the main shopping street at the conjunction of three roads. It is no coincidence that this was also where the stocks and the gallows used to be, just outside the present church gate. The church itself is a squat Victorian stone building with a clock and belfry, surrounded by eroded tombstones in a grassy churchyard. Opposite is a pub (handy for a swift half-pint after Sunday morning service) and behind it the Co-op supermarket. There has been a church on the site since the 11th century and Simon cherished its history, profoundly aware of the procession of monks and rectors who had gone before. 'There have been rectors here always, sometimes monks, sometimes puritans, but somehow always someone to keep the praying going, the baptising, the marrying, the burying going,' he wrote.[1]

He was acutely sensitive to the layers of spiritual history as well as the kings, battles and industry that had marked the land. It was this 'sacred in the scene' that Simon was to seek, and find, in this unbeautiful South Yorkshire pit village. He wanted to tap into the natural way people still turned to the church at ritual moments in their lives, and make it meaningful to them; a part of their community. He passionately wanted to recapture the ritual and rich imagery that had been thrown out after the Reformation: the processions and gilded images of saints, the holy water and candles, a sense of religion that had been lost when the altars were stripped, the walls whitewashed and even the lighting of candles forbidden.

Simon arrived in early December 1985, anxious to be part of the Christmas festivities in Dinnington, and keen to have all the family to stay at the Rectory for Christmas. We had our family Christmas, but it must have been a very strange time for him, harbouring this new information about himself, not knowing how it might affect us all one day. My memory of the occasion is Simon appearing unusually distant, our new-found intimacy seemingly evaporated. There was the usual fearsome argument between Simon and my father. Walter was the one person, Simon always said, who could make him really lose his temper. Their arguments usually revolved round what seemed to me to be some obscure point of theological doctrine, while the rest of the family groaned for mercy. On this occasion they discoursed furiously over whether Jesus had been a perfect child; more god than man, or more man than god.

The Rectory was a big solidly built fifties house, set back from the busy main road down a steep driveway overhung with yew bushes. The land had once been part of Dinnington Hall grounds and a fine old Elizabethan redbrick wall remained from the original orchard. Simon's study was a quiet room, with a vast old wooden desk carefully laid out with pens, blotter and notebooks. Two comfortable armchairs flanked the fireplace. Extra book shelves accommodated his growing library; theological books ranged from huge Biblical concordances and Greek dictionaries to Creation Spirituality. Another wall of shelves ranked poetry; George Herbert, Dante, R.S. Thomas, and art books ranged from Celtic runes to Matisse. There was an eclectic selection of fiction; G.K. Chesterton rubbed shoulders with Armistead Maupin, Sara Maitland with Joseph Conrad.

Soon after he arrived Simon decided he wanted to paint the entire house white and asked for volunteers from the congregation. It was Jenny Bott who arrived at the door, rolled up her sleeves and set to. Although she was one of the first people Simon became friendly with in Dinnington she had not previously been very involved with the church. She is a plump woman with strong arms, red cheeks and short blonde hair, always ready for a laugh and ever ready to buckle down. She was always in the kitchen at Simon's parties, making tea, opening bottles of wine, taking another batch of sausage rolls out of the oven. If you ask Jenny what she does she will say nothing much really. Then you discover she does a secretarial job three days a week, edits and types the parish magazine, did all Simon's typing and sewed several of his vestments. All in addition to fostering thirty problem children over a period of twenty years, along with bringing up two children of her own and adopting two more. She laughed, describing it to me, 'One year we had six babies, one went out of the pram in the morning and another one came in the afternoon!'

Simon and Jenny started painting and the Rectory rapidly began to acquire a whole new character. Soon even the floor-boards were white, windows were draped in white muslin and the walls hung with prints, colourful abstracts, photographs and a beautiful collection of engravings of waterfalls; here and there were framed haikus and quotations. There were candles everywhere, even the bathroom. A little room under the eaves was turned into a prayer room, with bamboo mats on the floor, a wall of icons, incense and candles. Natural treasures, prisms and crystals, shells and stones, dried heather and twisted branches, were gradually assembled and lovingly arranged. Simon had a passion for pottery, assembling a considerable collection of earthenware bowls, enjoying the symbolism of the bowl as a vessel. Small tables and shelves became crowded with tiny carved wooden boxes, Chinese lacquer caskets, alabaster pots and bowls full of tiny shells.

Simon once brought home fragments of earth from Bardsey, 'burial place of a thousand saints,' to keep in one of his innumer-able little boxes. This subsequently became a family joke, since we were all under the impression they really were the bones of saints. I recall my three-year old son, Theo, knocking the box on the floor and me hurriedly brushing the earth up along with a leavening of household dust. Then it transpired that other members of the family had done exactly the same. Simon never did think this was as funny as we did.

He took such pleasure decorating his new house. His note-book at the time is full of measurements, lists of curtain colours, coal scuttles, blinds, all the furniture required for each room. Then right in the middle, as if he has paused in his plans for the house to think of the future, is the first draft of the poem I read at his funeral. Then it was called, uncompromisingly, 'If I die,' and in it he pondered on all the things he cherished, all the things he hoped people would one day remember him by. It was dated in Simon's cryptic way, St Edmund, King and Martyr, which turned out to be November 20, nine days after he was told his HIV diagnosis.

Immediately, thankfully, the rhythms of the church year swallowed him up, embraced him as it always would. 'I felt more at home once I'd done a funeral . . . the need waiting to be satisfied, my place in helping to do that,' he noted in his journal. He did make changes, however, establishing a book stall and restoring the tradition of holy water using the ancient font which had been abandoned in the churchyard. He began to try and persuade the parish church council to remove some of the pews and create a more flexible space, explaining that in the Middle Ages there were no pews or seats at all, but this particular suggestion was always considered thoroughly outlandish.

Nor did he want his congregation to have their own choice of hymn at funerals. He was determined to excise the 'Old Rugged Cross', which he particularly loathed as mawkish and sentimental. It was not in *Hymns Ancient and Modern*, but had been so frequently requested that the previous incumbent had copies typed up and inserted. Simon spent an entire morning going through all the hymn books in church, gleefully cutting it out again. There are still some in the parish who haven't quite forgiven him for that, and I'm sure that later, Simon himself would have conceded the arrogance of it.

Sometimes his naïveté led to problems. A retired priest had been helping with parish duties before Simon came and there was a misunderstanding about celebrating mass together. The older priest took offence, and Simon was left bewildered. 'Insensitive, proud, disrespectful, "You have devastated an old man." Is that true?' he wrote in his journal. One of the parishioners still remembers it, 'Simon looked terrified. Something had gone on in the vestry, and he looked very upset. He read the wrong lesson, read the lesson for Easter instead of Christmas.'

Yet the congregation of St Leonard's welcomed him warmly, this scholarly new rector whose shy demeanour masked his fierce determination and commitment. They rapidly became aware of the issues with which Simon was most concerned. Women's ordination was at that time one of the most controversial issues in the Church of England, and Simon soon made it clear that it was a cause about which he cared passionately. Although the climate of opinion was changing in favour of women's ordination, there were still many in the Church of England who firmly opposed it, primarily on the grounds that a woman could never be a priest because the priest is supposed to represent Christ, and more pragmatically that it would threaten unity with Rome.

Simon argued strongly for the ministry of women, in his sermons and his writing, stressing the value of their contribution to the life of the church and their particular spirituality. He believed he had something to contribute, as he wrote in his journal, 'I feel as if I can do something for the women – something vicarious. I can stand at the altar for them – for the women who can't stand where I do, for the men who are so afraid of women standing there.' His filing cabinet bulged with newsletters, letters to Bishops, including his own, articles and correspondence on the issue.

In March 1987 women were for the first time ordained as deacons; traditionally all priests spend a year as a deacon before being fully ordained as priests. Simon attended the ordination to the diaconate of twenty-four women in Southwell Minster and he described it vividly to his parishioners in a sermon two weeks later, 'I was sitting near the front so I couldn't see the processions coming in at the back of that great Gothic church . . . the organ wasn't playing because it was Lent so we could hear every sound. We stood for the procession of the bishops and the ordinands and in the silence you could hear their footsteps coming in down the long nave. Women's footsteps in women's shoes.'

A year later Simon joined a protest outside Sheffield cathedral where the previous year's deacons were being ordained to the priesthood. All that is, except for the women. They stood silently outside the cathedral with a banner saying 'Women made deacons 1987. Women ordained priest: When?' and a banner for each of the women deacons in the diocese. They went into the church to exchange the kiss of peace with the rest of the congregation, and then came out again, forswearing communion. 'It hurt to do it – hurt the women very much.' Simon said later in another sermon.

Afterwards priests new and old, swarmed forth, in cassocks, birettas, and long black cloaks. Some were supportive, but there was also a lot of anger, and what Simon identified as fear, fear of the women, fear of the threat to their own male priestly power. He felt particularly saddened by gay clergy who rejected women and wrote in his journal, 'The great problem to me – and it hurts – is the antagonism, irrational and subconscious – of gay clergy . . .' By 1988 Sue Proctor began her training, at this stage for the diaconate, but, it was fervently hoped, eventually for the priesthood. Alma too was waiting. For the more conservative members of St Leonard's the idea of women's ordination was difficult to accept, but gradually they began to change, as they changed about so many things.

There was a core group who were already active as officials in the church, already running things, whom Simon identified early on as people who could develop their talents further, 'I remember the distinct feeling within a few months of arriving in Dinnington that some of the people in the congregation knew and cared about the church and the parish far better, far more deeply than I ever could. I thought about that a lot,' he observed in a talk[2] he gave on the relationship between clergy and pastoral workers. These key members of the congregation were to play an important role in the story. Sylvia and her husband, Jim Fairhurst, both members of the choir, were typical. Jim was a big, hearty man, a miner, very old-fashioned, and famous for his parsimony. He wore his old miners' boots till they dropped off his feet, and used his old cloth cap as an oven glove. Sylvia still roars with laughter when she tells the tale of the time he was mistaken for a tramp and given some sandwiches. He took them home and ate them. He and Sylvia met in Portsmouth during the war, where he had been stationed as a sub-mariner. Then she had been known as Tess, a much more suitable name for this big jolly, untidy woman with a smile which lights her face like the sun. But a previous Dinnington rector's wife had insisted that all the women in her Mothers' Union group had to wear hats and gloves and use their given Christian names, so Sylvia she reluctantly but obediently became. She worked hard to look after Jim and her five children in a house once lit by gaslight, but then went on to train as a nurse and do A-levels. She would still far rather read poetry than do housework, and always appreciated Simon's literary background.

Several of the parishioners lived near to the Rectory in a quiet little avenue backing on to the leafy grounds of Dinnington Hall; neat little houses with carefully tended gardens, especially that of Margaret and Walter Hawley. Margaret and Walter are the kind of couple who seem to have grown to look alike; both slim, and upright, with delicate features and silver hair. Walter grew up in Dinnington, the youngest of eight children, poor but happy as he tells it. His tales of family life still have Margaret weeping with laughter at stories she must have heard hundreds of times before, especially the one about his Dad fishing out a kipper thrown into the gramophone.

Walter went down the pit at fourteen, where he worked for several years on the coal face before getting a job on the surface as a pit electrician. It is impossible to imagine Walter down the pit, and even harder to imagine how he managed to maintain his lightness of spirit. He is a seventy-year old sprite, always affable and ready to help whenever necessary. Margaret, brought up a Methodist, started going to Dinnington church when her children did. She became verger and flower sacristan, responsible for all the weddings, funerals and especially the church flowers, her favourite task. She is a woman with a quiet authority that some find a bit intimidating, but she has an independence of spirit that appealed greatly to Simon. 'Some people find Margaret irritating,' he told me in 1995, 'because she's so efficient. She just gets on with things, and can be abrupt. She is like me in lots of ways, a bit of a perfectionist.'

Both Margaret and Walter are naturally artistic people with an unpretentious response to art and beauty. Margaret once described to me her pleasure at seeing a new painting of a Madonna in a church in the Yorkshire Dales, 'The Madonna was a proper Dales girl with rosy cheeks,' she said delightedly. They are contented, good people.

Kath Graham, a little, grey-haired woman who fusses like a mother hen over her myriad tasks was always one of Simon's most faithful adjutants. When he arrived in Dinnington she was one of the churchwardens, a key role which provides the link between church and diocese. She also distributes the parish magazine, organises christenings, and opens the church for regular coffee mornings. Kath ran the ironmonger's shop in the village for many years after her father died, and remains the kind of person everybody turns to, who always seems to know what's going on. She would shout, 'It's only me,' as she came through the back door of the Rectory, but her self-effacement concealed potential which Simon sought to develop, 'She is very efficient and a good organiser. Because she has been in the parish a long time, people know her and are ready to contact her without ever having to go through me. In another world – a very different world – she would be a priest.'

Joyce and Sam Robinson were also prominent members of the church, by now retired. Sam is small, dapper with a dry wit; Joyce is generous, maternal, and they have forged a close-knit marriage. He managed a shoe shop on the high street for many years, and is a well-known and respected figure in the village. He was one of the old school with traditional views – anti-women's ordination let alone homosexuals in the church, but here too Simon struck a chord, finding in Sam a willing supporter for his desire to bring back many of the old traditions of the church (though he was never able to persuade him about the pews). Gradually, Sam even adapted to the idea of women's ordination. Sam and Joyce retired to live in a sheltered housing complex at the other end of the village from the church where Joyce, who also worked in a hospice once a week, found a whole new constituency of people to look after.

Simon involved himself in Dinnington life – everyone remembers his enthusiastic dancing at the hoedowns – and the Rectory rapidly became a natural part of parish social life. They held cheese and wine parties, bring-and-buy stalls in the garden and regular evening meetings, such as the Learning Together sessions which introduced many parishioners to a level of spiritual reflection which was quite new to them. People welcomed the change from the previous rector whose family had precluded such an open house policy. Simon's talent for delegation meant he tended to leave the actual organisation of events, and the washing up, to others. Soon there was a regular team of women, most of whom seemed to be called Jenny or Margaret, making tea, bringing cakes, and popping in the back door the next day to fetch their dishes.

That first Easter Simon initiated the Easter celebrations, reviving ancient practices that he would continue every Easter in Dinnington for the rest of his life. Maundy Thursday before Easter was the traditional foot washing ritual, on this first occasion of the young people and of the choir, a gesture of respect and humility in memory of Christ's washing of his disciples' feet before the Last Supper. After this service the altar was stripped and the church shrouded in semi-darkness for the Easter vigil, recalling Christ's night alone in the garden of Gethsemane when he prayed, 'Take this cup away from me.' On Good Friday a large wooden cross was placed in front of the altar and seven candles lit to represent Christ's wounds.

On Saturday evening a vigil was held with quiet readings and silences, and then at midnight twenty-five people set out for an overnight walk to Roche Abbey. The ancient ruins of Roche Abbey, once the most important abbey in the county, are only a few miles away, nestled in an enfolding valley with a stream running through it, a fine site which was further landscaped by Capability Brown in the 18th century. It was founded by Cistercian monks in 1147 and the abbey church along with Canterbury and Wells is one of the earliest examples of Gothic style in England. The atmospheric ruins are a favourite place for quiet walks, picnics and open air religious services. The night-watch pilgrims returned to St Leonard's where the new kitchen was put to good use in a early breakfast of soup and sausages.

Dawn was the climax as forty people gathered in the dark to wait for the sun to rise. They clustered round the fire flickering outside the church and Simon lit the paschal candle. More tapers were lit as they entered the church and Simon carried the great beeswax candle to the altar. They encircled the altar table for the first communion of Easter, renewing their Baptismal vows as Anglican tradition decreed. People who participated in these rituals, most of them for the first time, found them moving and impressive. It was Simon's passionate conviction that people needed ritual in an increasingly secularised world to give their lives rhythm and meaning. For him this meant the daily rituals of prayer, the regular celebrations of mass and the Christian year, and the sacramental rites of birth, marriage and death.

Death especially required a familiar ritual to make sense of it. So an important task was also to talk about death, and he was familiar with it as only a priest can be. Not like a doctor with the responsibility to avert it but as someone whose profound responsibility is to help others accept it, and try to understand it. In his journal at the beginning of 1987 he carefully rehearses how to talk about death:

Talking with someone who is dying.
The more love there has been the 'easier' death is to cope with.
Everything is going to be alright . . .
There is nothing to be afraid of . . .
There is *no* punishment
Finding the sense of immersion in the universal human community – the unimportance of 'my' individuality, the unimportance of 'my' death, the little rivers that we are travelling to the vast undifferentiated sea.

He concludes, 'If I die, what's left? Memories. What memories? Tend, foster, cultivate the love in the memories.'

But there were those who were sceptical of some of Simon's odd ideas and the following year he responded rather waspishly in the parish magazine. 'Apparently some people have said that they're not coming to our church again because the Rector does silly things like washing people's feet.' He explained the symbolism involved, expounding on the bizarre nature of the entire Christian story, culminating in a body nailed to a cross – and added for good measure that the word 'silly' used to mean holy or innocent. People's reasons for coming to church or seeking religion were often very different as Simon observed in his journal, 'There are the "womb ones" and the "desert ones" – the ones who come to church to retreat into the safety of the

womb and the ones who come to push a bit further into
the desert, heading for the kingdom . . . and most of us are a
mixture of both.'

Simon at least was determined to pursue the journey, and
keen to take his flock with him. His beloved Bardsey was also
on the agenda that first year. It was the first of many such parish
retreats, many of them to other islands like Iona, Holy Island
and Lindisfarne, which he cherished for their Celtic past and
their still tangible spiritual atmosphere. He particularly
embraced the idea of a native tradition of spirituality rooted in
the landscape and ordinary people, and loved the lyrical beauty
of the Celtic prayers and hymns which made even the most
humble human activity into a prayer. These ideas were quite
new to most of his parishioners, and their parish holidays and
retreats were a development they always valued. Indeed, the
parish acquired something of a reputation for always going on
trips, but they were never just alternative social events, there
was always a spiritual focus to them. Prayers were always said
and the Eucharist offered, candles lit and saints remembered.
Everything was sacred.

On Bardsey, the little group walked and prayed together, sat
and watched the sea, the birds and seals, and held windblown
services in the little ruined chapel. Walter Hawley found it a
wonderful opportunity to pursue his artistic inclinations, making
his poignant, idiosyncratic sculptures of driftwood and stones,
several of which now adorn St Leonard's.

Sylvia and Jim Fairhurst and Sam and Joyce Robinson all
went on a retreat with Simon to St Oswald's convent, hidden
away in a fold of the Esk valley inland from Whitby, surrounded
by moorland of purple heather, stone walls, and wandering
sheep. It is a gentle place with a lovely hillside garden, which
was to become a favourite with the parish, though it took some
getting used to. Joyce remembered, 'after 9 pm compline it was
completely quiet . . .' and Sylvia laughed at the memory, 'We
had to keep silence from 9pm until after breakfast. Jim got
better at it than I did!'

Another favourite place of parish pilgrimages was the little
church of St John's at Throapham in the next parish to
Dinnington. It seems likely that St John's was built over a holy
well or spring, and was once the site of a pagan midsummer

festival, attracting many pilgrims, and only later appropriated by the Christians and dedicated to John the Baptist. The little church is now redundant. Cold and empty and usually in need of cleaning, anyone going there is always instructed to bring a coat and a cushion – and a candle. Here they sat on their cushions with their candles in front of them to sing Taizé chants. These ancient Gregorian chants were revived by the Taizé community in Burgundy – established in the 1940s only a few miles from their birthplace in the great Abbey of Cluny, famous in the Middle Ages for its Gregorian chants. Now the chants and songs are sung at Taizé by thousands of young people, and it is a practice which has been embraced by more traditional religious communities, as a different, more meditative way of worship.

Simon's parishioners responded naturally, instinctively to these new experiences. Margaret Hawley said, 'We began to have a much deeper spiritual life. Simon had introduced things like Taizé, and the learning groups.' She reflected, 'Personally I now have a deeper insight into what it really means to love one another and to love God. It has never been as deep for me as it has since Simon came.' Others felt the same, 'He was a wonderful priest,' said Joyce. 'He was a deep, loving, spiritual person, and he opened up our minds to lots of things, going on retreats, things we had never done before.' It was also at this time that they discussed and articulated their philosophy, and at a conference on Parish Life in 1987, devised the parish motto they were so soon to put into practice, 'Unlimited, unconditional, unquestioning love, freely given with no expectation of return: with comradeship and equality for all.'

As their spiritual lives developed so did their involvement in the church and community and gradually more people began to fulfill roles that would traditionally be considered the vicar's work. It was a new movement within the church, the Pastoral Workers' scheme, which fitted perfectly with Simon's idea of communal ministry. It was as if Simon was already training people, delegating his work, perhaps unconsciously, for a time when they would need to do it for him. He had observed very soon after he came that there were people performing pastoral tasks that he would never be able to do. 'One of the most important things for me was saying that you mustn't expect that your priest can do everything. Each of them had characteristics that I didn't have, and it was a way of affirming their gifts. This is what the church is about, not about a special priestly caste that does everything and you just lie down and worship them.'

As well as delegating practical responsibilities, he began to involve people more in the church liturgy, participating in the services with readings, prayers and administering the chalice at communion, something that often is only done by the priest. The way he recruited Jenny Bott was typical, asking her to help administer the chalice at communion very soon after he arrived, even though she was not at that time very involved with the church. He somehow managed to combine a certain ingenuous naïveté with a philosophy that was determined to let people find their own way of expressing their spirituality. Margaret Hawley remembered, 'He had a knack of putting ideas into your head without you realising.'

A small group began pastoral training; Walter, Kath, Joyce, Sylvia Fairhurst, and Derek Norbury, a gay man who had become more involved in the church since Simon's arrival. They began to hold regular Monday morning meetings at the Rectory, after morning prayer in the church. These were meant to be sort of ecclesiastical power breakfasts with all the spiritual refuelling already done, and practical application thereof to be sorted out. As a rule they would discuss the Bible readings for the next Sunday and its implications for them, for the parish and the wider world, and would also make practical arrangements for church activities such as funerals and weddings for the rest of the week. These meetings became for everyone a key moment of preparation for the week, and for visitors staying at the Rectory there was a comfortable routine to the familiar faces arriving at the door, Kath making the coffee, and everyone settling themselves comfortably on the sofas.

The pastoral work was a significant development for all of them and they shared the ideas they discussed with others. 'Joyce has been one of the most articulate about how important it has been to her,' Simon commented, 'using her gifts and finding out how much she could be stretched.' Indeed the Bishop of Sheffield had this observation to make when I talked to him in 1995, 'One of the most remarkable aspects of Simon's ministry is the creation of a significant number of people in his image and after his likeness, with a spirituality and prayerfulness and a concern for beauty which isn't really the hallmark of an average South Yorkshire parish church, I have to say. They may not even realise how unusual they are.' The relationship was one of mutual benefit as Margaret Selby, the diocesan worker responsible for pioneering the Pastoral Workers' Scheme and a good friend of Simon's, commented to me in 1995. She stressed that for Simon being a parish priest, working as part of a community, was of critical importance, 'I don't think taking him out to be a canon in a cathedral would have been right, he would have lost so much in a more rarified atmosphere, he might have lost his edge. Somehow he is fairly sure of who is, so he allows other people to be who they are. It all goes back to the Eucharist – the important thing about the Eucharist for Simon is that he lives in Dinnington. He does it there because he lives there.'

Nobody had asked Simon if he was gay when he was interviewed for the job in Dinnington. It wasn't really a conscious factor then, though in today's more sensitised climate, it would be a much more likely consideration. 'What about marriage?' they had enquired then. Simon had dissimulated, interpreting the question as one about a current topic of debate, the marriage of divorced people in church. He then added, with perfect truthfulness but a profound ambiguity at which he was to become adept, 'As for me I'm happily single but not celibate.'

Whether he should have told them he was gay remains contentious. He said in one of the 1995 BBC Everyman interviews,[3] that he chose not to, in part, because he didn't want to become a 'single issue' priest. 'It is an important part of my life but certainly not the main part. Being an openly gay priest in the Church of England would inevitably attract the kind of attention that would make it the major feature of your life.' So it is ironic that he was destined to become not just known for being gay, but for having AIDS as well.

In any case, most of his parishioners admit that had he told them he was gay when he applied for the job, they would undoubtedly have replied, 'Not in Dinnington thank you very much.' Sam Robinson, interviewed in 1995, was quite forthright, 'I've said before, Simon would never have been in Dinnington had he said he was gay, had he said I'm gay and

HIV – phew, they wouldn't have stopped talking for six months. Some people have said it wouldn't have made any difference. Well that's rubbish.'

It did not, however, take long for some people in the parish to realise that Simon was gay. On the whole it seems that those who did realise also accepted it. It didn't matter to Joyce Robinson, for example, 'We did know as soon as we had contact with Simon. But we mixed with the local amateur dramatic society which had a lot of gay people, and such a lot were our friends, so it didn't worry us in the least whether he was gay.' Margaret also recalled, 'I'm pretty sure I knew Simon was gay, probably from all the friends he had. But you didn't talk about it to other people. And Simon never would have flaunted it. Ninety per cent of people didn't even have the remotest idea, he never gave any indication, he was not effeminate, some gay people have got mannerisms and you know straight away, but Simon was just a young man living alone.' Kath too says she had always known Simon was gay. It had been mentioned at a meeting they both attended soon after he came to Dinnington. It didn't bother her, why should it?

Simon deliberately told a few people he was homosexual in the first year or two, as he said to me, 'One or two guessed though most don't seem to have. It was mostly women and not all that many of them really. It was always my intention to tell more and more people, slowly disseminate it as personal information rather than a public announcement.' Jenny Bott was one of the first people in whom he confided. Jenny and a neighbour, whom Simon had also got to know quite well, were sitting in Jenny's house, sewing new vestments, a gold chasuble, for Easter. Simon dropped in for a cup of tea with them. He recalled, 'They were two people I relaxed with very much and felt close to quickly. I felt like being that bit more open with people, rather than the straightforward priest–congregation relationship.' They didn't really say much in response to this revelation at the time. Simon said to me later, 'I would have worried if the relationship had changed subsequently, but it didn't.'

The women do seem to have found it easier to cope with, and it seems to have been their husbands who often found it more difficult, sometimes stopping church attendance altogether. It may have been more difficult on a personal level for the men to deal with homosexuality, but they also seem to have been more inclined to think through the moral implications of Simon's ambivalent position. People didn't always respond as expected, however. Simon told another woman when they went out for a walk, who said it didn't bother her – but, 'if you ever touched my son I would kill you!' It must have hurt. 'I think I said that the connection was a false one. So I had obviously got *her* wrong, and I discovered subsequently that she was really quite racist and homophobic.'

For several years then, Simon managed this tightrope of some people knowing, some not having the remotest idea, and nobody really talking about it. He continued to have regular parties at the Rectory, not just for the parish but for friends as well. He happily mixed everyone together, which meant there were often gay friends and our parents there at the same time. Jenny Bott recalls one occasion when Simon came into the kitchen and begged her to separate Father from an argument with one of his gay friends.

My sister Caroline, then seventeen, lived with Simon at the Rectory for a year between 1986 and 1987 because my parents moved to the South of England where my father become a Baptist minister once more. Caroline was about to start her last year of A levels so it was decided she would stay with Simon. She and Simon developed a close and deeply spiritual bond of affection, and it was during that time Simon told her he was gay, finding an opportunity after watching an episode of a soap opera with a homosexual storyline together. She says she was shocked then, that it was not something she had ever thought about before, but Simon gave her a novel to read about a boy growing up gay which helped her to understand. She more than any of us was able to share both parts of his life, although she was aware of the split between his parish life and his Friday nights out, dancing.

There was a small gay community in Dinnington when Simon arrived, centred round the Dinnington Players, a classic 1950s style theatre group. Derek Norbury, one of the few openly gay men in the village, was a keen member. They would have liked Simon to become more involved, especially since he was interested in theatre and they had heard about the mystery play he had produced in his previous parish. But Simon made it pretty clear that the Players was emphatically not the kind of theatre in which he was interested, and the poor Players ceased to function within a year or so of his arrival. Simon was invited out to gay pubs with them, but he said he kept them at arm's length because he didn't really want to be involved in gay life in Dinnington.

Simon and Derek never actually discussed their homosexuality, but once Derek realised the situation he was much encouraged by Simon's quiet presence. It had never been easy being gay in Dinnington, 'You get the sniggers and people laughing at you behind your back,' he said regretfully, and he had always felt tentative about his involvement in the church. He is a tall, well-built man with a neat blond moustache; he used to work as a foreman on a building site, but retired because of ill-health. He lives with a partner and two over-fed dogs, in a house stuffed with ornaments and pictures, the tiny well-tended garden full of gnomes and little statues.

Simon also took the step of telling one of his church superiors. Stephen Lowe became Archdeacon in 1988. He had a reputation as a liberal and Simon saw this as his chance to tell someone in the hierarchy. Stephen Lowe recalled, 'He took an immense risk, at that first meeting with a new Archdeacon. He told me he was gay, and we talked and shared for a long time. I had been weighed up very carefully. I didn't actually bother asking whether he was still practising – it's not an issue for me. But I didn't share that fact with the Bishop, who probably did have an inkling, till four or five years later.'

Despite these tentative overtures, Simon's homosexual identity was still a whole area of his life he was obliged to keep separate, as he wrote in his journal, 'I suppose the contrast from "outside" must seem stark – and I'm just so used to it (you can imagine the tabloid headlines "secret life of gay vicar") and yet for me there genuinely is no contradiction. What is the "gay scene" anyway except the place where I see and relax with friends – and where I can dance ... I would prefer both lives to be different – more open generally to each other, not just to me; they are both part of the kingdom for me.'

'the meaning is in the waiting'

*Experiencing the present purely is being emptied and hollow;
you catch grace as a man fills his cup under a waterfall.*[1]

Annie Dillard, *Pilgrim at Tinker Creek*

For some years Simon remained well, without symptoms,
returning for regular checks at the hospital, but otherwise suc-
cessfully putting aside the HIV diagnosis for most of the time.
The issue arose frequently enough anyway. Stories about AIDS
were beginning to appear in the press in the year or two after
his diagnosis. There was a great deal of fear and very limited
knowledge of the disease. Margaret Thatcher and her government were struggling with the issue, appalled by the prospect
of having to issue explicit warnings about unsafe sex.[1]

The first warnings which appeared in the press only served
to confuse people further. In 1986 came the famous tombstone
advertisement, intoned by John Hurt, 'Don't die of ignorance.'
This was accompanied by leaflets distributed to every household. Safe sex campaigns directed specifically at gay men did
not appear until 1989, and it is generally agreed that had the
government acted earlier when news of the disease first
appeared, they could have warned many more people and
avoided more deaths.[2]

In 1986 and 1987 there were many programmes and articles
about AIDS, and the tabloids exploited every angle. An Anglican
priest who was working as a prison chaplain died of AIDS and
the story made headlines, 'The Church has AIDS!' Official
church guidelines were issued on pastoral care for people with
HIV and AIDS. But confusion remained about it. In 1987
churchgoers at Kings College were urged not to drink from the
chalice but to dip bread instead. The chaplain insisted that it

was more for the benefit of those with AIDS, 'Carriers of the disease are more vulnerable.'

In Dinnington too some members of the congregation expressed concern about the safety of the chalice at communion. In the parish magazine in 1986 Simon responded, 'I am assured by the best medical authorities that there is *no* likelihood of catching AIDS this way. Despite the press, AIDS is not particularly contagious except by direct *sexual* contact. The chalices are as a matter of course carefully wiped while in use and carefully washed afterwards; this has always been done. The tragedy of AIDS is that there is no cure or treatment – pray for those who have AIDS and for all who are at risk.' Simon continued to drink from the chalice first. He did consider changing his order of service so that he would be last to drink from the chalice, but significantly he decided against it. It would have been the first step on a path of compromise which he increasingly found it impossible to follow.

In 1987 Simon wrote again in the parish magazine about AIDS. His subject was the promise of new life at Easter. 'One of the places where all this comes into focus for us at the moment is the spread of the disease AIDS ... It is life of this kind the church must be offering to our brothers and sisters who are suffering and dying of AIDS – and other similar diseases. "Perfect love casts out fear," says St John and our fear of death has to give way to love. We know now that the fear is irrational – AIDS is not easily caught, sex and blood-to-blood contact are the only ways, so our task is to let the love cast out the fear. For this reason it is vital – since it is safe – not to change our practice with the chalice at communion.* To change would be the sign of fear, shunning those who suffer: not to change is a little sign of solidarity with the suffering, a little sign of love and commitment. (If the predictions are correct in a few years time we will all find ourselves directly involved, knowing people who suffer.)' This, surely, was an intimation of trials to come.

Alma, then curate of Ordsall near Retford, had been on an AIDS training day at Westcott, and she gave a talk to St

---

* that is, dipping bread instead of drinking directly from the cup.

Leonard's about AIDS and pastoral issues after a parish council meeting in 1987. She remembers the occasion with wry hindsight, 'I didn't realise the dynamic, I knew he was *gay* . . . Simon said he had been getting questions about the issue; the church warden at the time was still concerned about the dangers of the chalice. All churches had received a directive from the Archbishop about AIDS and the chalice; the point was that under the rules of the church precious metal and fermented wine already minimises transmission, otherwise the clergy who finish up the wine would have every disease going, but for appearance sake, you always wipe the chalice and switch it round before the next communicant.

'I showed a Health Education Council video and gave out leaflets – I erred on the impersonal side, talking more about the disease, not so much about sympathy or pastoral care. One woman went for me and said I hadn't condemned immorality. I said I wasn't asked to do that, I was asked to talk about a disease. And Simon sat at the back, impassive . . . So I did rather look back on that and think what the hell did I say! Had I known I might have been even fiercer, I get so protective.'

The ironies for Simon were abundant. He taught a course for several years on making moral decisions as part of the annual pastoral workers training scheme, devising a role play between parents and their HIV-positive student son. The activity always raised many issues and generated intense discussion, but as Simon observed in a sermon, 'What it showed most sadly was that the people playing the parents were . . . so confused and insecure about sexuality in general that they never paid any attention to the person in trouble.'

One year two people were chosen to play pastoral workers, and were not told in advance of the problem with which they would be confronted; someone who was HIV-positive, who couldn't talk to his parents, nor to the vicar, but might come to them. Simon remembered it, 'It always challenged them; each year they went through all the classic things, some of them were very good, knew all about it, but one of them, after welcoming him into her kitchen, said,' Simon put on a broad Yorkshire accent, ' "Oh and I've just given him a cup of tea . . .!" She apologised afterwards – I don't think she'll react like that again!'

The most dramatic response was when Simon briefed the person supposed to be HIV, and they said they simply couldn't handle it. So Simon had to play the role himself. 'So I sat there saying I'm HIV-positive . . . I wonder if that particular group – who must have seen the papers and stories about me by now, see the irony of it . . . it certainly felt bizarre.' Then he laughed, 'But then they said I wasn't very convincing . . .!' As we giggled together it was one of those strange occasions when you wonder, how on earth can I be laughing at this? There is a catharsis in laughter as well as tears, I suppose. I wondered, I asked him, if it was a way for him to explore what might happen to him when he told people? 'I wasn't consciously seeing what it would be like for me. But I was very aware of it myself, and as an issue to explore. I suppose I was subconsciously working it through. But it was so unreal . . . it was a separate thing.'

He continued to keep his life in separate compartments. One night a week he would go out with gay friends to a pub or gay club in Sheffield, Manchester or Leeds, and what he most liked to do was dance. It was a truly liberating experience, 'There is something holistic – body-and-soul-together about dancing, something free and just responsive, relaxed and uninhibiting . . .' his journal records. His friend Andrew remembered how he would often spend an entire evening dancing with total concentration, all his energy focussed. It is an image I always treasure, that conveys better than anything else the idea of gay liberation.

There were several tentative relationships in those years, and some that actually lasted quite a long time, but always they were coloured by Simon's desire for autonomy and his encouragement of it in others too. He truly wrestled with the conflict between loneliness and independence. 'I am lonely though my odd pride prevents me admitting it – yet I also know, think I know, I couldn't live with anyone.' He was so determined to be self-sufficient. But his lofty aspirations always seemed to fall apart as soon as he met someone new, 'What is this overwhelming need for someone else. I want to be protected, sheltered, held, not at all possessed, but held . . .' he writes in his journal, but his conclusion is desolate, 'There is no consolation – we are each of us alone: and even in love we are shoring fragments against our ruin. You have to stand alone first before anything else.'

His relationships with lovers always seemed to founder over this problem, and I can't help thinking he must have been a difficult person to be involved with; so idealistic and so naïve at the same time. In one instance he split up with a long-term partner because he had not told him he was HIV-positive. It was only when his partner saw the drugs he was taking and guessed what they were for that he confronted Simon, finding it impossible to accept that he would not have shared something so important. I found it pretty hard to accept too, though it is the fact that he did not want to share the knowledge with someone he was closely involved with that I find most difficult to comprehend.

Nevertheless it raised serious questions about responsibility, and I questioned Simon about the issue. It was difficult since I had no desire to enquire closely into his specific sexual preferences, but Simon understood the need for me to discuss it. He said that there had only been one partner who might have conceivably been at risk before he was aware of his diagnosis, that he had contacted them, and that they had thankfully tested negative. Once he knew his diagnosis he said he had never put anyone at risk. For Simon this was a pretty unambiguous statement, and given his desire to be as truthful as he could be, and the degree to which he had already revealed many things to me, I believe this to be the truth.

Simon understood that his fear of intimacy and dependence was wrapped up with the fear of exploring his own pyschic depths, those nether regions of desire and fear which most of us, most of the time, keep well battened down. 'How far does one go in this following of instinct-need-desire?' he asks, 'More and more is exposed of the deeper psyche. It is a deep pool if you start swirling it around, you disturb all the water, not just the surface – and you stir up the sediment at the bottom so that it surfaces: especially in dreams. You may find out what is there but it can be alarming to do so.'

Consciously he devoted little time to worrying about his HIV diagnosis or his future prospects, but his dreams, which he increasingly noted down, reveal his anxieties. He dreamt about his own funeral: 'only I seemed to be speaking at it . . .' and dreamed often of his schoolfriend Ashok who had committed suicide. It was one event, one experience which was impossible ever to resolve. Perhaps he could learn to understand his own death, but he never understood why Ashok died, Ashok had never confided in him, and there was no way he was ever going to find out. It was perhaps one of the few wounds that always remained.

The unresolved conflict with my father is also revealed in his dream notes, most of all the degree to which Simon was still struggling to escape his influence and dominance. One dream was rapidly scribbled down in the middle of the night as soon as he woke, 'my father holding me and he was holding me tighter and tighter and I was saying louder and louder, "Let go of me, let go of me." ' I do not know whether it was Simon's vocation or his sexuality but he seemed to remain in thrall to my father to a much greater extent than the rest of us.

His journals reveal that he was slowly beginning to understand that coming to terms with AIDS meant he could not keep it separate from the rest of his life any more. 'It may be that HIV is a metaphor for myself – the dis-ease within that is about inevitable restraint in relationship . . . so conversely if I can begin to do something about that then the metaphor begins to be changed . . .' He realised he needed help, needed someone outside the parish to share his spiritual journey and perhaps, too, to provide support on the rocky path of illness looming ahead. So he began to see a spiritual director on a regular basis. The idea of a spiritual director is an ancient one, increasingly revived today. It is a relationship that differs significantly from that of a patient and analyst, since both director and those seeking direction know that they are on the same path with similar spiritual objectives. (The confidential nature of the relationship means that I won't identify the person who fulfilled this role.) Simon said he never found it particularly easy to articulate his feelings, but the opportunity nevertheless provided a critical buttress of support.

Despite the threat of AIDS, or perhaps because of it, he also began to explore further the connection between his spirituality – his priestly vocation, and his sexuality. He found several sympathetic people in Sheffield, in particular Nancy Johnson, a tall, earthy, Cornish woman who worked for the diocese on marriage and family issues and was the diocesan contact with the

Lesbian and Gay Christian Movement. She had little time for church convention but a lot of time for the kind of spiritual journey on which Simon had embarked and they formed an alternative spiritual group which was a very important focus for them both. Simon often dropped in to see her when he was in Sheffield, enjoying her warm family kitchen, the steep town garden with·its guinea pigs and rabbits, the company of her children, the youngest of whom was his god-daughter. Jim Cotter was another close and supportive friend in Sheffield. He too is a gay Anglican priest, and runs a small publishing company and retreat house in the city. His frank acceptance and celebration of his homosexuality helped Simon greatly. Jim also supported Simon's writing and published one of Simon's own book of prayers.

Simon began to crystallise his ideas about gay spirituality. Like women, gay people could transcend conventional sprituality, he felt. In his journal he reflected, 'The idea that not having a convention and tradition, a model for gay relationships, is an advantage – that hadn't occurred to me – but it surely is: you are alone to find your own way – nothing between you and God . . .' This was new territory, and he often invoked a phrase of Jim Cotter's about being 'God's spies' – pilgrims in a new land.

He began to write and talk more openly on the subject. At an LGCM meeting in Leeds in 1988 he gave a talk, exploring his ideas, 'Do gay people pray differently?'[3] He believed that what he termed 'gay prayer' should involve joining the ranks of the oppressed, a 'liberation spirituality', stressing, 'If we are going to pray like this we shall have to get our arms and our praying hearts around AIDS, around its huge burden of accompanying fear.' He valued the self-awareness that could result from the need to consciously analyse sexual and spiritual motivation, 'One thing this self-awareness seems to mean for many gay people is a deeper, stronger consciousness of the body (and indeed sex as part of the body).'

Perhaps most radically he believed the critical characteristic of gay spirituality was the threat to the institution of the family. 'It has to be shown that there are other ways of living than in family, other equal, possibly greater relationships. We could give so much to each other in a mutuality of sexualities – and straight people might actually rejoice in what gay people can give to their children.' He believed passionately in the idea of friendship as the paradigm human relationship, ultimately more important than family. 'The fact that Mary was a friend of Jesus was more important than that she was his mother,' he insisted. He often refers to friends (for example in the dedication to his book, *The Well Within*) and it is understood that this includes his family. And he was fond of reminding Mother of the moment when Jesus refuses to acknowledge his own family at the door, saying that everyone was his family now. (Poor Mother.)

Simon continued to think deeply about spiritual matters, refining his image of God as something deeper, wider, less definable than the orthodox patriarchal figure. It was the beauty of the universe which convinced him of the existence of some kind of God. And although his faith remained strong, it did not promise him life after death. Increasingly, he did not believe in it. 'It is a radical break not to believe in life after death. What I feel is the ease with which we evade the reality of death's annihilation.' What he wanted was to respond to the 'mystery in things' to apprehend the divine in every aspect of life. He starts from these epiphanies. 'It's the ability to recognise the numinous at any moment, however strange and unexpected, the spirit-laden moment.' He loved the image of water, waves, streams, waterfalls, the well, the sense of sustenance and renewal, depth and continuity, and the idea of the wave as an integral part of the whole. He was always taking photos of the sea, sunlight catching the waves. He loved the song in *The Tempest*, his favourite Shakespeare play, 'Full Fathom Five thy father lies . . .' and the line 'a sea change into something rich and strange', which is how he describes the possibility of prayer. 'The sea change of prayer is that moment, any moment, every moment when we see into the meaning of things, the heart of things.' The song was one of the readings he suggested for his funeral.

He loved holy places and the idea of pilgrimage, as he wrote in a series of talks on contemplative prayer, 'Pilgrimage seems to be growing again in our world – surely because we're sensing again the "serious earth", the significance of places, of prayed-in places, of people who have made places sacred.' In his talk on prayer he encouraged his listeners to remember a moment

of their own, 'Taste it again, whatever it was – in church, on
the sea, up a mountain, listening to music, with your partner, a
friend.' And he observes presciently that it may well be a sad
moment, a moment of suffering. 'The sense of the presence
often comes to us fully, more deeply there than anywhere
else . . . recall that moment, that time, recall the grace, observe
the shape and the feeling within you of what was then given to
you . . . and with it now quietly pray.' For himself he is learning
to wait, to find value in the waiting itself. R.S. Thomas expressed
it perfectly, 'Moments of great calm/Kneeling before an altar/
Of wood in a stone church/ In summer, waiting for the God/
To speak . . ./The meaning is in the waiting.'

His holidays were always an endearing mixture of pilgrimage
and tourism. He went often to all his favourite places: Whitby
and the Yorkshire moors, his beloved Celtic islands, Holy Island,
Iona, and Lindisfarne. He went to Ireland several times, revel-
ling in its rich Celtic history. He often went on holiday with
Alma, perhaps the person with whom he relaxed most; they
seemed to spark in each other a kind of camp humour and
relished the same absurdities. They loved to go shopping
together and shared an insatiable appetite for knick-knacks and
craft shops.

In 1987 Alma and Simon went on holiday to Greece, not
very sure of where they were being sent by Dinnington's travel
agent. They ended up on Ios, a slightly incongruous couple on
the beaches crowded with lager louts, but Simon went dancing
with great enthusiasm. They spent one Sunday searching unsuccessfully for a mass in which to participate, much as they would
spy out the kind of tea shop they liked in England. They
gazed longingly at a monastery perched inaccessibly on a high
mountain top, and the island itself became a metaphor for him,
'The pace has slowed so that somehow the place mirrors the
interior map . . . the sea fringe and its superficialities – and then
that barren interior, the peaks, the emptiness, the occasional
shrouding cloud and in particular that fascinating monastery –
or whatever – on the highest peak, inaccessible, intriguing,
unassailable . . .' But then sometimes, his own tragedy breaks
through. In Iona in 1987 there is a heartbreaking, brief note in
his journal, 'I seem to be permanently on the edge of tears.'

Towards the end of 1987, two years after Simon arrived in Dinnington, the storm clouds really began to gather. There was a lot of negative media coverage of homosexuality and AIDS, and at the same time the issue of homosexuality in the church was becoming more and more heated, and attracting more media attention. The notorious Clause 28, an amendment to the Local Government Bill, which forebade councils and their schools from promoting the acceptability of homosexuality, became a *cause célèbre* galvanising prominent homosexuals, such as Sir Ian McKellen, to declare themselves.

Then came the controversial General Synod of 1987, and the tabloids trawled for gay vicar stories. One particular article which appeared in the Sunday *People* the week before General Synod, was uncomfortably close to home. A vicar in the diocese had been set up by another priest who had secretly tape recorded their conversation. The vicar believed his colleague had come to discuss his own problems, but he was tricked into advising on homosexuality in a way that could be interpreted as speaking of himself. His remarks were deliberately twisted and headlined in the *People*. The cleric in question did not resign however, and was supported by the Bishop of Sheffield. But it was much discussed in the diocese – how must Simon have felt knowing this was the treatment meted out to gay clergy by the media?

Both AIDS and homosexuality were on the agenda of the General Synod in November 1987. The subject of AIDS was debated and although great concern and pity were expressed, the issue inevitably fuelled the homophobia of the fundamentalist faction. The following day Tony Higton's controversial motion condemning homosexuality was discussed. He proposed that 'homosexual acts' should be regarded as 'sinful in all circumstances' (and that clergy should adhere to that as a condition of being in office.) Rev. Malcolm Johnson, an openly gay Anglican priest, was then running the St Botolph's centre in the city of London for homeless people, and organised support groups for gay clergy. He proposed (unsuccessfully) a motion that would give acceptance to all committed relationships, regardless of sexual orientation, 'The essential of the Biblical message', was that 'human love is a reflection of divine love and should be characterised by the permanency and commitment of relationships'.

Although Higton's motion was rejected, the Synod did accept the motion that 'homosexual genital acts' fall short of the ideal of sex 'within a permanent married relationship'. It was the first time the Anglican church had made such an explicit statement of its position on homosexuality, and meant that many gay priests were totally compromised. It polarised an issue which had previously been quietly avoided, and which continued to become more and more of a challenge to the church.*

Simon reacted to the Synod vote with great anger. The following Sunday he preached a sermon on the church and morality which to this day is still referred to as That Sermon in Dinnington. He began dramatically, instructing his congregation to imagine very different headlines in the morning paper's after the Synod vote. '*Church says to adulterers, fornicators and homosexuals – "We do not condemn you."* All the leader writers and the rent-a-quote MPs would have frothed at the mouth at a church gone so trendy and sloppy, no backbone, no fibre, no moral sense any more. Well they didn't need to worry of course because the church in its debate on sexual morality on Wednesday didn't say anything of the kind.'

He made a comparison to the occasion when Jesus was confronted with the woman taken in adultery, 'The report in the papers then would have been *"Teacher says to adulteress – I do not condemn you"* and then he emphasised his point, 'The first and over-riding principle in christian morals is not the making of clear rules and sharp dividing lines – the first principle is "No

---

* It is generally believed that a sizeable minority of the clergy of the Church of England are homosexual – estimates range from 15–30 per cent, with some suggestion that a far larger proportion of Anglican clergy are homosexual compared to the rest of the population.

A study of clergy and stress, by Dr Ben Fletcher suggests several reasons for this; the church may provide homosexuals with a channel for parental instincts of caring; being homosexual results in subtle and explicit emotional persecution from an early age which may develop into greater concern for those in a vulnerable position; some may turn towards the spiritual and religious in an attempt to understand their sexuality, or to channel their frustrated sexual energies.

Dr Fletcher paints a sad picture; he concludes that homosexual clergy are more likely to suffer stress because they do not have the benefit of being able to live with a partner, and even have to distance themselves from the parish community, as well as other friends, clergy, etc. They are also more likely to suffer from problems of identity, psychological isolation and societal pressures and face deep questioning about their own sexuality

Moreover, he says the very vocation of the clergyman may also require a homosexual clergyman to become a central figure in the lives of a community who share a different set of sexual and moral values. This is particularly likely in the case of the parish priest. The community focus of the job, which provides a great basis of support for the heterosexual clergyman can therefore be a major source of stress for the homosexual.

It is interesting therefore that in Simon's case it was the community that actually provided the support.

condemnation" – christianity is not about guilt but about this sigh of relief – "not condemned" knowing that we find ourselves free to set about making that good life, living better.'

He paused in his sermon, while the Sunday morning congregation sitting in the pews looked up at the pulpit, wondering what on earth he was going to say next, 'What is it that makes us so anxious to lay down laws for other people's lives – especially their private sexual lives? Why do we so completely fail to trust them to have consciences of their own? Why on earth do we believe that pronouncements of the church will make the slightest difference except to harden people's attitudes to an increasingly moralistic institution? There is some deep seated and disturbing insecurity in us, an insecurity about our own identity and our own behaviour that makes us want to legislate for others, to dictate how they must behave even in private – we hanker for a power over others that we don't have over ourselves ... This does not remove from the church any role in discussing and guiding in morality though it does basically alter the approach. We cease to lay down laws and declare ourselves "not like other men", rather in this way we join with the "wounded surgeon" who knows how to heal because he is wounded himself...' He ended, 'The new radically free Christian behaviour is best summed up in the stark, glad, risky, freedom of St Augustine's phrase, "Love and do as you like." Now there's a headline for the *Sun*.' Although Simon did not explicitly declare himself gay, most people got the message.[4]

Sylvia Fairhurst still remembers it well, 'Simon was so indignant about the Synod vote. You could have dropped a pin, nobody coughed, there was complete silence, everybody clicked. I was absolutely shattered, it wasn't something I'd ever really thought about, I thought to myself – how can he be a vicar if he's homosexual? But the sermon was good. It altered attitudes, it made you think.'

After the sermon several people came and told Simon that it was the best sermon they had ever heard, the most helpful and thought provoking. To his surprise no-one expressed disagreement. But the next day at the Mothers Union jumble sale there was passionate discussion and very strong disapproval. A meeting was arranged to discuss the issue of homosexuality and the church, which became very heated indeed with a stand-up row between two of the parishioners. Derek Norbury's name was also brought up, and this caused further shock, as some people hadn't even realised Derek was gay.

Simon himself was most appalled that none of the dissenters had felt able to speak to him directly about the sermon. So two weeks later he abandoned the raised stone pulpit, and thereafter preached his sermons from a simple wooden lectern close to the congregation. In his sermon that first time he declared, 'I want to make a crack in the power of the clergy, the kind of authority that comes with standing up above you; the pulpit for me is a powerful symbol of separation and authority and I want that to end ... I am no different from you, not holier, not stronger, not better. I continue to believe that I am set apart, I strive to hear what God says to me for you, but I'm not perfect, not special, but trying like you to be a clear channel of grace.'

Increasingly Simon was becoming frustrated by the traditional authoritarian role of the priest, and he constantly questions it in his journal, 'so unrealistic, so inhuman, so pious, so "pure" ... I want to be allowed to be me.' One woman beseeched him to return to the pulpit, as he described in an article he wrote subsequently for the *Church Times*, 'It's where I belong, I am above them, she said ... For me it was a little sign, a gesture. The empty pulpit is now an eloquent symbol to me of vacated power ... How am I going to persuade that woman – and the rest – who want me back in the pulpit? Strong, thinking, free people who still want me six feet above them? I think she has to know that I can't stay alive (alive for them – and for me) trapped up there; she has to know that I'm as human as she is; I laugh and I cry and I swear – and eventually she has to see that being in the Body of Christ together means there is no room for power and dominance and that kind of authority.'

The move from the pulpit was another step in his journey to meet his parishioners in humility as the wounded healer. This questioning of his role as a priest helped him adjust when the time came to become the cared for instead of the carer, a step so hard for a priest or anyone whose primary role is caring for others.

Meanwhile the day-to-day realities of parish life went on; the church roof was leaking, the flag was stolen from the top of the flagpole, both the youth club and the choir were declining in numbers (though the scouts and brownies were thriving.) In 1989 a curate was appointed, a reflection in part of the Bishop's estimation of Simon's ability to train others. Bob Fitzharris, a warm-hearted family man, given to embracing Simon with bearish hugs, cheerfully shared the work of the parish. Simon was relieved from some of the day-to-day burden of parish work, and could concentrate more on other work, especially writing.

He increasingly found a need to express himself more directly through writing. Poetry was his great love, and often he develops an idea from the journals into a poem. Several poems were published in gay and Christian anthologies.[5] He continued to write articles, for the *Church Times* and other religious publications and occasionally for the *Guardian*, recounting some ironic tale of parish life. He also published two books of prayers which have sold steadily ever since. He took up calligraphy and the 'self-forgetting' required to concentrate fully was to prove a very therapeutic activity.

He also began writing a book, a biography of a controversial Anglican monk, Dom Gregory Dix.[6] Simon was suggested as a possible author by another monk, Brother Kenneth of Mirfield, who had always encouraged his writing. Dix was both monk and scholar, a member of the first Benedictine Anglican monastic community to be established in Britain earlier this century, and an influential figure in the Anglo-Catholic movement. In his writing Dix stressed the value of contemplation, the centrality of the Eucharist, the importance of Christian community and of involving laity in the church liturgy. All were concerns close to Simon's heart. I am sure his close analysis of the spiritual life of another must have helped his own self-analysis, although the fact that Dix himself died of cancer at 51, at the height of his career, must always have been painfully apparent as Simon wrote.

Although it was a difficult subject and research material was rather sparse, Simon was delighted by the opportunity, and immersed himself in the study of liturgy and church history that the subject required; it gave him the opportunity for challenging academic study which he had missed since leaving Cambridge.

His appreciation of monastic life and the value of retreat also increased, as he visited the various monasteries and colleges where Dix had lived. He spent a lot of time at Elmore Abbey, the Anglican Benedictine monastery in Hampshire, where Dom Gregory's community was now established. The Abbot of Elmore soon became a dear friend, and Simon cherished his unorthodox habits, in particular his fondness for walking round with a mobile phone clamped to his ear. Simon enjoyed regaling us with tales of the monks, their fondness for television, the food they cooked for themselves. He loved the tradition of eating in silence while one of the brethren read to the community; although sometimes the books, 'so piously chosen' as Simon observed, proved somewhat surprising in content.

I had always wondered if Simon might end up a monk himself, and to me it is still one of the surprising things about him, that with such an obvious means of escape from the potential problems of developing AIDS as a parish priest, he did not retreat to monastic sanctuary but chose instead to remain very much in the world. Instead his study of the work of Gregory Dix deepened his sense of Christian community.

The book also provided a good opportunity to travel more widely. Dix had spent some time in the USA establishing a sister monastery there, so Simon followed in his footsteps in 1988. He went to stay with an American woman soon to be an ordained priest in Long Island. They went sailing off Montauk, and in the photos of him then he looks so healthy, almost a jock with his new cropped hairstyle, shorts and t-shirt. Then he went by bus to the monastery in Michigan into 'the slow rhythm of the Benedictines,' as he put it. No-one with his passion for waterfalls could fail to visit Niagara Falls, and it fulfilled all his expectations, 'It has that steady pull downwards – down and down, so oddly inviting – it's like the sea in a waterfall.'

The spiritual metaphors were never far away; even a long wait in a bus station produced spiritual imagery, 'the night hours at Albany were the most tedious and yet the most symbolic – the waiting, the "sounds of night".' Manhattan simply overwhelmed him, 'I was flooded with it – autumn leafy light, Central Park, St Thomas' Church, the quiet contrast . . . and the people, so many quietly begging people.' Most poignant was his visit to the Museum of Modern Art, where there was a photographic exhibition of people with AIDS, 'the pictures of the AIDS victims' posed – so ironic, and yet blatant, brutal but inexorable'.

Simon continued to visit the clinic at the Royal Hallamshire Hospital on a weekly basis; he always went regularly (though often people who are HIV-positive but still healthy, prefer not to be monitored.) In December 1988 he agreed to participate in the Concorde trial of drugs for HIV-positive patients, which assessed the benefits of AZT while patients were still healthy. Results of the trial, published in 1995, now suggest that the benefits are limited if any. AZT may even have a negative effect, so as the evidence emerged we began to think it was possible that Simon's participation in the trial may have had an adverse effect. As it turned out he was given the placebo in the trial.

His consultant throughout his illness remained Dr George Kinghorn, whom he had met when he was first diagnosed. Kinghorn, tall, brisk, with a hint of a Geordie accent, is now clinical director of the Department of Genito-urinary Medicine at the Royal Hallamshire Hospital. He had decided to specialise in genito-urinary medicine because it was an area where medicine could be curative, finding people before disease occurred, rather than palliative. The advent of AIDS was thus an ironic development; suddenly they had patients who were going to die. 'It was an emotional challenge as well as a clinical challenge to look after patients we eventually lost. It seemed rational to me to give complete care from the time of diagnosis till death.' Kinghorn explained to me.

In the early days there had been a degree of competition between disciplines as to who would treat AIDS patients, since once the disease is well advanced it exhibits such a variety of symptoms, from skin problems and parasitic infections to bronchial problems and pneumonia. Patients tended to vote with their feet, however, and went where they felt comfortable, not surprisingly to the genito-urinary department, which was already used to treating people suffering from sexually communicated diseases with discretion.

It was still very early days when Simon was diagnosed in 1985, Kinghorn explained. 'All that was known was that it was likely to be a life-shortening illness, but there was no therapy, no physical treatments, it was pre-AZT. We could do something about lifestyle factors that could exacerbate the condition and we could try to harness the psychological element.' Support was essential, 'We had to be there to help carry the load. It took us into difficult territory – with this condition the end point was death and doctors find death as difficult as anyone else.' The need for secrecy in many cases was particularly awesome; in this medical situation more than most it implied an element of the confessional more akin to the priesthood, 'You look after somebody for many years, sharing what is often a secret, a very important secret.' Kinghorn emphasised.

According to the medical notes Simon was still finding it very difficult to face the fact that he was HIV-positive, and he was reluctant to tell his Dinnington GP, although in the end he was obliged to when he had to call him out for something else. Dr Kinghorn lives very near to Dinnington and knows the village; he understood Simon's reluctance to tell a local GP and acknowledged that he had been worried about the reaction in the community if and when Simon's condition became known, 'I was concerned about how he was going to cope within the environment. Dinnington is a tough place, full of tough miners.'

In the spring of 1989 Simon's visits to the clinic revealed the first AIDS-related symptoms. He noted in his journal around this time, 'Everyone needs someone to hold them, even though we have to stand on our own two feet.' It is as if he is beginning to acknowledge the possibility of the need for others, for support. The opportunity to move on, to communicate, presented itself, all too easily, all too bleakly. His friend Andrew was also diagnosed HIV-positive in November 1989. He was very anxious about the results of the test and he asked Simon to go with him to the clinic. They sat in Simon's car together afterwards, rain drumming on the windscreen, and Andrew told him the result. Then Simon confided his own secret. Andrew remembered the occasion well, as he told me, 'Simon told me the same day, I was very ill, very nervous. In my own head I was thinking, that's it, I'll be dead the next day. Simon said, "I don't know if this is a good time to tell you" . . . but he did. And I felt relieved – he looked as healthy as me. It was a shock, but it felt nice; a real weight had been lifted off my shoulders.' They drove back to the Rectory in the pouring rain – and they talked. Andrew said, 'Even though I knew a little bit, I was thinking how many days have I got left. I had never had a sexually transmitted disease in my life, and now I've got the only you can't get rid of.'

It seems entirely characteristic that Simon should finally have told someone else his own diagnosis not in order to enlist support for himself, but in order to support them. I suppose that was his professional role, to find a way to make something positive of his own afflictions as a way to help others. It was not so much that he was being selfless but rather fulfilling the vocation that for him, made the most sense of his life. It was certainly a path he was to follow increasingly as his own illness progressed; using his own illness to articulate the pain of others. It was a path in which he was encouraged by his spiritual director, as his journal makes clear, 'It was suggested I take HIV sufferers etc., as a special burden, a private intention, always at mass – to carry them, and it, openly with me then. I can at least do that. What would it mean to befriend HIV/AIDS? To accept it, welcome it – stay with it? Can you do that?'

Simon continued to question his role as priest, and when his four-yearly Episcopal review came up in the autumn of 1990 he wrote in his report for the Archdeacon (who has particular responsibility for local clergy) about his desire to challenge the perceived power of the clergy, 'I want to find some way in the near future of encouraging a sense of "independence" in the parish. I'd like to see them launch out into control of their own world, in which clergy then really would be servants.'

The Archdeacon Stephen Lowe, then submitted his own report on Simon to the Bishop. He expressed his appreciation of the work Simon was doing in developing the pastoral work of the parishioners themselves, 'Simon has undertaken a remarkable piece of work in the development of lay ministry in Dinnington . . . his is a well-ordered, effective, caring and spiritual ministry.' Lowe particularly praised his gifts in liturgy and writing and described him as, 'a priest of integrity, hard work and self-discipline'. And he made a proposal for the future, 'I can see Simon blossoming as a residentiary Canon, having responsibility for the liturgy, music and artistic life of a Cathedral and having time to write. He is highly intelligent and will be a credit to some of the great Cathedrals of the country in this role and in five years' time or so maybe his next move should be in this direction.' It was not to be.

Instead Simon set to work developing the artistic life of Dinnington. He sometimes said that art was almost as important as religion for him; indeed at one point he mused, 'If I had to choose between art and religion I might choose art . . .' quoting William Blake, 'Christianity is art not money.' He took great pleasure in music and painting but perhaps most of all saw art too as a way of connecting the community and bringing people together, another way of deepening their spiritual experience. These thoughts led him to the idea of creating a memorial in the church for all the miners who had died down the pit. He had always been concerned that St Leonard's had no visible evidence of Dinnington as a mining community, that the pit had somehow been kept separate from the life of the church. The parish and the miners in particular responded eagerly to the proposal and Simon was determined that the work should involve as many members of the community as possible, as he had done with the miracle play at Norton.

He summarised his ideas in an article in the *Church Times*, which took the form of an open letter to the artists commissioned to create the memorial.[7] He argued that the ordinary working world and the church had to be connected, 'In the past some would have disputed the connection. Church was to escape the ordinary world, they might have said. I passionately oppose that view. A parish church should be woven into the fabric of ordinary life, and from there suggest other possibilities, hopes and longings.' He argues that the church had to be part of its local setting, 'The church as a place of depth in the community; a kind of well, a place of breathing.' The pit, he stressed, 'That hard, hidden and dangerous place that has so extensively fashioned and marked this village is not incidental to its life and meaning. It is not an accident but where this community finds an identity.'

That winter Peter Barnes first appeared. He was a local boy, only twenty, but had recently come out of prison; a glue-sniffer, burglar, convict, truant. He was also a poet. He first turned up on the doorstep in the middle of a snowy winter night, and asked to sleep in the garage. Simon was at home alone with three spare bedrooms so he invited him to stay. He gave him money and tried to help him, in particular through listening to his poetry. Then Peter would disappear – off to London, 'begging' he said, only to return again a few months later. Simon became very fond of him, and clearly felt an enormous responsibility. Simon's dreams turn this importunate stranger into a metaphor for AIDS, 'The stranger within – I dreamed very realistically of someone in the house – footprints, noises; they were "living" in the little room (I call it the "secret place"). It turned out to be Peter. It's obvious really – the stranger within, the rejected one . . .'

In early 1991 symptoms started in earnest as Simon began to have night sweats. 'I don't understand why I'm not much more frightened than I am,' he wrote, 'It's every gay man's fear . . . I have it and I seem to watch it detached from a distance. Is it just that I don't admit it? or have I faced the devil and seen that there is nothing there: nothing to fear?'

Meanwhile, the rest of the family was more preoccupied with birth. My son Theo was born in October 1990, and we had discussed the possibility of Simon acting as a birth companion for me, an idea we both liked very much. In the end it was hardly practical since we were such a distance apart. My sister Jackie was able to come, however, and support me along with my partner. She was pregnant herself and I remember resting my head during labour on her soft rounded belly, but I regret that Simon wasn't there. He would have got so much out of it, I realise now. And it would, perhaps, have brought us closer, made it easier for him to tell me before he did. But I can't help wondering – would he have told me then he was HIV-positive? Shouldn't he have in those circumstances? It is perhaps unfair to speculate about a hypothetical situation, but it focuses the issue of responsibility again and how much it was fair to keep his diagnosis so entirely secret. I don't know the answer.

I went to the Rectory for a family Christmas, with my new son. There is a photograph of Simon holding Theo and one of Simon watching me breastfeeding. Now they make me sad as I wonder if he thought about the fact that he would not see this child grow up. Then my sister's baby was born, in March, but complications meant that Jackie was very ill afterwards and we were very fearful she might even die. It was a very frightening period – , in retrospect the first intimation of mortality for all of us. Father characteristically begged her to come back to Jesus. Simon sent her a strange, harsh little poem, 'It was your life suddenly – /real as a slap to the face,/sharp as a twisted thorn's cut/to the stooping brow./

Forgotten the Suffering Sermons,/the pious talk of Carrying Your Cross, Your life/suddenly – /real/ as a nail through the wrist. (SPB 5.4.91).'

It was almost as if he was saying, now you know how it feels.

Then in June the hospital decided Simon should switch from the Concorde trial to open AZT. A significant drop in immunity (usually measured as the CD4 count) had been recorded. He wrote his reaction in his journal, '(The anniversary of my priesting . . .) Today I went on to AZT. It's like a gate, a new journey, a steeper bit of the path . . . with the test/trial I could pretend I was "helping the medics" now I'm "undergoing treatment".' He noted a quotation from Kafka. 'My fear is my substance, and probably the best part of me.' We talked about that moment later, that moment when Simon stopped helping them by participating in the trial, and had to take the drug to help himself; the moment when he stopped being the carer, and began to be cared for. It highlighted the whole issue of who cares for the carers, and how they have to learn to allow themselves to be cared for, too.

It was still a busy time for the rector. There was a parish visit to Cambridge, and Simon arranged for them all to visit Westcott House, his old theological college, where they ate their sandwiches in the college quadrangle, surrounded by the deep fragrance of wisteria. The principal of the college celebrated the Eucharist for them in the chapel, and afterwards someone commented to Simon that it was clear that was where he got his approach to liturgy; the gestures, movement and silences that characterised Simon's particular style of conducting services. The Rectory continued to be a centre of parish social activity with a cheese and wine party followed the next week by a parish garden party in the Rectory; lots of stalls with cake, games, bric-a-brac and refreshments. That summer there was a parish trip to Cumbrae, an island in the Firth of Clyde on the main shipping route to Glasgow. It has the smallest cathedral in Britain, the Cathedral of the Isles. They rode bikes and tricycles round the tiny island, which Simon found exhilarating, 'The Inner Circle they call that road – a journey within, a circling, a spiralling: I begin to talk to myself, to converse and to go on a little further along the way . . .'

Then that autumn Simon finally told Mother he was gay. My journal records her visit to me in London soon after and spending a lot of time discussing it. Of course she had known really, but now she knew officially, and wanted to talk about it. She was perhaps most concerned to work through the different theories – and hopefully deny the Freudian that my husband so firmly held. As a biographer (Barry Miles) of two homosexual men, Allen Ginsberg and William Burroughs, he has always been convinced that homosexuality is, fundamentally, traumatic. In each case he suggested it was possible to identify a specific traumatic experience which laid the basis for homosexuality. This seemed a bit different from Simon's perception of his homosexuality as a gift from God (well, maybe not – Simon would no doubt have figured it in somehow.) Whatever, I felt I had to tread very delicately. There seemed no point in Mother searching her soul for what she might have done wrong. The best thing for my mother it seemed was to believe that it is something you're born with and quite natural; as Simon often put it, like being right or left-handed. Now recent research seems to confirm that there may well be a genetic factor in homosexuality, and that about 5 per cent of the population inherit homosexuality as a biological trait. But we didn't know that then.

She had asked Simon then if he had had an HIV test, and he replied with his by now consummate ambiguity, 'There is no need.' It was not a lie but it was misleading, and if she had reached the point of asking him should he not by then have felt it was time to tell her? I asked him too at one stage if he should have a test, and his reply to me was equally ambiguous, 'I'd rather not.'

We then had the problem of Father. I realise now that he didn't want to know about his son's homosexuality, and the last thing to do would have been to force the knowledge on him, although there was a current of feeling in the family that Dad should be made to face it. In trying to deal with it he too would have agonised over whether it was in some way his fault. But until Mother knew officially she didn't have to feel she was deceiving my father. It could remain an unvoiced suspicion of her own. I think I had visions of Dad denouncing Simon. As it turned out there was no need to worry about Dad for long.

Ironically, as Simon noted in his journal, 'In a strange sort of way I've become a "role model" – a sign that you can be a parish priest and intellectual and imaginative, can be gay and an incumbent – I'm not sure that makes me very comfortable.' The idea didn't make the Bishops very comfortable either. In December 1991 the House of Bishops put out a statement called Issues in Human Sexuality,[8] which was an attempt to respond to the 1988 Lambeth Conference request that over the following decade all Bishops should undertake, 'a deep and dispassionate study of the question of homosexuality'. The statement drew the conclusion that monogamous, heterosexual union was 'the setting intended by God for the proper development of men and woman as sexual beings'. It made a sharp division between the behaviour of lay Christians and clergy. It specifically challenged the idea that same-sex love 'equally represents God's perfect intention for human sexuality', but it did acknowledge the integrity of lay homosexuals in faithful, permanent partnerships. However the clergy were called upon not to enter into active relationships and it urged 'support and affirmation for homosexual clergy who choose to live a life of abstinence'. Simon and many like him were still out in the cold.

The future looked bleak for Dinnington too. It was earlier that year that the pit closure was announced, adding ironic poignancy to the plans for a Miner's Memorial. In October St Leonard's held a service to mark the closure. The church was packed. The Mayor came. The Bishop came and preached the sermon. Before it began the pit buzzer sounded. It was always used to mark the change of shift at the mine but it hadn't been used for many years; it sounded more like a warning siren as the congregation shivered in collective memory.

The service began in darkness and the church bell tolled 89 times for each year of the pit, on and on relentlessly, as three little children made their way to the front of the church carrying miners' lamps. Children from the primary school performed a

'Chorus for Coal', and the National Union of Mineworkers banner was dedicated, to be kept in the church thereafter. Miners and families shared their stories. Sylvia Fairhurst described the anxiety of waiting for Jim to come home from his shift, the anguish when he was late, of not knowing if he was safe.

And then at the end, the glass screen at the back of the church, where the Miners Memorial screen was planned was illuminated, showing silhouettes of miners heads and lamps and the great pithead wheel. It was a dramatic moment, one which Simon in particular cherished, effective drama and, he believed, a moment of light in the darkness and hope for the future. But that year even the Dinnington Christmas illuminations were cancelled.

love comes quietly

Love comes quietly,
finally, drops
about me, on me,
in the old ways

What did I know
thinking myself
able to go
alone all the way.

Robert Creeley

Father died suddenly at the beginning of 1992. He and my mother had retired to Selby, near York; his last years had been frustrating, but he remained undaunted in his campaigns, especially against unemployment and Margaret Thatcher, for whom he reserved a particular loathing. He had been distributing leaflets for the Labour party one freezing cold Saturday morning in January, when he had a heart attack and just keeled over in the street. For him it would have been the end he wanted, what he no doubt would have described as straight to Glory. Reports in the local Selby papers paid tribute to his 'passionate belief in social justice'.

He had mellowed somewhat as a parent, and indeed Caroline my younger sister had a much more affectionate and closer relationship with him than any of her elder siblings. She hardly recognises the stern patriarch I portray. He accepted many things that would have been unthinkable in earlier years; grandchildren born out of wedlock in particular. But Simon's homosexuality was never discussed.

His death was a shock for all of us of course. For Simon there remained always, 'the sad image of him falling, alone and

dying, in the road . . .' Simon had been staying at Elmore Abbey
researching his book on Dom Gregory Dix, and it was the
abbot who told him. He had been well ensconced in the gentle
monastic rhythm; work, rest, chapel, walk, letter-writing. But
he returned immediately and arranged everything; how familiar he was with the procedures of death! It seemed natural to
hold the funeral in Dinnington; I was ignorant enough of his
parish then to suggest I might arrange the flowers. I realise now
that to have anyone but Margaret Hawley do the flowers for a
funeral was unthinkable. The coffin stayed in church overnight,
surrounded by Father's favourite daffodils. After an evening
service I went back to the church with Simon to light candles,
appreciating perhaps for the first time the opportunity created
by these symbolic rituals for mourning and reflection. The
funeral next day was packed with people, and Simon delivered
a brilliant eulogy for his father. Among the congregation only
Andrew knew about Simon's own condition. Simon included in
the service the familiar family prayer, the collect for purity,
'Unto whom all hearts be open and all desires known . . .' I had
probably not heard it for twenty-five years or so. Simon who
was standing behind me at that point, noted my shudder and
attributed it to the power of prayer, which in a sense it was, but
for me it was also the power to revive unwanted memories.

Of Father Simon wrote in his journal, 'Now he has let me
go – what I asked of him in dreams and in the unconscious: it
feels as positive as that.' After the funeral Simon returned to
Elmore Abbey and the company of the monks. Almost immediately he began to get ill. 'I became so tired last week, the strain,
among other things, of acting almost all the time in "automatic
mode" . . . and now I feel ill – another effect.'

It was the start of cryptosporidiosis, the parasite which lodges
in the intestine. Slowly he began to lose weight. He told me,
'The first real symptoms I was conscious of were after Dad died
when I went back to the monastery. I noticed that the stomach
upset and diahorrea didn't seem to go away.' The food at the
Abbey, cooked by the monks themselves, was uneven, 'I put it
down to their food, and it may well be that somewhere there I
picked up cryptosporidiosis.' It may be that there was some
fundamental connection between Father's death and the onset
of illness, that Simon unconsciously felt that he could now be

ill, that he had somehow suppressed it while Dad was alive, unable to cope with the idea of him knowing.

Simon was beginning to look ill by this time, and a few people guessed the reason, although he was still telling everyone that he had this dreadful stomach bug that wouldn't go away. Joyce Robinson remembers going to a formal regimental dinner with him that April. They sat at the high table with the other guests of honour, and Simon could not eat a thing. Finally he had to leave and one of the other guests enquired curiously about his illness, suggesting that he looked as if he had AIDS. But still he told no one.

He wrote about it though, at least obliquely, in a couple of articles developed from talks he had given at St Leonard's, called Fragile Body. The title comes from the first verse of the 15th century Latin hymn, 'Light's abode, celestial Salem'.

O how glorious and respendent
fragile body shalt thou be
When endued with so much beauty,
Full of health, and strong, and free,
Full of vigour, full of pleasure,
That shall last eternally!'

He writes about the fragility of the body, about sickness and weakness, and of course he is speaking for himself, 'We watch bodies fail in sickness and age and we realise how fragile they are . . . Death – the body's end is just a breath away. Our world will not let us escape try as we might, from the fragility of our bodies, from the relentless reminder of cancer, or from our impotence (rage though we may) and fragility before AIDS.'

Not that he necessarily believes in the reassuring resurrection message of the hymn, but he finds something else in it, a glory in the body now, not in some heavenly promise, 'I am not quite sure what I think about resurrection bodies, or even about the resurrection body of Jesus, the contrast with pain and weakness, and fragility.' He concludes, 'The point is not about escaping the body but going further into its realities, its pains, its passions.'

Father's ashes were scattered in Billsdale on the Yorkshire moors in May. Again Simon organised everything, keeping the ashes in church until the time came. Simon helped Mother with the practical tasks, including sorting out Father's beloved books.

How hard it must have been for Simon to comfort Mother, how we all assumed he was the best person for the job, took it for granted. In a sense he was. He had such courage. He took the responsibility very seriously, and began looking into the possibility of her moving to live near him in Dinnington. He felt sure it was a community where she could feel at home. He returned to Elmore to his Dix research and wrote Mother a tender letter, how he would remember her daily at mass and reflecting on how he felt about Dad's death.

Now I think Simon would in any case have put off telling the family, and especially my mother as long as possible, that it was easier to tell friends first, but Dad's death only made it more difficult. The idea of further adding to Mother's burdens was terrible to him. Nor could he bear to tell Alma, even though they went on holiday together to Whitby that spring. She remembered him being particularly remote. 'By the end of the holiday I was going to call the relationship off. I could have had a dummy in the car. He even read books in restaurants! I am not easily offended, so I just got a book out myself. It was concentrated alienation, this thing in restaurants was a switch off from really being quite scared . . .' In May, Simon was finally diagnosed as having AIDS. His CD4 count, the measure of immune deficiency, was by now down to 70.

Mike Cameron the new curate arrived in Dinnington in June. He was to prove the lynchpin, the key factor that meant that Simon was able to stay in the parish. Simon at this point could not know, and I don't think even attempted to think through the implications of his illness, and what would happen in the parish. 'It wasn't really in my mind – perhaps it should have been – but I wasn't thinking like that then.' It was pretty clear to Simon when Mike came to see him for the first time at the Rectory that he was the right person for the job.

It remains entirely typical that Mike has always insisted that it was the best possible first curacy that he could have had. He is a man in his fifties, who came to the priesthood after a successful career as an executive in the steel industry. He grew up in London, his father was an old-time music hall comic (Mike appears to have inherited his skills, judging by the reports of his juggling at parish picnics), but moved to Yorkshire at the age of ten, and left school to go into the steel industry. It was the parish motto that attracted him to the job, 'Unlimited, unconditional unquestioning love . . .' It was quite obvious that a young inexperienced curate – someone indeed like Simon himself had been, would not be right. Even in normal circumstances Mike would have been a perfect choice as a complement to his own talents. As it was Mike fitted the space perfectly. He is a short, stocky, handsome man with a generous smile and a kind of grounded earthiness which was a perfect foil to Simon's more ephemeral spirit. I always think of Mike Cameron as Mr Greatheart from Pilgrim's Progress, a humble, medieval pilgrim always ready to carry others' burdens. Even his own wife describes him as the most unselfish person she has ever known, and he cheerfully described himself as the vicar's mate to local schoolchildren. He was always a bit impatient with the smells and mumbo-jumbo of which Simon was so fond. But they shared the same attitudes on fundamental issues such as women's ordination. And Mike had the conviction of someone coming to something late in life that they feel very confident of wanting, and very grateful to have found. Simon valued him enormously, 'It came naturally to him – the pastoral concern, the camaraderie, a genuine concern for people. Although I share a lot of that I find it more difficult to express.'

Simon had always been frustrated as a curate himself by how restricted his own contribution was allowed to be. His approach, once Rector himself, was quite different and as soon as Mike arrived he was thrown into the deep end, immediately asked to celebrate funerals and weddings, the public sacraments more usually reserved for the vicar. Effectively, Simon shared the work load without any concern for heirarchy from the start. The parishioners noticed and approved, Sam Robinson confirmed, 'It was a wonderful place for anybody to come as a curate. Mike had only been here a week and Simon said, "Would you like to do that wedding?" and Mike nearly fell off his chair, and that's been the pattern ever since.'

Simon was beginning to feel physically weaker, and the reality of it really hit him when he went to Bardsey that year in June. No longer could he clamber over rocks and streams as he had always done, 'I wept yesterday for the first time – at the restrictions that begin with this disease, If this "malaise" is permanent then there are all sorts of things I love to do which I'm not going to do ever again ... "ever" is a long time and it does make me cry.'

His journal continues, 'This is my body – I love it, I want it. I'm not proud of it, but I'm not ashamed of it either. I want to cherish it, to hold it, hold on to it. I feel sad for it with this presence inside of it.' He wrote a chapter of the Dix biography, and spent a quiet birthday, sitting in the sun sheltered from the wind. 'Can I go quietly? Find the Deep Peace some-where and let it all go? I like the feeling of not leaving a mark, but I think I'm a long way off yet ... I know there's so much more in there, stories especially.'

He was groping towards metaphors to articulate how he was feeling; no longer was it the island he could somehow feel in control of, no longer could he perceive all from a superior vantage point. The great ocean of the subconscious was encroaching, lapping at the shore. According to Carl Jung, dreams of the sea stand for the unconscious bursting through into consciousness like a flood: 'Such invasions have something uncanny about them: they bring about a momentous alteration of the personality and produce something similar to the illusions and hallucinations that beset lonely wanderers in the desert, seafarers and saints.'

Simon felt as if he was wandering in a desert, 'It is a wilder-ness I live in ... on its edge only, I still don't know what to do with it, how to explore it: a wild place, I'm sure with a dream time to it ... as I begin to slow down what else can I do but confront it?' He began to see he could explore his experience, try to understand it through writing, 'It's stories I need to find – as simple and as difficult as that: parables ...' He was unsure where to begin, unsure of the form, and it was not until he began to get ill, and began to struggle with AIDS both physically and metaphorically that the stories began to emerge. 'There is a part of me waiting to be "uncovered" – a lid lifted off – and it's the mythic bit, the story telling part. I'm sure it's waiting to be opened up, released, to come "on stream" – how I get there I don't actually know.'

Slowly he began to accept that he could not do it all on his own, that he must begin talking to friends and family about the illness and the future. And then sweet Caroline, littlest sister, sent him a poem by Robert Creeley, which was so apt, so sensitive, I wonder how she knew ... He copied it out into his journal:

Love comes quietly,
finally, drops
about me, on me,
in the old ways

What did I know
thinking myself
able to go
alone all the way.

She was very close to Simon and she seemed to have a certain capacity to touch him – to insist I think on being allowed in, to get under his skin a little. Meanwhile, my sister Jackie had already guessed the truth. She was still working as a nurse at that time and had become curious about the medication he was taking, 'I was puzzled by this bag full of drugs he took everywhere, just looked them up once when I was on night duty, and realised immediately. I just shouted it out, I couldn't help it,' she remembers, 'My brother's got AIDS!'

By September the physical symptoms were worse, and Simon could hardly swallow due to his ulcerated oesophagus – which may in fact have been due to the drugs he was taking. He noted on a trip to Cornwall that he was virtually delirious with the effect of new tablets. But life in Dinnington went on as usual. There were parish outings and pilgrimages, Harvest Suppers, jumble sales and Christian Aid collections, and problems with the unsatisfactory repair of the church bell. Derek Norbury was made a reader in September, which meant he was licensed to preach, take funerals and assist at communion. Simon was firm in his support, but there were mutterings from others who did not like the idea of a gay lay preacher. According to Derek, 'Some people didn't think it was right for me to be in the sanctuary, giving communion.' He offered to resign, 'I said to Simon if it was going to cause any trouble in the church that I should resign. But Simon said no, the church is for everyone, it's there for you and if you resign on this point, I shall resign also.'

The Miners' Memorial project was slowly developing as the

artists, Janette Moon and Russell Morris, worked on designs for a great etched glass screen and supervised small groups of parishioners working on mosaic inlays. Simon spent a lot of time with the artists, delighting in the developing connections between art and spirituality and continuing to think of ways in which he could relate art to religion, and indeed art to Dinnington. He met David Bingham, a dancer, who was looking for rehearsal space for a new piece for his dance company Side by Side. It was about AIDS, specifically a gay couple waiting for the result of an HIV test, and their response. Simon offered the Middleton Institute, the old village hall, as a rehearsal space, and then suggested in return that they should perform the dance there.

It was a very raw piece, and would have been considered innovative anywhere let alone Dinnington. But they turned up every week at the Institute, slotting their rehearsal in between WI meetings and OAP meetings, making sure the cutlery and the cups were tidy in the tiny kitchen afterwards. Nobody knew what the reaction would be when they finally performed the piece with two gay men facing the reality of a HIV diagnosis and embracing on the floor. Most of the audience were older people with just a sprinkling of gay friends, but they reacted sympathetically, nobody left and everybody clapped. There were bemused comments, however, and it certainly became a topic of conversation in Dinnington afterwards. After the performance there was a party at the Rectory, one of Simon's typically unlikely combinations of parishioners and gay friends.

Simon had introduced the performance and given the audience a rough outline of the story, using it as an opportunity to talk about HIV awareness. He was not looking well himself. He had been losing weight rapidly, which he still officially attributed to his ulcerated oesophagus. He described the dance at a conference on Spiritual Direction the next day, 'It was moving, affectionate, violent, erotic, touching, beautiful, strong, tender, dramatic, intense: it made you very aware of bodies, of wordlessness, of expression, and of our deep, deep reluctance to communicate. AIDS has surely become a powerful metaphor for all that we are most afraid of within, that darker interior, the fearful place. A metaphor for all that spirituality meets as it struggles to bring its justices together, inner and outer; a metaphor for our attitudes – our "spiritual attitudes" to our bodies, our sexualities, our selves in their darkest aspect.'

It may have helped Simon confront his own struggle with exposure. But he soon began hesitatingly to tell a few close friends. There is a list in his journal: 'Those who now know': it includes several close women friends, Jenny Bott, Nancy Johnson, Sue Proctor, Margaret Selby, as well as Mike Cameron, the curate, and five gay friends – three of whom including Andrew were themselves HIV-positive. 'Those still to tell' include his family and Alma.

It was a measure of the fear of AIDS at that time that he nearly always said he was HIV-positive first, and then that he had AIDS. In fact at that time he still used the term AIDS Related Complex, a term which has since been abandoned as misleading by the medical profession. The fact was he did have AIDS by this stage, but somehow to tell people initially he was HIV-positive made it gentler, then you could think ahead to AIDS as the inevitable outcome, rather than be confronted with it as the stark reality.

But it was to Jenny Bott that Simon went first, just as he had when he first talked about being gay seven years previously. 'It was one of the times when he came back from the hospital and he decided he'd got to tell people, and he came to our house and sat on our settee, and said I've got something to tell you. I'm HIV. I mean it's just letters to start with, it doesn't sink in. I just said if you want anything we'll be here. Good grief what can you do, you know they've not got a cure. It was him being ill that I thought about. I didn't even think the church council might make him leave, or the Bishop will make him leave. I never thought of him leaving Dinnington until he died. But it didn't even cross my mind that he was going to tell everybody.

'When he went I thought I was going mad, I didn't sort of jump and get the cups out of the way, we'd gone through all that ages back about the chalice. But you don't know enough, and you've got to believe what the doctors tell you. That side of it never frightened me, I could go and clear up after him, I'd never be sick. But I could see how it did frighten people. I didn't know who to ask about it because nobody else knew. So I rang Terrence Higgins. I just said I was a friend. They sent a great big envelope, so I read it, and read it, and read it. Because you don't understand it all.' When I talked to Jenny two years later she was still carrying round the envelope of information from the Terrence Higgins Trust, jammed into her overstuffed handbag.

She went round to the Rectory later that week, and told Simon she would be willing to talk to other people once they knew, understanding how important that was. 'I think we thought things were going to happen a lot quicker. People were stopping me in the street. You didn't even know if they knew he were gay, they was wanting to know what was the matter with him. I didn't tell anybody what was the matter.' Jenny was most concerned immediately that the family didn't know. She insisted to Simon that he tell his mother.

Soon after that Simon told Sue Proctor, who had by this time begun her training for the priesthood and was deacon in a nearby parish. They sat together at the kitchen table in the Rectory. 'He asked me to go over because he wanted to talk and I knew what he was going to say,' Sue told me. 'He was so sick, so thin, I was waiting for him to tell me, for some reason we didn't ask, I don't know why, probably not wanting to face it. I had already been feeling sad, but it was a shock to hear it said. But I think you have the right to tell people in your own time.' She was very concerned about the implications both for Dinnington and the diocese, 'I thought what is going to happen, the lid's off now . . . I knew people like Jenny would be alright because they all loved him so much, but the community, the diocese . . . I wanted him to tell more people than he did at the beginning, but they would not necessarily have been sympathetic. We got to a stage where a lot of people knew, and lot didn't. It was a messy few months.'

Then it was Mike's turn. He and Simon went for one of their regular quiet days together at Jim Cotter's retreat house, high on a hill overlooking Sheffield. It was an opportunity to talk away from the parish. He first told Mike he was gay, and then that he was HIV-positive, 'Mike was hit with a whole new future. He was most concerned about me, what I wanted to do about it.' I asked Mike if Simon should have told him he was gay when he first came to the parish, levelled with him, as it were. Mike was adamant, 'I'd never thought about it – whether someone is homosexual or heterosexual isn't something that

1982. Simon at Norton parish church, near Sheffield, after being ordained as a priest in the Church of England. He moved away from the fundamentalist teaching of the Baptists and was confirmed at twenty-one. He said it was the most significant choice he ever made. 'It felt like I'd come home.'

Above: 1985. Simon receiving his Masters degree from Emmanuel College, Cambridge.

Right: Simon in Montauk, Long Island, on a 1988 research trip to America.

The Bailey family at Dinnington Rectory, 1987. From the left, standing: Jackie, Caroline, Simon (with nephew Laurie), Rosemary, Martin. Seated: Walter, Irene (with granddaughter, Joanna).

Vicar dying from AIDS

The Rev Simon Bailey: dying from full-blown AIDS virus

Village rallies round tragic gay reverend

VILLAGE vicar Simon Bailey is dying from AIDS.

The gay reverend, who has been rector of Dinnington, near Sheffield for the past nine years, is on a drip feed at his home.

People living in the tight-knit community are giving him their full support.

They learned of the 38-year-old clergyman's condition some time ago after the HIV virus developed into full-blown AIDS.

EXCLUSIVE
BY DAVID CLARKE

Teams of parishioners have helped him continue his church services and often stay overnight while he is connected to the drip, which helps him fight off infection.

A TV documentary about Mr Bailey's continuing ministry will be screened in the new year.

A spokesman for the Bishop of Sheffield said: "He has known about his condition for about 10 years and it is now full-blown AIDS," he said.

"The support shown by people in his parish, which is a very tough and down to earth former mining community, has been tremendous."

His deputy, lay preacher Derek Norbury, said Mr Bailey was a "wonderful caring man full of good ideas" always helping others.

Mr Norbury said he knew his friend was gay but was "devastated" when he learned about his illness.

"He kept it to himself for some time but when the virus became full blown he told his family and people at the church and now practically everyone knows about it.

"Simon decided to come out and talk to the TV cameras not for himself but to help others in similar circumstances.

"There is a lot of discrimination against people with HIV and AIDS in other places, but I think people round here are more caring and understanding," he said.

The news comes during a turbulent week for the church as homosexual group Outrage threatens to "unmask" 10 bishops as gay.

■ **Star Opinion: P6**

The news broke in the Sheffield Star *at the end of 1994. 'Some people think I should have kept my head down,' said Simon, 'kept it as secret as possible, not disturb the "peace of the church" yet again. But I can't keep living and at the same time keep this a secret.'*

Far left: 'If there had been any pastoral breakdown, or threat of it, I would have gone. If people had said, "He's not baptising our baby", then yes, I would have gone. But it hasn't happened.'

Left: Simon with Rev Sue Proctor, after her ordination in 1995. She is now rector of St Leonard's in Simon's place, their first woman priest.

Left: Simon with Rev Alma Servant in 1995, after he preached at her first eucharist: 'We did it! We have women priests... it is a breath of fresh air, a sense of real possibilities.'

Below: Simon with Walter Hawley, ex-pit electrician and parish pastoral worker, surveying what remained of Dinnington pit for the Everyman TV programme in 1994. Walter: 'When we learned of Simon's illness we closed ranks.'

Presiding at communion became the central focus of Simon's life. 'At what point of ill-ness would I feel impelled to resign, unable any longer to be a priest? I want to die as a priest because life includes being hurt, ill, in pain, dying... There's something significant, isn't there, that I as a "victim" of AIDS preside at the eucharist, offer the sacrifice?'

Above: Lunch at the Rectory. Simon with his niece, Martha O'Carroll.

Left: Ashness Bridge, Derwentwater, 1995. Simon and Rosemary on a nostalgic trip to the Lake District revisiting childhood haunts.

Simon robing up in the vestry at St Leonard's. No other profession has such concealment of the body.

Greeting parishioners after Sunday morning service at St Leonard's. Suddenly they had to think about homosexuality and AIDS in terms of a person they loved and respected very much.

Simon lighting a candle in the quiet room at the Rectory. On the flyleaf of his journal he inscribed a quotation from Milton on his blindness. 'So by this infirmity may I be perfected, by this completed. So in this darkness, may I be clothed in light'.

On suffering: 'I don't think there is a point to it. That's just the bottom line I have to work from. It's a mystery but there's no reason why I shouldn't experience it like anyone else. Why not me, after all?'

seems important to me. The first thing I thought was this awful gloomy thing – death, death, death ... I wasn't shocked. My main concern was for Simon and to help him carry on here.'

In the midst of all this gloom, however, was a moment of great joy for Simon. The General Synod were about to take a final vote on whether the Church of England would allow women to become priests. Near the beginning of November he wrote in his journal, 'The vote. Oh God, it can't fail, it just can't ... for Alma, for Sue ...' Then, '1.11.92. We did it! We have women priests ... it is a breath of fresh air, a sense of real possibilities, the C of E need not be a dinosaur, we can reflect a bit of the kingdom! I said to Sue "the tide is coming in" and that image has stayed with me ...' The images somehow coalesce, the tide had turned for women, but it was also coming closer for Simon, the tide that would sweep him out into his great ocean of nothingness, of love ...

On a visit from Liverpool to London my sister Jackie told me about the AZT drugs. What other explanation could there be? I had heard dreadful stories of people with AIDS retreating into isolation and rejecting their families – for some reason at that time I believed this was somehow an inevitable part of the progress of the illness. Simon meanwhile was still trying to find the right opportunity to tell Mother. According to Sue Peters, the Health Advisor at the hospital, one of Simon's greatest anxieties was the family, how we would cope, indeed how we would react, and his guilt at the burden he would inevitably inflict on us all. It is still immensely sad that he could not feel sure of us.

At the end of November he finally told my mother, the day before he was due to drive her to London to stay with me. He called me beforehand and was very insistent that I must encourage her to move to Dinnington, where he had found sheltered housing for her. We all had dinner together that night, including Caroline who was then living in London, working as a church volunteer on the Isle of Dogs. Simon and Caroline drove to her house for the night, and he told her then. Mother waited till the next morning to tell me, which was kind since Theo was teething and I was already sleeping badly. Although the news came as a shock, it was also a confirmation of our fears. We sat and talked and wept together for hours. Somehow we assumed that it would be impossible for her to live in Dinnington after all, because Simon would not be able to look after her, and she might prove an added burden to him. I feel obscurely that I somehow betrayed Simon in responding that way. I don't know what we thought would happen. Mother also felt unsure whether she could cope, 'I envisaged everyone pointing and talking,' she recalled later. We had no idea how the church would respond. It was a dreadful time – perhaps still the worst, nothing ever seemed quite so bad after that, nothing could ever be as bad as we anticipated.

(*My journal.*) Mother says it was the worst weekend of her life, even worse than Dad dying. She was in utter despair, and there was so little one could say in comfort. After Mum told me, I remember thinking she was already speaking this different language – he was HIV and had ARC, Aids Related Complex. It wasn't yet AIDS – somehow that was very important . . . Simon arrived at my house the next day, and I greeted him with a hug and a cup of tea. I said things which now seem so pompous – I said how sorry I was and what a full life he had already had and how life expectancy until recently was only 37 or so anyway. As if he was already dead. He said for him it felt as if he was growing old very quickly.

It was like an iceberg all of us sitting together. There was so much more under the surface, not expressed. I was acutely conscious of Simon's physical contact with my son Theo, (then two years old) knowing with my rational mind that there was no danger. Simon seemed to be making a deliberate point about it as well, offering Theo a drink from his glass of water.

We then had to tell the rest of the family. I told Jackie over the phone, merely confirming what she already knew. Mother and I had a terrible week of exhausting emotional talks. For a while it was all we thought about; it was the burden you strapped on when you woke in the morning. Of course the fact that it was less than a year since my father died made it all much worse for Mother. She said she and Dad had faced some dreadful situations but they had always been together. Now she felt so alone. She then had to go on to Devon to stay with my brother

Martin and tell him the news. Telling people is hard, the bearer of the news inevitably has to provide emotional support, and it was good that we managed to unload some of that burden from Simon. There were many reasons why he chose to keep his diagnosis secret for so long, but I for one feel almost grateful that he did. In this instance a burden shared is not a burden halved, it is doubled with every person you tell. And perhaps it would have made it much more a reality for him to have others enquiring anxiously about his health all the time.

For Simon there was an added dimension, as he explained in the BBC Everyman programme, 'There is inevitably still always this lurking shadow deep deep down about AIDS as a self-inflicted wound, something I could have avoided, something I've brought on myself rather than a straightforward disease for which one can't be held responsible. At the stage when I must have contracted it there was no way of knowing about it . . . and yet that's there for people, whilst no one says it, it must lurk in the background for a lot of people that . . . this is my own fault.' Alma too was devastated when he finally told her one weekend soon after when she was visiting him. For Simon it inevitably added to the pain to inflict the news on people he loved. He had to cope with their reaction, and their struggle to control their own feelings as they offered sympathy to him. 'Alma was very difficult,' he remembered, 'She was very good, she came and hugged me and we talked about it at length.' Afterwards she said she had spent the following night in tears, but had felt she had to restrain her own feelings when he told her. Alma remembered, 'The thing that slayed me was that he had had to cope with it on his own for seven years, that I could not get my head round. I told him I felt I had misjudged him all this time – "You're not the man I thought I knew – now I don't know what was really you and what was you coping." '

Alma, by then also waiting to be ordained and working as a university chaplain, had grave misgivings about the likely response of the church. 'I was very concerned at first he would get thrown out of the Rectory. I gave him a key to my house in Manchester, though I said if he came there we would have to get married for appearance's sake!' She had heard a rather grim tale of another young priest who had died of AIDS in Wales. He had kept his homosexuality and his illness a secret from his parish, and when he resigned, the parish were not even told where he was going. The parish apparently was told that the priest had gone abroad on holiday, had a road accident followed by a blood transfusion and then suddenly a few weeks later he was ill with AIDS.

As soon as Simon told us he was HIV-positive my initial (perhaps distancing) reaction, as a journalist, was to 'research' it and I tried to call everybody I could think of from the Terrence Higgins Trust to the novelist Sara Maitland and the academic and AIDS activist Simon Watney for advice. It was considered necessary to be terribly discreet at that stage, and I often didn't even use my own name, let alone Simon's when I called. Nor did I feel able to talk to many friends, and for another eighteen months or so, kept the knowledge from all but one or two of my closest friends, as did my siblings. It was far too easy a story to leak. We all had to learn to live with the secret together.

We were particularly concerned about the media, and how to handle it. Stories about celebrities with AIDS continued to be tabloid splashes, and they were often pursued without mercy even when they were very ill. There was a tendency for people with AIDS to come out and tell their own story before they could be outed by the tabloids. In many areas people were still unable to tell people at work about their HIV status.

At the same time the whole issue of homosexuality within the church was becoming more and more criticial. If the ordination of women had caused a split, it was nothing compared to the divisiveness of the homosexuality issue. The fundamentalist wing of the Church of England was becoming stronger and more vocal in their condemnation of homosexual priests. On the whole opinions of Simon's prospects if his condition became known were bleak. Simon Watney who has written extensively on AIDS and the media, warned me that a vicar with AIDS would very likely be considered good copy. I also talked then to Father Bill Kirkpatrick, a priest who works with AIDS sufferers. But Simon was a different case – a priest who needed help himself. It emphasised further the whole issue of carers who are themselves in need of care.

It slowly became apparent that the issue was not an unfamiliar one to the church. Malcolm Johnson, one of the people I contacted, is now the Bishop of London's advisor on Pastoral Care, based at St Martin-in-the Fields. For many years he ran the St Botolph's centre for the homeless in the city of London. He was openly gay himself and ran a support group for gay clergy so was often the first point of contact in a crisis. I was much encouraged by a frank interview he gave to the *Guardian*, about the time Simon told us he was HIV-positive, in which he defended homosexuality as 'a gift of God' and criticised the cruel attitude of the Church of England to its gay clergy. When I talked to him after Simon died, he told me about the first case of a priest with AIDS, back in 1983. He had been a prison chaplain and was taken ill, and diagnosed, and died almost immediately. The case became a tabloid scandal with his picture on all the front pages. 'That made people say the church has AIDS,' said Johnson. This, then, had been the atmosphere in which Simon discovered his own diagnosis.

Another young priest who was HIV went to see Johnson in the mid-eighties. He decided he wanted to leave his parish, but he died before he could. He had told no one in the parish. Johnson preached the funeral sermon, his first AIDS funeral, 'It was very difficult because the parish felt that while the vicar was so ill he had pushed them away, he wouldn't let them visit him, hadn't wanted them near, hadn't wanted them to know. That had caused tremendous hurt, and all the energy which should have been devoted to fighting the disease was devoted to hiding the situation, and lying.'

At the end another priest had come to look after him, a friend not a boyfriend, and nursed him to the end and he died at home. In this instance then the parish wanted to know, perhaps would even have accepted it. And the Bishop involved was also very supportive, taking particular care of the man's aged father. There had also been another case of a priest who stayed in his parish in North London, though Johnson remained unsure whether people knew what he had died of. But in all the other cases of which he was aware the priests involved had taken early retirement.

Johnson realised in the early eighties that the church needed to anticipate the problem of clergy diagnosed HIV-positive, and went to see Graham Leonard, then the Bishop of London. Johnson was asked to speak at a staff meeting of Bishops in

London, and warned them that there would soon be several cases of clergymen with AIDS in London and they needed to decide what to do about it. Johnson also went on a fact-finding visit to San Francisco, and persuaded Bill Swing, Bishop of California, to speak to the London bishops during a visit to the UK. In San Francisco of course things were rather different. The splendidly named Swing actually appointed a priest with AIDS as a residentiary canon in the cathedral in San Francisco.

It had been agreed to draw up a package deal for early retirement and accommodation, and guidelines were established for rural deans for when their clergy showed signs of HIV. A group of hospital chaplains and clergy already involved in the HIV field was also established, and HIV training days were held at St Botolph's. Critically though, this initiative had to remain discreet. It could not be publicised; the church was far too sensitive about homosexuality within its ranks, and had the media known about it, the very care offered would have been disparaged, no doubt. Johnson now says, 'I wish we had let more people know.'

By the time Simon began to tell people in 1992, he must have known that there were other people out there in a similar situation. But I don't know if he had any idea of these London initiatives during all the years he kept quiet. Perhaps it would have helped him. There is something especially sad about the fact that people in these situations have to be so shrouded in secrecy that they can't even talk to each other. It took many years for Simon and several friends who were also HIV-positive to confess their diagnoses to each other.

But there were a few points of light in the darkness. David Randall was one of them. David Randall was another Anglican priest who had been diagnosed HIV-positive in 1985. He had been an openly homosexual priest in London for many years, and declared his HIV status not long after his diagnosis. In 1988 David started CARA, a programme providing education about HIV/AIDS and a network of pastoral care. He talked publicly about his life, his partner who had AIDS, and his own HIV-positive status in a television programme in February 1993. His courage and openness was enormously encouraging to us and to Simon, who wrote to David, though they never met.

Randall, however, was in London, and had stopped being a parish priest, so his situation was less delicate.

A couple of weeks after Simon told us, I went to spend a few days with him, taking Theo, my son. I rushed round, making bread and filling the freezer with meals (which Simon never ate.) I always seemed to be Martha, the one who bustles about in the kitchen and complains about her sister Mary just sitting listening to Jesus. But finally I sat with Simon on the sofa in his sitting room and simply hugged him. I tried to ask him how he felt, how it felt.

We had the first of many conversations, difficult to initiate but very intimate once we got going. It seemed odd that I would now become so much closer to him, in a way that might otherwise never have happened – only to lose him. Despite being so different we seemed to be on the same wavelength. We talked about Bruce Chatwin, the song lines, people as nomads, trying to relinquish everything. He said he felt like a man walking in the desert, into completely unknown territory. It became the subject of the first story he wrote, which began, 'As he gazed the desert was daunting, forbidding, frightening, but the more he contemplated it, the more it intrigued and held him – the sheer emptiness, the vast space, unexplored, untouched, unattempted.' He was beginning to see that creating metaphors, stories for his experience would help him understand and articulate it. To speak as a dying man to those who are dying – 'well, I can do that,' he reflected.

We talked about Mother and he expressed such sadness at Mum's initial reaction to him when he told her, drawing her hand away from him. While I was there she came to stay for a few days, in order to look at the bungalow Simon had found. At that stage they both found it very difficult to talk to each other, and I remember one grim occasion when Mother was sitting weeping on the sofa, and Simon sat next door in his study, his face impassive. I went from one to the other begging them to talk to each other. Mother was trying to decide whether to move to Dinnington; she felt, understandably, that it would be hard to cope seeing him every day. She was particularly worried about how the family would react; both my father's family and her own were very upright, old-fashioned Christian people, though the Bailey side tended more towards fundamentalism, and were very strict. We could not know what would happen, and Simon was no more capable than anyone else of working out what the future might hold. Indeed he survived in part by not thinking about it too much, 'To think too much, to give in, to work out too many scenarios would be to enter the void, to live with chaos, but it means I don't integrate the thing, I live with it as a shadowy stranger behind me – but always just over my shoulder,' his journal noted.

But he did want Mother to be in Dinnington, and reluctantly she accepted that she too was to be drawn into this frightening uncertain future. I can't really remember if I consciously thought about whether I should get involved. I hadn't been particularly involved with Simon before. We got on well, I visited him occasionally, sometimes even went to church, but I didn't really know him any more. He had retreated again after that brief moment of connection. But getting involved in other people's lives has always been in my character; sometimes it is a failing, but not always. There was never really any choice. Perhaps there wasn't any for Mother either. Finally, in February 1993, she moved to Dinnington.

By this stage Simon was visibly weaker and thinner, but in the spring he managed a visit to London. I tried to cook things he would like but he ate very little. He enjoyed himself though, going to bookshops and art exhibitions. There was inevitably the feeling that this might be his last opportunity. I, in my wisdom, suggested we went to see Derek Jarman's *Wittgenstein*. It is a fine film, but it is about AIDS and death, and not exactly a barrel of laughs. It was only later I realised how insensitive I was in some ways, so keen to try and understand and explore what Simon was going through that I almost never just provided amusement, entertainment.

I remember later on being with my sister Caroline and Simon watching another hilarious, camp film on television, *Priscilla, Queen of the Desert*, and watching them just relax and enjoy the movie together, laughing. Why don't I do that? I thought. The next time he came to London then (and yes, there was a next time) I had learned better and we went to see *The Madness of King George III*. Well, I thought, that was more lightweight.

Simon was determined to finish the Dix biography and went

on retreat to Holy Island in order to write. It was very cold and bleak, 'I went for a walk to the sea today and the wind was just so fierce and cold I ached and cried.' He was nearing the end of the biography, and there were uncanny echoes for him in Gregory Dix's final illness; when Dix was diagnosed with cancer, he was in the middle of a lecture tour of the United States, fund-raising for the sister monastery there. Simon wrote:

'[Gregory] was sure he couldn't tell the Abbot, because he would be called home and the money would never be raised in time, but he said, determined to stay, "I was very frightened ... the really horrid thing was not being able to consult anyone", In addition to all the other pressures of the situation Gregory was living with this most alarming and secret pressure of all: the pain of illness and the thought of dying.' Rarely can a biographer have identified more closely with his subject.

It was becoming clear that it was time to tell more people, and in particular the church hierarchy. Telling the Bishop became a sort of refrain. We had no idea how the church would react, and Simon was understandably reluctant to tell them. Crucially he had to decide whether he should resign or try and brave it out. 'I keep saying, I want to stay in control of who knows what; but "control" is a two-edged thing – it's about self-sufficiency and proper pride and integrity, but it's also about fear of dependence, loss of dignity, a more unattractive kind of pride ... the vital thing is not be a victim – that's what the "control" thing is about, defining oneself as far as possible, accepting the very real boundaries of that, and then being "for oneself".'

Mike Cameron for one had great faith in Dinnington, 'I felt these deep reservoirs in people, deep compassion, I could not imagine any other response from Dinnington folk. I trusted that.' But at that time he did not trust the church, 'It sounds terrible. I could trust Dinnington and not the church.' But the moment could be put off no longer. It was time to tell the Bishop.

the wounded healer

Priests have a long way to go. The people wait for them to come
To them over the broken glass
of their vows . . .

R.S. Thomas

As it turned out the Bishop already knew, or at least had guessed. Stephen Lowe, the Archdeacon, had wondered for some time. Nancy Johnson confirmed his suspicions, although she now has no memory of doing so and Simon himself expressed surprise that she would have betrayed his confidence. Stephen Lowe's approach was clearly quite subtle, 'I think Nancy didn't deny it when I asked her directly. I think she said you ought to talk to Simon, at which stage I knew.'

Stephen Lowe, portly and impressive, particularly in his ecclesiastical robes, is a liberal, progressive churchman, and keen to be seen as such. His responsibility as Archdeacon is the pastoral care of the clergy in his diocese. Simon knew how much he owed Stephen Lowe for his careful background handling of his delicate situation; interceding with the Bishop, holding the fundamentalists at bay and later on, persuading Simon to make a BBC television programme. (Lowe's powers of diplomacy were to be put even further to the test only a year or so later when the news stories about the Nine O'Clock Service broke in Sheffield and the Rev Chris Brain was accused of sexual relations with his devotees.)

Stephen Lowe had enormous respect and affection for Simon, and had been particularly encouraged when Simon took the risk of telling him in his early years at Dinnington that he was gay.

But in the end it was the Bishop who would decide Simon's

fate. David Lunn, Bishop of Sheffield, is a gentle, unworldly man; his sleek silver hair, slight lisp and courteous manner seem to speak of another time entirely. He is traditional in his views, and was an outspoken opponent of women's ordination. But despite his occasionally intemperate utterances, he is a realist in practice. He once publicly announced he would resign if women were ordained; everyone who heard him knew that by that stage it was almost a fait accompli and that he was bound to be embarrassed by his threat. In the event he stayed in office.

He did go and visit Simon, 'The Bishop came round to see me in another context, about his local history studies,' Simon said. It was only later he realised that he must have been checking him out. It seems likely now that the church may well have known even before the family did. At the time we saw ourselves as central to the drama, but now I realise that Simon put off telling us as long as he could, and when he did neither he nor any of us were fully aware of the larger picture.

Simon always argued that informing the Bishop officially was unnecessary until he actually became ill. He really did not know how the Bishop would react. He knew he would be sympathetic to the illness, but how supportive he would prove to be was another matter. Simon might well be asked to resign. That he did not want to do, as he explained in the video journal he made for the BBC Everyman programme, 'The obvious answer is to resign, so that all the issues would go away. But of course they wouldn't. They remain here and they remain in the church. The church's reaction is usually to resign and go away. I'd really rather face the issues.'

At the end of April Simon's spiritual director persuaded him the time had come, and volunteered to talk to the Bishop on his behalf. Simon recalled Stephen Lowe calling him soon after, 'The Bishop had rung him up in what sounded almost like a panic, he said he was on the verge of tears. I found it moving really.' He is an emotional person, according to Simon, 'He is curiously naive in some ways, given to tantrums; major crises have often been because he has had a tantrum.'

But when I asked him the Bishop maintained he had already known, 'It came as a grief to me for Simon's sake, but not a great shock, partly because Simon looked as though he had AIDS, one didn't have to be particularly astute.' Lowe also insisted, 'It was never a shock to him or I, we had already guessed. We had actually prepared . . .' Apparently there had never been any question of Simon leaving, 'Partly because of the sheer integrity and quality of Simon's ministry and partly because Dinnington was a model church. We really didn't think of doing anything else but carrying on loving him through it all.'

They were naturally concerned about the media, and the possibility of scandal. Lowe said: 'We were always slightly nervous, so fairly soon after we knew formally, we had press releases prepared. We worried that we would get a big blow up, and we needed to be ready to move quickly. My real worry was that somebody would be so shocked they would ring up the press and say the village is in turmoil, *News of the World* revelation stuff. That's what we were terrified of.'

The Church of England debate on homosexuality was becoming increasingly heated and the Bishop and his staff would have been expected to affirm the agreed policy of the House of Bishops on the subject. As Lowe put it, 'You can see the whole blooming edifice which is pretty shaky anyway, come crashing down every time a bishop breaks ranks.'

In fact the Bishop remained sympathetic to the complexities of the issue and was not inclined to be judgemental. He has always insisted that there was no question of Simon resigning. In an interview with me he said, weighing his words carefully, 'I suppose we could have brought moral pressure on to Simon, and I'm told some bishops would have done, to avoid scandal. I can't speak for other bishops, but apart from moral pressure there was no real way Simon could have been made to resign. It's a bit absurd, even if he had been having orgies every night in the house, there would still have had to be the whole business of a court case.' Technically, the Bishop explained, there were only two things that could have led to a demand for resignation; a breakdown of pastoral relationships with the churchwardens and Parish Church Council (PCC); or if someone had brought a charge of immorality.

Anyway the Bishop felt this was a decision he could take unilaterally, 'I share some of that North Country bloody-mind-edness. It never crossed my mind to consult other people outside the diocese. I felt perfectly able to take whatever decision I wanted myself. It would have been difficult I think if there had been a great clamour from the PCC that this terrible man be got rid of, but there never was.'

He added hesitantly, 'I would have found it very difficult if there had been a campaign for a full sexual life for homosexuals as being compatible with the priesthood in this particular case. If he had had a partner, I would have found that difficult.' But the issue was never discussed with Simon, 'I had no desire to discuss it. I have no knowledge whatsoever of what sexual experiments our clergy indulged in before they were ordained . . .'

'Or after?' I interjected, aware that this was after all the entire issue at stake.

'Or after. It is a matter for their own conscience – well, not entirely their own conscience – because there is an element of local scandal, acceptability and hurt to other people. There is no problem when clergy sin and repent, but the problem arises when they do things that I and other clergy consider sins, and they don't.' But he declared reluctantly, 'If challenged I would not have been able to say that it was acceptable for a priest to have a continuing physical relationship with someone to whom they were not married.'

The Bishop has always maintained that sex outside marriage, homosexual or heterosexual, is the problem, 'I am not sure any of us has a right to a physical sexual relationship that is wholly unconnected to responsibility to others, marriage and children.'

He seemed to suggest that since many people enjoyed sex for other reasons than procreation there was no reason why this should be denied to homosexuals, 'I find the whole debate about homosexuality extremely difficult because it seems to me it's neither here nor there. The quality of people's relationships with each other is of crucial importance. The claim is made widely now that a human being is not complete unless they have a sexual relationship. That is the claim I resist. But if you accept that claim then it is very difficult to deny a similar sort of sexuality, for amusement as it were, rather than for family life, to the person who is a part of the so-called gay community.'

He agreed that Simon's homosexuality could have contri- buted positively to his work as a priest, but only in as much as he was celibate and committed to his work. 'There is possibly a dedication to others which is achieved by the laying aside of the trappings of home and family. There is in some people a readiness to give themselves wholly to the needs of others, which can put immense strains on their marriage. It is difficult to have more than one relationship which is total in its commitment.' This was certainly a tension with which I was familiar, having watched my parents struggle to balance the demands of God and family. Simon probably did in many ways commit himself more to the priesthood because he did not have a traditional family to care for as well.

David Lunn also felt that AIDS should not be treated any differently from other terminal illnesses, 'I could never see, still can't see, why the nature of this illness had anything to do with the present, why the fact that it was AIDS was any different than if it had been cancer ... or any other distressing illness, likely to be fatal. It didn't really matter whether he was or wasn't gay ... There were questions I don't ask because I didn't think it would be fair to enter into a breast beat. It was something that had happened some time previously, and when you think about justifying the ways of God to man, it was a ludicrously inappropriate result.'

For Simon the conjunction of Stephen Lowe with his liberal views and David Lunn with his combination of compassion and bloody-mindedness, was fortuitous. Some, indeed, would claim divine intervention though if so it seems somewhat capricious. Lowe also sought advice from Malcolm Johnson in London, 'Malcolm said you will be the first to actually hold on to him. There had been perhaps five or six cases before and they had been quietly retired, given a sort of golden handshake and encouraged to go into a hospice or whatever. I said well that's totally wrong, and quite impossible in this case. I was determined to hold on to him if we possibly could.'

With the whole-hearted support of the Archdeacon and the at least tacit support of the Bishop it was much easier to discuss widening the circle of knowledge. It had become clear early on that the telling itself was a burden that could not be carried wholly by Simon. So Simon and Mike Cameron, the curate, shared the telling. They chose to do it slowly, usually talking to people individually. Both maintain that it was the only way it could be done; this was not something that could suddenly be announced to a large group all at the same time. 'People really needed time to adapt to the knowledge,' said Mike.

Simon felt that he was closest to his team of pastoral workers, and resolved that it was time to tell them. The obvious time was at one of the regular Monday morning meetings, and it was decided that Mike would tell them all while Simon was in hospital for tests, the first time, in fact, he was on the ward as an in-patient, and the first time he had been in hospital since he was a child. The cryptosporidium parasite had been definitely identified and despite treatment he was still suffering diarrhoea and nausea. His weight had dropped to about seven stone.

Margaret and Walter Hawley were going on holiday the following week, and Simon realised they had to be told before they went. So, on Friday morning he phoned Margaret and said he needed to talk to her about something personal. Margaret walked round to the Rectory. Later she told me sadly, 'When Simon told me it was no surprise. I had worked it out some time ago, but you don't want it to be, you push it to the back of your mind. I could see he was not getting better, and you just use your own common sense. I felt upset for him, but worried what the repercussions would be, how we would cope with it.'

She told Walter, and later that day she walked down the High Street to see Joyce Robinson, a friend of many years. Joyce could see immediately from Margaret's face that something was up. Margaret didn't beat about the bush, 'Joyce, what do you think is the matter with Simon?'

'Well actually I think he's got AIDS,' said Joyce matter-of-factly. There, it was out. After months of rumour and gossip, they had said the words. For none of them was the information a complete surprise, and yet the confirmation of such dreadful news remained a shock. It became necessary finally to accept it, and confront the implications.

Although some of the pastoral workers had their private suspicions about Simon's illness, no one had discussed them with each other, and it wasn't even clear that everyone necessarily was aware he was gay. Once out in the open the news fractured their world – no-one really knew how anyone else would react, or how the rest of the parish would respond. Margaret and

Walter were particularly concerned about Kath, worried that in her admiration for Simon she would be especially shocked and devastated.

They met on a Monday morning towards the end of May; the little group that day included Joyce, Kath, Derek and Sylvia. Mike began by saying gravely that Simon had given him permission to tell them he was HIV-positive. He asked them to keep the information to themselves, though they could tell partners if they wished. He also warned them that there might be some negative reaction, possibly vandalism against the church, when the news did come out. Accounts vary oddly of that meeting; some remember Simon as being upstairs rather than in hospital; some can't remember exactly who else was there; even people's reactions were interpreted quite differently.

Sylvia was shocked. 'It had gone round the village a bit that he had got AIDS. But I just thought he's only a slender lad, and if he's had diarrhoea as well . . . Well of course we would support him like.'

It was devastating for Derek, being both gay and seriously ill with diabetes and with what was later diagnosed as motor neurone disease. He really seems to have had no notion of Simon's illness, despite the fact as a gay man himself he must have been more aware of the possibility than some. 'That morning when Mike told us, it was like a dream. I couldn't take in what he was telling us. I cried, honestly, I just couldn't hold it back. Simon was the last person in the world I expected to hear about.'

Kath's reaction astonished everyone who thought of her as a naive and unwordly person, and she appears to have thoroughly enjoyed surprising them all by insisting that she already knew and accepted that Simon was gay, 'I started putting two and two together. But I didn't say anything to anybody. People said, "Oh dear it'll upset Kath . . . what will Kath think?" And I said, Kath doesn't think anything, I just accepted it. I said it hadn't the slightest effect on me – I knew he was homosexual you see.'

For Kath it was perfectly clear what they must do, 'We just said to him when he came out of hospital if there is anything we can do we'll do it. We definitely wanted him to stay, we didn't think he could possibly go anywhere else. He had to be where he was known.' For the women especially their reaction was dominated by their affection for Simon. Their response was intuitive, emotional at first, and they formed their opinions on the basis of experience, rather than principle. For Joyce it was the most natural thing in the world to support him, 'Even though he looked so ill at that stage we wanted him to stay here, it was probably a motherly thing with me, we just wanted to do what we could.'

But it was the men of the church who were perhaps most surprising in their response, since most, despite their reservations or outright condemnation of homosexuality, still responded first to Simon's predicament. Sylvia was surprised by her husband, Jim's reaction when she first told him, 'He just says, what a shame, he's so young, he has so much going for him. He never suggested not going to church. We didn't see it was our business.'

Simon commented afterwards in the Everyman programme, 'I think the hardest thing people have to work towards is the realisation that they can't separate my sexual identity from the rest of me. The person they've grown to appreciate as their parish priest, from whom they might feel they've learnt, who they might feel has helped them to grow, isn't separable from this person who is also gay.'

Simon's formal interview with the Bishop was overdue and had had to be rearranged due to his hospitalisation. Finally, at the beginning of June Simon went to the Bishop's large official residence in Sheffield. 'He was very pastoral,' Simon recalled, 'But he managed not to mention HIV or AIDS in the course of an hour. I think that showed more a fear of illness than anything else.' When I later suggested to the Bishop that it must have been a difficult encounter he said he couldn't really remember. A week later the pastoral workers group went on a day's retreat to Rievaulx Abbey. They did not discuss Simon's illness specifically, but as they strolled individually and together through the ruined choirs of the Abbey they took the opportunity to murmur their support and affection for Simon, and their coherence as a group was affirmed as they sat together in silence meditating on flickering candle flames, and participated in what Simon rather charmingly described as a 'Eucharistic picnic'.

Simon was in no doubt about what he wanted, 'It was important to me to carry on because it is such an important part of my life. It does mean extra burdens for people here and for the diocese in supporting me. But they said you set the agenda, we'll do what you want. It was immediately suggested that I ought to stay here, not find a hole to hide in ... and carry on till the end of my life.'

He was determined to deal with AIDS as something ordinary, not special, preferring not to engage with the 'professional' AIDS community, believing this was something people could learn to cope with as part of being ordinary, caring human beings. I was still trying, unsuccessfully, to persuade him to get a buddy, a counsellor, anybody else (as I now think) to share the burden. I was especially concerned for my mother, who although she could talk to me and her other children at length, I found increasingly difficult to really support adequately. She proved as reluctant as Simon, however, to seek outside or professional help. In June she came with my family to the French Pyrenees. We didn't talk about Simon at all.

For the small team of people who now officially knew about Simon's illness the most difficult part by far was keeping it quiet, or prevaricating when others enquired about Simon's health. It was asking a lot of these honest, forthright Yorkshire folk to dissemble so profoundly. My mother couldn't tell her next door neighbour with whom she had become very friendly and she hated having to sidestep the subject when anyone enquired. For her it added a whole new dimension to the burden of moving as a recent widow to a new place. Although everyone respected Simon's discreet approach and mostly accepted that it was the right way to do things, they were uncomfortable with the need to mislead people about the cause of the illness.

Offically then, he had a intestinal parasite which wouldn't go away, causing weight loss and diarrhoea, and an ulcerated oesophagus. All this was true, only the reason remained undeclared. It was an adequate explanation if someone asked, 'What's wrong with your vicar, then?' But if they said, 'Has your vicar got AIDS?' outright lies were the only answer. Sylvia laughed about it as she rehearsed the catechism, 'Well you'd say he's got a crytosporidium germ in his bowel, and an ulcerated oesophagus. And they'd say oohh, it's not cancer then? But if they say has your vicar got AIDS . . .?' she trailed off.

Margaret also found it difficult, 'The hardest bit for me was having to try to think up an answer when people said, what is wrong with him? I didn't feel at liberty to say because he didn't want everybody to know at first. It goes against your nature. I couldn't even tell Doreen my close neighbour, because I didn't know how she would react. She was the organist and I was the verger, as well as being neighbours. That was my burden, not being able to communicate with Doreen.'

Eventually Margaret talked to Mike Cameron about it, 'Simon was really really poorly, all these questions were flying around, and I was finding it more and more difficult day by day by day.' Mike went to talk to Doreen, and although she is considered to be traditional in her views, she made no comment, but carried on faithfully playing the organ Sunday by Sunday. Still, Margaret never felt it was too much to ask of them, 'I'm sure Simon knew exactly how to do it, he was right, it filtered through slowly so we had no dramatic, oh what's happening at Dinnington? We really dreaded the newspapers getting hold of it.'

For Joyce her family proved the most difficult. She is very close to her daughter who lives nearby. 'She asked at a very early stage what was the matter with Simon. Once she'd gone I said that's the first time I've ever lied to her, and I couldn't cope with that. I said to Mike I shall have to tell my daughter – and she was a terrific help when I could tell her.' Sam, however, was convinced it was the only way to do things, 'Simon couldn't just say I have got AIDS – he would have had to vanish into obscurity. But it would be naive to think that people didn't know, or didn't tell anybody. I mean if it had been cancer or TB you would have said so straight out.' Or as Walter Hawley put it, 'Folk are not daft. They had begun putting two and two together.'

Stephen Lowe was typically diplomatic. He insisted that it simply didn't matter whether Simon's policy of telling people slowly and individually was the right way, 'I think it was important for Simon and that's all that matters. To control as long as he possibly could a disease that is actually out of control, in a situation where you need desperately to hold on to some sense of dignity about your position. To be able to control something is psychologically very important.'

On July 4 that year Michael Cameron was himself ordained priest. The ordination took place at St Leonard's instead of Sheffield Cathedral, the first time there had been an ordination in the seven hundred years or more there had been a church on the site. Mike knelt in front of the Bishop who was joined by all the other priests present who laid their hands on Mike. Simon preached the sermon, and Stephen Lowe was fulsome in his praise. 'Simon is one of the best preachers I have ever known. You really remember maybe three or four sermons over the course of your life, and that was one of those sermons. It was absolutely brilliant.'

It was in many ways a perfect summary of Simon's own feelings about being a priest and indeed presaged many of the issues which were to become so much more real as Simon's health dwindled away. He spoke in his usual even tone from the lectern, the pulpit long since abandoned. 'Being ordained sometimes feels like being singled out and separated and made to stand on a pedestal, different, somehow not so human any more. But in actual fact it's about going further in, being immersed in community, submerged in the Body of Christ.'

He addressed Mike but spoke from his own heart, 'You want to draw into prayer . . . the unseen church in a community like this – the people whose faith follows a different path . . . all the thousands who never or rarely come to church but who grope and long for something, whose spirit is open and searching still.' He continued, 'Priesthood demands that before you announce forgiveness for others you experience it yourself. It demands that you enter deeply into the lives, the pains, the pleasures of other people. Sometimes the pain you share will be almost intolerable, sometimes it will make you so angry, sometimes you will not be able to hide the tears.'

He described the image of Jesus blowing on to his disciples, 'He breathed on them and said, "Receive the Holy Spirit." For centuries the church included in the rite of baptism a continuation of this event. Insufflation it was called – the priest blew into the face of the candidate, blowing out the evil spirit, blowing in the Holy Spirit . . . I think it's the very gentleness of this image that has struck me . . . the disciples, huddled and hidden away in fear were no doubt hoping for power and courage and strength (rushing winds and flames, perhaps). Instead, Jesus gently blows on them – all the forgiveness of God, all the ministry of reconciliation is in that gentleness. Priesthood is not about power and domination and control. It's about this gentleness, like the breeze in your face on a mountain top, like blowing a butterfly off your sleeve, strong enough to move it, light enough not to hurt it . . .'

And finally he emphasised the central importance of the Eucharist, 'This gentleness comes alive in one of the other great privileges of priesthood – the Eucharist. You are ordained to preside at a meal – as domestic, as local, as gentle as that: forgiven people, reconciled friends sharing together around one table, as we shall do this evening. Presiding at this meal – is not about arrogance or pride or power or superiority, it's just about this gentleness, this humanness, this involvement, immersion in these people, in all we feel, in all we share, in all the ordinariness we bring here until it feels that gentle breath.'

The next morning was Mike's first communion as a priest. It was quite an initiation, just as his curacy had been, since it was also a service of healing, held for Simon among others. The roles were poignantly reversed as Mike performed the laying on of hands and Simon received his blessing. There were about fourteen people in the church, most of whom knew what was wrong with Simon, except for one rather bemused church army student who quickly gathered that the Rector was terminally ill.

Again Simon spoke, briefly, this time more directly about himself, trying to articulate his attitude to his illness, 'This service is not about "making me well" so much as about a different kind of wholeness – the wholeness that can accept affliction as itself a "path to God" and to life in a richer, fuller way . . . and in the mystery of suffering discover a different kind of healing. I have to say, frankly, that I haven't got there yet . . . affliction is not for me (yet . . .) a way to God, I don't know what the mystery of suffering means for me and I don't know at all what to do with this dying business.' He expressed his appreciation of the support he had received, 'What I do know is that the real mystery and miracle of life to which I've become very sensitive, is friends. I've never felt so deeply the sheer presence and support of the people who love me and that's what this service is about for me.'

It is remembered as a very emotional event; people's clothes were soaked with tears. But it was also very important. My mother certainly, despite the sadness, found it of great comfort. Sue Proctor came to the service, 'It was devastatingly sad. It gave me an awful lot to think about. It wasn't long before I was priested, and it brought all the suffering side of priesthood and sharing the pain, all that home to me. He was caring for us and we were caring for him. It was a turning point for me, thinking about healing and who is receiving. It was incredibly moving, there were so many tears, but it was deeper than that. It was a privilege to be part of it all. There are not many moments like that in your life.'

He spent a week with Alma and another priest in a cottage in Teesdale, shortly after. Simon asked that Alma should anoint him with healing oil. They devised a special ceremony for the occasion, after which Simon blessed his companions; after his own anointing assuming the role again of priest himself, and minstering to others. It was a moment of great significance for Simon. He went to one of his favourite waterfalls on that trip too; High Force, two dramatic fissures cascading water round a great slab of rock, and wrote in his journal, 'I thought about it as the place for my ashes to go . . . and that made me cry as I thought, "I don't want go . . .", so I sat with tears dripping on the rock and that terrific sound in my ears.'

By this time, July 1993, Simon was very, very ill. I missed a weekend visit because I was ill with flu, and my mother stressed that I really had to visit soon, before it was too late. A measure of the way Simon and Mother had learnt by then to communicate and accept each other was the poem Simon wrote for Mum. She had told me about the moment when she stood by his chair and he simply leaned his head against her. He told me about it too – for him I think the moment when she just – accepted him, it. She remembered the occasion, was so moved by it, and he recorded it in a poem, yet significantly neither of them ever spoke to each other about it. Now it is a sacred, enshrined moment.

Rest. For my mother 29.6.93

Will death be as soft as this?
My head comes to rest
against you – where you stood and I sat –
under your breast,
against your womb,
warm and cradled
in your arm.
The air was framed with an edge of tears,
but the sun was shining
and I rested
for a moment on you.

Like a sunlit icon of the Child
in the arms of the Bearer of Wounds
we were still,
we rested.
Can death be as soft as this?

It was the most precious gift he could have given her. He
included it in the book of his poems he made for her birthday
in July that year, all hand-written in the elegant calligraphic
script he had typically, perfected, each poem juxtaposed with a
picture or postcard. He included an old picture of himself,
smiling and healthy as he wanted her to remember him. This
book has turned out to be the first of many commonplace books
Simon painstakingly produced for family, god-children and
friends; each one a personal memento filled with pictures, quotations and poems and infinitely precious. I'm sure he had no
idea he would have time to write so many.

In August I went to visit.

(*Journal, August 1993*) It is amazing that I no longer feel that
terrible burden of responsibility to change things here, affect
relationships between Mum and Simon. They are so much
further down the road now than I am, I can only say teach
me. I know it will get more difficult, but I sometimes feel so
privileged to be part of this, the possibility that we can make
something positive out of such a tragedy. We now seem to

be able to talk openly. Simon has talked about making a will, even the cost of the funeral . . . making it easy for us to talk about it, and giving us a language with which to cope. I suppose Simon's experience of advising others about death and dying, I mean how many funerals must he have taken by now . . . it all gives him a language, a way of articulating his experience.

All this without the professional AIDS community to help – Simon had to do it his own way . . . I was so anxious for him to have a buddy, to be hooked into the carer system . . . he was so determined not to be, that his life, his community could handle it, perhaps even should be able to . . .

I feel so close to him and yet so different. Simon is going deep, me, I always seem to be spreading myself so wide. I feel there are things that I can discuss with Simon that fill a gap, that he feels I understand better, which is such a privilege.

Talking to Simon of last things; Mozart's Magic Flute, The Tempest, TS Eliot's Four Quartets . . . He seems to be striving for irony, detachment, those are the words he used, but how long does he feel he has got, I suppose it doesn't matter, since if he feels this way it will enhance the time he has. He talks of savouring colours and smells, not thinking about tomorrow, but savouring today. It is so unlike me, everything seems so superficial in comparison, even my relationship with Theo, there is always an agenda, getting him to bed, off to nursery, whatever. Tonight he read the *Ten Little Mice* book with Simon. Simon sat with his arm round him, and Theo accepted it completely, didn't worry where I was at all.

We were thinking about colour, the colour blue, the Mediterranean, International Klein Blue, Derek Jarman; Simon is surrounding himself with colour; abstract paintings and prints. Matisse, lovely sunny yellow jumpers. He is so thin he needs to wear thick clothes partly for warmth, partly to disguise his gaunt frame. He loves to buy clothes; every time I visit he has new things. I like that.

But his health was deteriorating further; his weight was down to about six stone, he had constant diarrhoea and appeared to be retaining no nourishment at all. It seemed to be hopeless. None of the drugs seemed to be working. My sister Jackie kept asking why his doctors didn't put him on an intravenous feed? We worried that he was not getting proper care, that perhaps he was being treated as a guinea pig, and began to discuss alternative therapies. Simon did consider the idea but eventually decided that he had invested too much in conventional medicine and more importantly in the people treating him. He also felt that he would need to be in London for the best alternative treatment, because so little was available locally, and that he did not want to do.

It fell to Mike Cameron to shoulder much of the burden of telling more and more members of the church about Simon's illness. 'It had to be done individually – it would have been wrong to tell everybody quickly. People needed to be supported to explore it fully for themselves, and then they were in a better position to tell others. They couldn't any longer say I don't know what's wrong with Simon. The problem of the press was secondary, the first thing was genuinely to support each other.'

Some people did find it very difficult, some because it was the first they had learned about Simon being gay, and some who simply could not equate the two, those for whom the idea of a gay priest was simply contradictory. In almost every case, however, the response was chiefly one of sympathy. Sometimes this led to deeper understanding of the issues, sometimes not. For some it caused family dissension. One woman who ran the Mothers Union still went to church, although her husband stopped going when he discovered Simon was gay. Another who later became one of Simon's carers had problems when her grandson got married because his fiancée's family decided they did not want Simon to marry them.

Some people were hurt that they had not been told earlier. Sue Rafferty for example, who became one of Simon's closest and most supportive friends, told Mike. 'People did feel very strongly that they had been hoodwinked. I wish he'd told me before, so I could have supported him, I felt as if I'd let him down. When my dad died Simon was wonderful, and I'm going on about how afraid I am of dying and all the time he was dying and I didn't know.' Her reaction highlights one of the many dilemmas for Simon, that once people did know they were less likely to want to burden him with their problems, which was after all, his job.

Sue is a brusque, forthright woman who talks non-stop, and her zest appealed to Simon enormously, as he described to me, 'She has a sense of humour, an enjoyment of the world, there's nothing prissy or puritanical about her at all yet at the same time she is very serious, the two go together in a very rich sort of way.' He once described her as having a 'prayerful voice' and when she leads prayers you really can hear a whole other dimension beneath the harassed housewife, mother and teacher that is her usual persona. Her husband had been a miner and Sue herself was working in the supermarket when Simon first came to Dinnington, but later she trained as a teacher.

Sue Rafferty recalled ruefully, 'I'm so naïve – it never even occurred to me that Simon was gay. I had never really thought of him as anything sexually, I thought he's a nice chap, a really nice fella. He's got a lot of female attributes – compassion and understanding.' The news came as a great shock to her, 'To find out on the same day that he was gay and that he'd got AIDS! It wasn't that he was a priest – I'm quite happy for anybody to be gay. Nobody's ever asked me what we do in bed, I look at it like that. He's a person before he's a priest, before he's gay.'

By August it was obvious that it was necessary to spread the information further. There was particular concern that the churchwardens, Steve Kohut and Ann Corlett, did not yet know. They were both new to the job. Simon really did not know how they would react. But their reaction was crucial since the church wardens are empowered to complain to the Bishop if they are dissatisfied with the behaviour of their vicar.

Their role is to represent the lay members of the congregation and, technically speaking, everyone in the parish is entitled to vote for the churchwardens. They have the responsibility of keeping order during the services (including the right to tell men to take their hats off) and traditionally they had the power to arrest anyone causing trouble.

Whether it was instinctive or Machiavellian, Simon clearly wanted a sturdy stockade of support around him before they got to know. He acknowledged that perhaps the order people were told in was wrong and that perhaps the churchwardens should have been told before the pastoral team. However, had the churchwardens set the agenda, the situation might have turned out very differently. And had they felt Simon ought to leave (after all, the more usual and predictable response to such a situation) others may have been much less inclined to go against the wardens in order to support Simon.

Stephen Lowe said, 'Mike was trying to manage who knew at any given stage, and there was a vast sense of relief among the people who had known, that we were sharing the burden. Particularly that the Bishop's staff knew and weren't going to do anything dramatic.' But Lowe felt Simon was wrong in not wanting to tell the churchwardens, 'They were new, and he wasn't quite sure about them, but because they didn't know, he was vulnerable if they guessed or found out and reacted badly. So I asked to see them and went one evening to meet them in the church. They didn't know what was coming at all.'

They were stunned. Lowe remembered, 'I shall never forget that day. Steve Kohut just sat totally silent and I could see it all going through his mind, all his emotions, and Ann was just crying, but women always find it easier to cope . . . Then they asked to see me again to go over again how we would react and respond.'

Steve Kohut is a small, neat, man who tucks himself up as he talks, sucking his teeth as he weighs his words carefully. He is a music teacher and freelance musician, often travelling to gigs all over Britain. Although he had not previously been a churchgoer, he started going to St Leonard's occasionally, 'Usually I'm performing late on a Saturday night so I don't really feel like getting out of bed on a Sunday morning, but it was enough to get me out of bed . . . Simon's a very good preacher, I like listening to him.' His voice cracked slightly, 'I would say he has been the main person as my spiritual guide.' By becoming churchwarden he felt he could 'put something back'. For Simon, Steve's value was precisely that of someone 'speaking from the outside world'.

Steve seems to me quite cynical in many ways, the only one who has stubbornly viewed my involvement as 'getting a good story', but in many ways his distance and his refusal to be steamrollered into unthinking compassion have provided an invaluable counterpoint to the devotion of others. And in his

challenge to Simon he has fulfilled perfectly the task entrusted
to him as churchwarden.

After the Archdeacon came to see them, Steve recorded the
sequence of events in a journal.[1]

Wed Aug 4 1993. 7.30 Had a meeting at my house with
Anne Corlett, we both agreed that this news could have
serious consequences for Dinnington and St Leonards . . . It
was considered that to keep it secret for much longer could
also be dangerous.

Later in conversation with me, he recalled the encounter
with the Archdeacon. We had an emotional little chat. That
finished with a little prayer. That was all very nice, and then
you've got to start thinking about the problems which aren't
quite so nice. I brought up potential problems with the Archdeacon, pointing out that it would not be unreasonable to expect
acts of vandalism against the church. His reply took me back a
little. He said, 'If that is the price we have to pay then so be
it.' Basically he said if the church gets burnt down then that's
the price.

Steve was anxious to explain his anxieties, 'The kind of people
who are going to throw a brick through the church window are
just yobbos. Er, what shall we do now – oh, vicar's a bit queer,
let's go and throw a brick through the church window. It was
certainly one of things we thought possibly could happen.
Strangely enough we never have had any trouble. But they were
quite legitimate anxieties. It was better to look on the black
side, than hide your head in the clouds while everything is
destroyed around you.

'The Archdeacon said they would always be prepared to help,
just give him a ring and he would come round. He hadn't
volunteered what kind of help, but that was fair enough. He
made it perfectly clear that this is new territory. There's been
gay vicars before, there have even been priests with HIV before,
but they've all been put out to pasture. This was the first
instance of a priest wanting to die in office as a gay priest with
AIDS. It was basically get on with it, sort it out, we'll monitor
the situation.'

Ann Corlett said she thought she had had an inkling about

Simon's illness, but Steve was devastated. 'I am naïve, I deal purely with facts, so I never try to read between the lines, so it was a revelation. I came home from the church, and rang Simon and asked to have a chat, and I went straight round there.'

The news came only two months after Steve had taken on the churchwarden's job. What he had seen as a fairly easy job had suddenly become a potential nightmare. A task that appeared to be a mere formality had suddenly assumed a reality and the implications were very worrying. 'I was supposed to be the link between the parish and the church, the Bishop . . . I must confess my first thought then was to resign. I could do without it. I had a full diary. I didn't need this. It was too hot to handle.'

If Simon had expected Steve to be more sympathetic he was mistaken. As far as Steve was concerned, 'The clergy don't play by the same rules as the rest of us, they are ruled by the law of God, that's why they are different. They have their own rules, I don't think they should corrupt them. I expect them to be God's representatives here.' For Steve, although he had no problems with homosexuals outside the church, and in his profession he was likely to meet rather more than most Dinnington parishioners, he could not accept the idea of a gay priest. As far as he was concerned if those were the church's rules they should be obeyed.

It was as if because he felt himself an outsider, someone who had deliberately come into the church rather than just grown up with it, he could not handle the idea that it was not as simple and separate a place from the rest of his life as he had expected. Nevertheless, Steve like so many others supported Simon because he respected him as a person. 'In Dinnington our priest is well loved, and it's sad he has to go through this turmoil, hiding his sexuality, when I'm sure that deep down he would want it to be known. He's a man of great intellect and I'm sure it's hurt him to hide this away.'

Thus began a determined campaign by Steve to make the knowledge more widely known in the parish. 'It would be nice to have known that he could have trusted more people earlier on. He's getting a lot of support . . . and I'm sure he would have got it earlier had more people known.' On September 1, Steve Kohut organised another meeting with Mike Cameron.

Steve wrote,

Mike, as was to be expected, pushed the compassion issue, whilst Ann and myself pushed the more general issues involved, mainly whilst at this point there was plenty of support for Simon the man, you could expect less support for having a gay rector, even less for having a gay rector with AIDS. I was still adamant that more people should know. Mike was not so sure, the more people who knew the more problems would accrue.

Steve explained how he felt to me, 'It was interesting at this time that Simon said he wanted to be in control of who knew and who didn't . . . that we were the last of the people who ought to know. I was against both statements. I considered Simon to be in the public domain and therefore fair game for the parish. I thought that this information was very dangerous, with only a few people knowing and if the story gets out and into the wrong hands then there were few people to show support. Then there was the potential of a large hostile mob. Dinnington has been a macho town, to a certain extent still is, mining has a tough tradition . . .'

Meanwhile the church authorities stayed well behind the scenes. There were several people in the parish who felt that they did not get enough support, and reckoned they could have had explicit direction rather than just tacit acceptance from the diocese. Joyce particularly felt they should have received more support. 'I felt very strongly about that – I just felt they buried their heads in the sand, I really do, because I kept saying, what does the Bishop think? I kept bringing it up. I think my bug was that they weren't concerned. Probably it was right we got on with it – but did they ask, how you are coping?'

As someone who was already used to working with AIDS patients as a volunteer worker in St Luke's Hospice in Sheffield, she believed that some people really needed counselling. 'There were times when we felt as though we were drowning in AIDS.' Both she and Sam are keen walkers and regularly join other members of the church and friends for long hikes across the countryside, difficult if you can't talk to people openly. 'It was a tremendous relief to us when we could talk.' But then of course the subject took over, 'Sometimes from the beginning of a ten mile walk to the end it was the subject of discussion.'

She was especially concerned that Mike Cameron was over-burdened, 'Simon was so ill at one time it must have been a tremendous strain. Mike was just thrown in at the deep end. We've often said weren't we lucky we got an older man as a curate. If he had been a younger curate he couldn't have coped. Nobody has really given Mike the praise he deserved.'

But Mike insisted that the diocese had always been very concerned that he felt able to cope with any increased work load as well as the emotional turmoil many of the flock were experiencing. 'I believe the diocese gave this parish as much help as we asked for. It was cleverer to let people get on with it.'

Simon considered Mike Cameron's support absolutely crucial; the situation was one which would indeed have been very difficult for a callow young man to handle. And Mike welcomed the need to think through the implications for his own work, and what it meant to be a priest. He was indignant that sexual orientation was considered so critical, 'A priest can be anything, greedy, uncaring – and heterosexual. But if you are homosexual, you can be the most beautiful person in the world but not a priest . . .'

During the last week of August there was a parish retreat to Iona, and everyone remembers how ill Simon was then. I don't think anybody expected him to last much longer. My mother wrote about the trip for the parish magazine, no doubt with Simon's gentle persuasion. They stayed in the Bishop's House, close to the beach, overlooking a dramatic sea of ever changing colours. My mother wrote, 'Iona has been described as "a very thin place – only a tissue paper separates the material from the spiritual." ' There were walks, quiet talks round the fireside and communion celebrated every day. She described a trip to Fingal's Cave and an evening boat trip around Iona, but she is discreet about Simon's enfeebled state and her own sorrow; the only indication that he, like her, was unable to walk very far is her reference to their tour of the island by pony and trap.

There was one occasion everyone remembered when they all went paddling in the sea. Simon rolled up his trousers too, and his painfully thin legs brought home to everyone how debilitating the illness was. Alma had also joined the retreat and the worst moment for her was when she and Simon conducted a service together. 'Simon was so weak, he was only just holding it together.' She came out of the vestry after the service to find Mother sitting there alone, 'I think she was crying, and I went and sat by her. Then Simon came out. He just looked at us and walked slowly out, it was terrible.'

Simon finished the Gregory Dix biography while he was in Iona. Stephen Lowe observed that he seemed to be putting off writing the final chapter for a long time, as if finishing it would somehow signal the end for him too. Given the similarities, that is hardly surprising; the last chapter has a detailed account of the death of Gregory Dix. It must, surely have been excruciating to write. Simon notes the last Good Friday address Dix gives, 'There is only one way: to let go of self, to give oneself to God out of love,' He quotes from Dix's writing a year or so before he died, describing death as, 'a ritual act, an act of worship . . . an act of adoration. Supremely it is an act of sacrifice to God.' The Father Abbot of Dix's community wrote a detailed account of his last days; working to the end, insisting on a meeting with his publisher, dictating final revisions to a passage about St Mark. And then he describes the final moments; the morphine, the prayers for the dying, the crucifix and lighted candles at the end of the bed.

The last two or three pages of the biography evoke a typical moment in Dix's life, saying mass in the early morning, and you know Simon is writing poignantly from his own experience, ' "Domine, non sum dignus . . ." he said, bowing over the altar before his communion, and there was perhaps a twinge of pain in his stomach? – a reminder, a warning: "but speak the word only and I shall be healed . . ." ' One of the reviews of the book commented that Simon's description of the last illness and death of Dix was the most moving and effective part of the book. Simon asks in the biography, 'Did Gregory have time, while he was ill, to sort out his papers, to remove controversial or sensitive material, to organise material that had potential?' Would Simon?

Simon seemed to be the only one by this stage who wasn't anticipating his immediate demise. He remained sanguine as ever. I asked him about it later, 'Well the growing weakness wasn't really that rapid, I kept reconciling myself to it and the clinic wasn't particularly alarmed,' he said, 'But when I heard one of the doctors talking about malnutrition, that struck me, it was an accurate word for it. But I wasn't anticipating imminent death.'

Indeed he even managed to go off for a holiday to Tuscany with my sister Caroline, to stay in a villa retreat near Florence where she had been working. It was a beautiful large Tuscan villa of mellow warm stone, with terracotta roof and bleached green shutters. He slept and sat in the garden and wrote poetry. Caroline remembers talking to him in the shade of the olive trees, talking about how he was learning acceptance. In one of the poems he writes,

> I lie in the quiet house
> and hear Mozart
> beyond the doors.
> It is late in the afternoon.
> The music gathers
> to the fingertips on the piano,
> gathers like a distant spring
> in a stone fountain
> soon to overflow.
> It falls.
> There is a soft cascade,
> the spread of water,
> a cadence.
>
> So the sunlight gathers
> over the pale hills
> through the reaching trees.
> It gathers, soon to burst gently
> on the dark edge of its setting,
> spreading down the mountains
> to fall softly into night.
>
> So I am gathered too.
> The fingertips precipitate the cadence,
> ready for that overflowing
> for that soft fall.

They spent a day in Florence, but Simon was exhausted, and

retreated to the Duomo for an hour simply to rest. In the photo Caroline took of him sitting in front of Santa Croce he looks terrible, so gaunt and thin, cheekbones prominent, the short sleeved check shirt accentuating the thinness of his arms. I don't think he ever looked that thin in the face again. He had to make his own way home, which he says was terribly hard, he was so weak he could barely lift his luggage. It looked like being the last time he would travel abroad.

Suddenly when it didn't seem as if things could be worse than they already were, everything else was overshadowed by the great SUN cloud that appeared. It was mid-September. Martin Sharp, an experienced regional reporter for the *Sun* for over twenty years, turned up on the doorstep. The *Sun* had received an anonymous phone call from someone in the village, saying that the Rector was dying of AIDS.

When I telephoned him a year or so later about what happened, Sharp was defensive, 'It isn't easy to turn up on somebody's doorstep and ask if they are dying of AIDS.' Simon invited Sharp in and they sat in Simon's quiet, book-lined study. 'I said I didn't want to pry, but if there was any truth in it it was a matter for him.' There was a long tense pause, and then Simon responded cautiously, 'I think it is extraordinary for someone to ring a newspaper and say something like that.'

Sharp then suggested that this might a good opportunity for Simon to tell his story. There was another long embarrassed silence. Simon said, 'I don't want to do that.' Then Sharp left, leaving Simon devastated. As if dying wasn't enough now he had to suffer torture by tabloid as well. Simon remembered it as probably the worst moment of his life.

One of his parishioners, who had just been told his diagnosis, turned up on the doorstep, hoping to offer comfort. 'She found me in tears when she came, in huge turmoil. Then Sue Proctor rang up and I burst into tears again on the phone and she too drove over straight away. Mike came round immediately too.' There was a real sense of panic. Simon remembered, 'Mike said it was the lowest he's ever seen me, and I couldn't stop crying!' he told me later. He called me that day too to let me know what we had dreaded had occurred, and then we waited. I

volunteered for the unpleasant task of buying the *Sun* every day
to see if they had run the story.

chapter 7

the little boat

The sea is so wide. My boat is so small.

Breton fisherman's prayer

Two weeks or so went by and I stopped buying the *Sun*. For whatever reason they had not pursued the story. Sharp told me later he knew the story would stand up, 'From the way he looked and what he said it was pretty obvious that it was true. And I could have gone to the churchwardens and done the story that way. But it would have had terrible repercussions. I don't want to destroy somebody's life. I took the view if he had wanted to talk I would have opened my notebook, but otherwise it would have been a gross intrusion. And I only live three miles away, I live next door to a vicar myself.' After my phone call to him a year or so later he came round to see Simon again, and offered to let him write his own story for the *Sun*. Simon declined.

Although the *Sun* never published the story the threat remained, certainly as long as Simon's illness remained a secret. It was imperative to tell more people, especially within the parish, and a series of stormy parish meetings took place that autumn. Simon finally talked to the churchwardens at a meeting in September. Steve Kohut still felt strongly that more people should know, that it was wrong to try and conceal it, 'Simon was not an ordinary citizien entitled to privacy.' He persuaded Simon and Mike that at least the rest of the parish council ought to know, and those who already knew shared the responsibility of telling the others, in advance of the regular monthly Parish Church Council (PCC) meeting in October.

The attitude of the churchwardens was crucial at this point; had they been unsympathetic Simon might have had to leave

the parish. Steve continued to keep his journal of events, and
recorded a visit to Simon the day before the PCC meeting,

Met with Simon at the Rectory, to discuss the present situation and how to approach the subject for the first time at
PCC level. I brought up his support for women priests and
asked if his support for them was more a sympathy vote than
a cause, because his own cause could not be promoted. He
agreed there was some truth in this.' Simon clearly reassured
him, since he concluded, 'Talked for about an hour and
concluded that the future did not seem too pessimistic.

The PCC encompassed a wide range of people; some like
Jenny Bott and Margaret Hawley, who were already involved,
others, especially older men, who held traditional views about
homosexuality, especially amongst the clergy, and some at least
who had not even known that Simon was gay. Geoff Gillard,
who had been away on holiday, was one of the last to know. He
is a tall, bespectacled, ponderous man, headmaster of a local
primary school. Gillard was also the Synod representative and
was well aware of the church's official position on the matter,
'It seemed to me to be a reasonable compromise at that time.
I don't think at the moment the majority of people in the
church could accept a practising homosexual being ordained.'
Nevertheless Gillard welcomed the opportunity to think the
issue through, and says that he never felt that Simon should
resign. He went to see Simon, 'It must be my non-comformist
background I suppose – but I think what I hoped for was Simon
to say he was repentant. It would have made life easier, then
we could forgive him. But of course Simon's point of view is
quite the opposite; this is how God made me – and because he
has got such a strong view on sexuality and God it makes it
almost impossible for his stance to be acceptable to the church.'
It was not likely to be an easy parish council meeting, and
in the end Simon himself was not there. He was by this stage
weaker and thinner than ever and had been suffering severe
fatigue and dizzy spells. Drugs had failed to combat the cryptosporidiosis and he was admitted to hospital, to see what could
be done to deal with the severe nutrition deficiency.
It was perhaps a good thing he was not at that meeting;

perhaps it was better for everyone to be able to discuss the situation without him, since they would feel more able to express their real feelings. The members of the PCC sat in a semi-circle of chairs as usual in the lobby of the church and worked through the written agenda. The issue of Simon's HIV diagnosis was discussed at the end. People were shocked and very dismayed, but Joyce in particular was strong, and encouraged everyone to believe they could cope with whatever happened. Sue Rafferty remembers how emotional it was, 'We all held hands and prayed together.' Steve Kohut continued to stress the need to spread the information further, but he realised how difficult that would be, 'Whilst there was tacit agreement to disseminate the news the people in the room knew only too well how difficult this task would be. You can't just say the Rector's got AIDS and leave it at that.'

Kohut has always expressed astonishment that the issue never made it on to the official PCC agenda, and was never recorded in any of the minutes. 'There are no records – I find that really amazing, considering it must be one of the biggest things that has ever happened to the church in Dinnington.' Another PCC meeting followed in November, 'I had to bring up the state of our Rector's health once again during any other business . . . The PCC in general had a head in the ground approach to the situation.'

Talking to me later Steve acknowledged that his anxieties may have been unnecessary, 'But when there is no path, when you're laying it as you go along . . . you're not even really quite sure which direction you're going in.' He was surprised at the lack of hostility, 'If one person had stood up and said, get that gay bastard out of the Rectory there would be a few more who would say, yeah that's a good idea, yeah . . . but nobody has.' But, as Kohut complained, there was hardly a clear lead from the Church of England, 'The church should decide whether homosexuality is acceptable or not. You cannot have homosexuality that is acceptable but without sexual contact. It can't be partially all right.'

Even now undoubtedly there remains a great deal of ambivalence within the parish about homosexuality in general, especially gay clergy. At that stage it was something new for them to consider, not an issue that most of them had ever had to deal with; most would just have assumed it was wrong without considering the implications. Now they had to think about homosexuality in terms of a person they loved and respected very much. There seems little doubt that their response to Simon was dominated by his illness and would have been less sympathetic if he was simply telling them he was gay – and healthy.

People clearly needed to know more about the subject, so a day was organised with the social responsibility officer for the diocese to discuss homosexuality. Simon wrote an account of his personal experience, hoping to be able to read it to the meeting himself. In the end he was in hospital and Derek read it for him. In it he described his early sense of his 'difference', the guilt and confusion he suffered, and how he gradually had come to reconcile his faith and sexuality. He told them he had had several relationships, but that more and more he valued singleness and deep friendships. He admitted, 'There have been partners in my life in the last few years while I've been in Dinnington but never "living-in".' It was a crucial admission, that he had contravened the current position of the Church of England, that homosexual clergy should be non-practising. But he went on to stress that he considered his homosexuality to be, 'a God-given part of myself', and emphasised, 'I'm the person you know because I'm gay.'

Nor did he resist a bit of sermonising – it was a good opportunity to use his own story as an example of what he had been trying to teach them about the broken healer, the flawed priest. 'I've wanted to tell the story for a long time and principally because it underlines what I've always stressed, that priests are human beings – living with tension and conflict and their own turmoils ... They're not virtue-machines or heroes on pedestals ...'

He concluded defiantly, 'I'm not here "sharing a problem" and asking for sympathy and tolerance. God lovingly chose to make me as I am, he called me to Dinnington as I am. I believe passionately that God wants me here and wants me to be as honest as I can be.' Certainly Simon did not want them to avoid the issue by feeling sorry for him. Derek too took the opportunity to talk about his own homosexuality at that meeting; for him, too, it was the first time he had discussed it with most of those present.

This time the discussion was a lot more heated than at the previous meetings. People had had time to consider the implications of a rector with AIDS, and attempt to come to terms with their feelings about homosexuality. Simon and Derek had given them plenty to think about. Someone said they would have to ask any future rector if they were gay. When Derek asked why, the response was, 'Well, some of us have got children – we wouldn't want anything to happen to them.' My mother was there at that meeting, and at this she reacted with great asperity, 'You don't mean to tell me you would have the audacity to ask them that question,' she expostulated. But people were understandably shocked and distressed, and Jenny Bott, for example, was sympathetic to those who had only just been told, 'To some it was a double shock, finding out that Simon was gay, and then that he was HIV, to cope with that in the same week. One man had only been told that same evening.' She insisted, 'It was gutsy of him to express his fear.' she said.

Meanwhile Simon was in hospital, as Dr Kinghorn and his team struggled to save him. The cryptosporidium and diarrhoea meant that he was retaining very little nutrition, so he was effectively starving to death. He underwent a whole series of tests and treatments, and it was eventually decided that he needed drip feeding to survive, Total Parenteral Nutrition, (TPN). This would need to be administered five days out of seven for a period of seven hours a night. On November 11 the TPN was started, fed through a permanent tube in his chest, the Hickman line, which is used for delivering nutrition and drugs directly to the bloodstream. Simon had no idea if it would be permanent, or how long it would last.

Initially the team administering the TPN insisted that Simon would have to be admitted for the treatment. But according to the hospital notes Simon was, 'vehemently opposed to this, since it would mean he could not continue working'. Quite a battle ensued since the TPN team considered it impossible for a patient to administer the treatment themselves and there was, say the medical notes, 'much deliberation'. The main sticking point was that Simon had no-one to help him at home. Sue Peters, the hospital Health Advisor, discussed the problem with

Walter, and there seems to have been no hesitation about whether the parish would look after him. It was simply taken for granted. Margaret recalls sitting in Simon's hospital room one day with Mother and Joyce while the issue was still under discussion by the hospital authorities. She assured him in her quiet way, 'Oh Simon don't worry about that. I'm sure there are a group of us who are willing to do it. It would be no problem for me.' She said later, 'It was the natural thing to do.' She felt in a way that she had been prepared for it.

She had already spent several years of her life caring for her parents. 'When it's somebody you love you do it,' she said simply. Kath Graham also had cared for her mother in the last years before she died, and for Joyce Robinson too, caring for sick and old people was a natural part of her life. Despite her husband Sam's negative views about homosexual clergy, he too felt it was a completely natural reaction, 'If somebody were ill, if somebody were knocking on the door you would have done likewise. You wouldn't say, well, that's their fault, end of story. You've got to care for them haven't you?' In the small community of Dinnington they still took care of relatives and friends in the old way, and it seemed to be the most ordinary thing in the world to look after Simon.

The original team of carers consisted of Joyce, Margaret, Kath Graham and another woman friend of Simon's who was training for the priesthood in Sheffield. They went for training sessions on the ward at the Hallamshire Hospital and they were instructed how to administer the feed and medicines through the drip. In fact, Simon always did everything for himself, but they still needed to be there in case anything went wrong, or simply to answer the door once he was hooked up to the drip.

Finally Simon was allowed home. It was a reprieve, though more perhaps for those around him than for Simon himself. In his journal he notes a prescient observation from Jim Cotter, 'I don't think the artist has finished with you yet despite the darker colours.' Frustrating as the hospital sojourn had been, it gave Simon pause for reflection, perhaps an important period of preparation for whatever future he had. 'It's becoming like a retreat, this hospital stay, my head is full of things I want to write, to think, to talk, to express . . . I want to pray! No doubt it's to do with the feeding but there's also something in the restriction of being here that makes space for a different kind of liberation . . .' He began a new journal, inscribing it with words from Milton, writing about his blindness, 'So by this infirmity may I be perfected, by this completed. So in this darkness, may I be clothed in light.'

It was almost Christmas by the time Simon came home, and was able to take his place at the altar again, still Rector of Dinnington. A few changes were necessary at the Rectory, but it retained the same calm, ordered atmosphere. On the upstairs landing a vast fridge was installed for food bags and medicines, and regular deliveries of food and drugs became part of his life. Simon rearranged his bedroom to accommodate the drip stand and medicine trolley, but the room never took on a clinical aspect. It was a lovely quiet room, the window looked out across the old gardens of Dinnngton Hall, now a neglected orchard which the owner wanted to develop as housing and which Simon had thus far managed to block. Beyond were a few new red brick houses and then a curve of green hills. It faced east and the mornings were beautiful; cold orange dawns and insistent birdsong. The room was painted white like the rest of the house with white muslin curtains and bamboo blinds, white furniture, a crucifix and icons on the wall; Simon's passion for colour and especially yellow alleviated the austerity with a cheerful yellow quilt on the bed, bright gold dried chysanthemums and a series of small Matisse collages on the wall.

As ever there were books, candles and cairns of stones, meditatively arranged by Simon, and reverently dusted by his long-suffering cleaner, Janet. It was a room that would increasingly become the centre of his life, and he always cherished it. It was all part of his dignity, the way it always looked so fresh and neat, and he took great pleasure in buying new things, a bright new rug, a vase, cushions, and always new pictures. Mind you, there was always a cold little bit of me that thought, 'All this stuff and he acquires more daily and I keep thinking, Martha-like, what will we do with it all?' He saw it himself, too – he commented one day to Janet when she was cleaning, 'I don't envy whoever has to clear this lot up when I'm gone!'

Somewhat dubiously we planned a family Christmas at the Rectory. For the family, we were into extra time. We thought we had nearly lost him. There was joy in his survival but also anxiety. How long could he cope, how long could we expect the parish to care for him, what roles should we be playing, how much care would he eventually need. Potential tabloid headlines reverberated . . . vicar dying of AIDS, Yorkshire vicar in AIDS scandal . . . It was not clear how any of us could contribute much more than weekend visits. Although Mother was now living in Dinnington she could not be a regular carer because her own arthritis meant she found it very difficult to climb the stairs in Simon's house. She found this terribly hard, feeling that there was nothing she could do to help him.

There were many issues to discuss; the practical issues of contact, and physical care, but also the emotional responsibilities involved. How could we balance our responsibilities between our 'chosen' families and friends, and blood relations. And other family relationships inevitably were neglected in favour of Simon. For two or three years I hardly ever visited my other siblings, all the time was devoted to Simon, and we inevitably talked more of Simon than anything else when we did meet. Of course it had brought us profoundly closer too.

We had to ask ourselves whose needs came first – did it always have to be Simon? In the end we decided not, that we also had to think of our own needs and our own families. Indeed Simon needed to think of others too, not just in his priestly capacity, but as a brother, as a human being. It became clear early on that if he wanted us to visit with children, he had to accept a certain amount of mess . . . I have an image of him as we say farewell after a weekend visit already re-arranging the bowls, the little boxes, contentedly but determinedly. And however much we begged he never ever put away anything to safeguard it from the children, so things did get broken. But I suppose it was all a part of him trying to keep his life as normal as possible, not having to compromise.

It was to be our final family Christmas with Simon. It certainly felt final and although in fact Simon was still around for the next one, we didn't all try to get together again. For me at least it was a profound strain. Family Christmas is not easy at the best of times and definitely not recommended at the worst of times. All the immediate family came to the Rectory or stayed nearby, including Martin and Susan and their four children from Devon.

Although Simon was getting most of his nutrition from the TPN he still sat down to meals and attempted to eat, but he often felt sick and found he had lost his taste for many things. Fresh fruit was ill-advised and often all he could stomach was sweet, innocuous food like tinned pears. He ate lots of sweets though, and the children were delighted by the constant supply of jelly babies. They adapted more easily than the adults to the strange new routine, snuggling up with Simon in bed once he was attached to his drip.

What to tell the children was of course an issue, and we all approached it in different ways. Theo was four by then, and quite used to Uncle Simon being ill; he used to enjoy examining all the dials and flashing lights of the drip and pump. He was obviously sensitive to the situation without being specifically told much detail. At the time I felt he would absorb as much as he could understand, and would ask if he needed more information. For Theo, especially, who ended up going to church rather a lot I think there was an inevitable and somewhat bizarre conflation of Simon and Jesus on the cross. He couldn't understand either of them – and I couldn't really explain them either.

My sister Jackie was much more upfront, and told her son Jack who was then eight, more or less straight away. He was already at school and had heard of AIDS, and he was a sensitive child and very attached to Simon. She felt he needed time to prepare himself like everyone else. Her daughter Martha, a year younger than Theo, also knew and was refreshingly matter-of-fact about it.

For my other brother Martin there was the critical problem of distance, as they lived in South Devon with four children, and this obviously coloured their response. Nevertheless, they chose not to tell the children, the oldest of whom was by then eleven, and none of the children visited Simon for the last two years of his life. I think they preferred their children to remember him, 'as he was'.

I think there must always be a temptation to make someone a scapegoat in a situation like this, and we had to resolve early on not to do that to Martin; everyone had to be allowed to respond to the situation in their own way. We were of course fortunate that because of the parish support we could afford to be delicate about each other's feelings. Had there only been family to look after Simon, then the pressures would have been much more difficult.

Children do need to learn about death; in other societies it is much more an ordinary fact of life than it is to us, and in many ways they can cope with it better and more directly than adults. They haven't learned to be squeamish. Indeed, there were occasions when they were the best possible antidote to our gloom both in their understanding, sensitive if inarticulate, and the sense they gave of the continuity of life. I know Simon took pleasure in their visits, despite the disruption. He cherished the moment when Theo said that Simon was another Daddy for him and I have a memory of them playing together with Simon's ancient toy soldiers. The soldiers were lined up in formation, pointing their guns at a little figure of a priest.

Despite the family's desire to support Simon, there were some unbridgeable gulfs that Christmas. The main thing I remember apart from vast amounts of cooking and washing up was Simon's refusal to say grace for us when I asked him, because 'we weren't on the same wavelength'. I was hurt, and he explained that he didn't want to impose religion on people who didn't share his beliefs – and with two atheist brothers-in-law present perhaps he had a point. It never became a critical issue as we always strived not to involve our partners more than necessary. But it was certainly true, apart from Caroline and my mother, that the family was not part of his spiritual journey.

He was very aloof, remote, with a provoking kind of detachment a lot of the time. A parishioner once commented that for Simon 'community' was a bit like walking through a forest of trees. It was like that with his family too. He wrote a poem about his three sisters, 'Just occasionally I hear murmuring voices – women's soft and distant: when I stop to listen there's nothing there; it may be my own breathing, or even traffic but it has an air of the mysterious.' Sometimes it seemed it was like that, we were no more than background murmuring. Certainly, although he was concerned for others in a wide sense, had inherited my father's tremendous compassion for people in need, sometimes he seemed to barely register individuals close to him.

Not long after Christmas Simon noted a dream of a large house, full of the family. Beneath was a cellar and a long way down a well, 'clear but remote'. It was his 'well within', the resources within himself which he was beginning to discover and develop. There is some comfort now in feeling that perhaps the family were a part of that.

People soon began to feel comfortable visiting him upstairs, and he added an extra chair for visitors, or people would perch on the bed if necessary. Occasionally they even held meetings up there. It was certainly a good house to adapt to such needs, and Simon was immensely fortunate in that. He was looking much better, his face had filled out a little and he had lost his cadaverous look. He was still very underweight, but in winter especially, he wore thick sweaters that disguised his thin limbs. He established a new way of life, with five nights a week of TPN, trying to get away for overnight visits or evenings out when he was off the drip. He needed to start about 7.30 pm. Sometimes if he was tired he would go upstairs to his bedroom, or he set the drip up downstairs and carried it up later. Everyone got quite used to him sitting in his usual corner of the sofa, while life went on around him. Although the team of carers had been trained to administer the feed and drugs Simon always did it all himself, a painstaking, lengthy and inevitably tedious routine that had to be followed religiously. Hygiene was critical because any infection of the Hickman line could be fatal.

The carers established a regular routine taking a particular night a week each, occasionally relieved by visiting friends or family. One of the spare bedrooms was set up with an alarm system, and Margaret even bought a little brass bell so Simon could ring for her if she was downstairs. Sometimes they would sit upstairs with Simon to chat or watch television, or they would settle themselves downstairs, Margaret with her embroidery, Kath sorting out the christening rota or the parish magazine distribution. Whenever Joyce had spent the night, there were always flowers on the table; she always got up early and went out into the garden to pick some fresh flowers before she went home. Simon's demands were never great; a flask of water and a drink of hot Ribena before bed. You always wished you could do more.

Although many more people in the parish knew the Rector had AIDS by this time, it was still important to be discreet and we remained very anxious about the media. Still it was an open secret in the village by now, especially as people got to know about the home-care system. On the whole the village was friendly and supportive. Joyce recalls somebody shouting to her in the high street, 'Are you going to Simon's, Joyce? How do they know I'm going to Simon's?' – it just goes on the grapevine in a place like this.'

There was one unpleasant episode, which upset Simon greatly. He had always gone to a hairdresser in Dinnington because he always liked to patronise the local shops, but his hairdresser told him he might put off his other clients. It was a cruel rejection. His garage in Dinnington was wonderful on the other hand and proved immensely helpful, coming to pick up his car from him and return it when it needed repairs, since Simon did not have the energy to walk back himself. This was increasingly often; his Renault 5 had originally been bought with a loan from the diocese and really needed to be replaced – there were the most awful clanking sounds when Simon drove it out of the garage sometimes. But it hardly seemed worth it. Which would go first, Simon or his car?

Meanwhile Stephen Lowe was struggling to contain the problem within the higher echelons of the church. Initially he had no idea after talking to the churchwardens what the parish reaction would be, but he firmly denies that any pressure was brought to bear on them. He felt there were several key reasons why the parish reacted as it did, one of them being the women involved, 'I've got the impression that the real powerful leadership in Dinnington is female, and the women seem totally unthreatened by it.' Then there was Simon's own spirituality, 'Simon's holiness and spirituality makes him more difficult to criticise than if he had been a trendy radical, his spiritual depth makes it much more difficult to throw stones at him. He really is a holy man.'

But the Archdeacon was considerably less confident of other clergy in the diocese, 'We never had any formal debate about the issue. I suspect because both the Bishop and I were a bit nervous about letting the others get their fingers on it.' The deanery, a regional sub-section of the diocese of Sheffield, was pretty conservative and Simon had never fitted into it particularly well, although Stephen Lowe points out that he always had a significant ally in Sue Proctor. She was about to be ordained and take over a new church in the deanery. But people had their suspicions, 'Two of the rural deans sniffed around, I wasn't sure how to handle it, when I knew and they didn't. I said he had stomach problems, and they half bought that for a period. I didn't have great confidence in either of them handling it, though they have never been publicly critical.' And there was one fundamentalist parish in the diocese which was infamous for its constant inveighing against homosexuality.

By the middle of February it was becoming clear that Simon's eyesight was at risk. I remember the spine-chilling moment I picked up a book in his car about coping with blindness. It was one of the things he dreaded most, not being able to read, and not being able to drive. He was also developing a few patches of Karposi's Sarcoma, though they were not particularly visible. Small mollusca – like little white warts – appeared on his face but were usually removed. But CMV Retinitis was the greatest fear, threatening his eyes and eventually the entire nervous system. Further medication was added to his home drug regime, but his right eye continued to deteriorate, and he had to be admitted and given the drug as injections directly into the eye. This had to be done once a week for four weeks and was certainly the worst treatment he was to undergo. 'Simon found these injections very traumatic,' underlines the medical notes. His journal says, 'Of course, I know how precious my eyes are and yet it was the way I automatically picked up something to read with my eyes dilated after the tests. I couldn't read a word and I burst into tears.' I learnt later that patients who contract CMV rarely survive beyond six months.

Derek Jarman died then, February 20, 1994. 'I admired him for being so open and brave about AIDS quite apart from his art. He led the way.' Simon wrote. Gradually in his writings Simon began to address the subject of AIDS and his death more directly and frequently, trying to find a way to understand it, come to terms with it. He wonders whether living in the present, trying not to look at the future is the right way, or whether he is denying reality. But he cherishes the days when is able to

enjoy the present moment fully, the 'kingfisher days' of a
favourite R.S. Thomas poem, one that he included in the commonplace book he made for me, 'There is an August within us;
aeons of preparation for a few kingfisher days.' He acknowledges
fear, but it is fear of pain, disability, dementia, rather than fear
of death. 'I can rationalise it away – everyone dies, other people
suffer more, I have done some of the things I wanted to do
– but it doesn't seem to somehow counter those bleak dark
waters . . .'

He continued to write his stories; having finished the Dix
biography this became an important creative project, another
way to find a continuing purpose and articulate his experience.
They are short, pithy little metaphorical parables and sometimes
he would deliver them as somewhat unorthodox sermons; the
discovery of a well, an artist searching for the perfect yellow,
sailing a coracle across a lake. One was an account of climbing
a mountain, the exhilaration of getting to the top, and it was
published in the parish magazine, 'On top of the world it
seemed, full of far horizons in the fading sun, breathtaking in
the breeze.' Although mountain-climbing was something he
could hardly expect ever to do again, it was ironically a metaphor
for coming out on top which he sorely needed.

He had given himself two years, a sensible span he explained
one day (sometime around the middle of 1993) long enough
to feel that it was worth planning ahead, planning holidays,
improvements to the house, parish events, but not so long as
to be unrealistic or to lose the sense of urgency, of limited time
that kept him going. 'They keep saying my attitude counts for
so much,' he wrote in his journal. The time had come again
for his four-yearly Episcopal Review. Simon submitted to
Stephen Lowe a succinct description of his situation, 'My
guiding principle has become "living as normally as possible for
as long as possible" . . . though I have to say that I don't really
know how to deal with this "affliction." ' He described his parish
work, his writing projects, and his growing involvement with the
retreat movement. He emphasised the increasing importance of
the liturgy both for him and the parish; even if he does nothing
else they want to see him presiding at communion and leading
worship.

Partly because of his illness, he said, lay ministry had

increased with much greater community involvement and a deepening spirituality in the congregation. 'Opportunities to help develop people's spirituality become increasingly important; quiet days, retreats, personal consultation and direction, but without setting myself up as a "guru".' As far as the future was concerned, he wrote, 'I think I am going to have to continue to learn a ministry of being served as well as serving. I still find it difficult to be still and receive help . . . maybe I ought to think about some ways of "sharing the experience of AIDS".' He concluded, 'I've never had much of a sense of "career" or "ambition" so there's not much hardship in drastically shortened horizons. I would like to stay where I am as long as possible.'

In his assessment of Simon for the Bishop, Stephen Lowe wrote, 'I made no notes during this interview as it is difficult to conduct a traditional Episcopal Review with somebody who is working with the effects of the HIV virus and who is simply ambitious to be alive in three years' time.' The Archdeacon wrote that he had encouraged Simon to think about sharing his experience of AIDS with others. 'He is still remarkably active and I think his inner drive and commitment not to give up are keeping him alive . . . his ministry is being marked by his continued search for beauty and creativity.' He recommended, 'I would like to feel that Simon could stay in the parish until the end of his life. He has been extraordinarily good for them and they have, in return, been very good to him. The presence of his mother, living in Dinnington, and the exceptional gifts of Mike Cameron and the Pastoral Team have meant that something very loving and very Christian is happening in Dinnington. There is no judgement, simply warm, caring, mutual ministry, which I have found very moving to observe.'

That Easter was a particularly poignant affair and I was beginning to dimly perceive what extraordinary things were happening in Dinnington. Simon was there before us, robed and ready, despite the cold, to light the Paschal candle as he had always done. His loyal parishioners, perhaps thirty or so people, followed him into their church to celebrate the great Easter Eucharist with him and re-affirm their commitment, both to the Church and to Simon.

The great change for Simon and his parish was his need for

care from them. He found that difficult to come to terms with, despite his determined past attempts to demystify his priestly status. Simon said in one of the BBC video journals, 'Expecting the clergy to be more holy, more pure than anyone else, the idea makes me extremely uncomfortable.' In his journal, Steve Kohut recorded a visit to Simon in hospital, a classic example of the desire to see priests as set apart, not like ordinary mortals, 'Simon was on new medication and he seemed to be alright. He was in a single room with his own colour TV and I was surprised to find him watching Gladiators. I passed no comment.'

It was a key issue; could people learn to accept a flawed clergy, learn perhaps to be less dependent on the priest, and more self-sufficient. Simon was being given an opportunity to expose the full extent of his flawed humanity, 'It is certainly a change of role to accept people's ministering to me,' he reflected. 'In beginning to think about this issue of gay clergy and a vicar with AIDS people have got a great distance to travel . . .'

Simon's own vulnerability was brought home to him when he prepared a service of blessing for the relationship of two women, one of whom was dying of cancer. She knew Simon through working in the diocese and they asked him to conduct a service for them, meeting several times to discuss exactly what form the service should take and also discuss what they wanted for the funeral. Sadly less than two weeks before the blessing was planned Val began to deteriorate rapidly. Simon visited her in the hospice and it was clear she would not be able to go home again. It was agreed that that night, when everything was quiet and undisturbed, he would say a proxy blessing for them. Pauline sat with Val and said the Lord's Prayer. The following morning Simon took them a card on which he had written the words he had used the previous evening. Then he held their hands together and said a short prayer. Val was barely conscious by this time, and she died four days later in June 1994. Afterwards Simon helped ensure that the music and readings Val had wanted were included in her funeral service. In a moving letter to my mother after Simon died Pauline wrote, 'The memory of that ministry and the knowledge that thanks to Simon our relationship did receive the blessing we both wanted is of enormous comfort to me.'

Simon talked about the experience himself at a Healing Service held shortly afterwards, 'It suddenly struck me, sitting with them the other day, that this was the blind leading the blind, the sick ministering to the sick, the dying to the dying. But what else can we do? We are all dying – all crippled and diseased, all struggling to live. The wounded surgeon, but not yet too wounded to go on, ministering somehow perhaps, I don't know how, from the wounds.' He stressed the universality of pain, 'We are all in this together. It is a community of need and pain and decay – and so also a community of healing and growing together and love as unlimited as we can make it.'

He carried anointing oil for the sick in a tiny phial, and he talked about the uses of oil in anointing and healing, reminding them of Jesus in the olive grove, 'His determination to be ready for sacrifice, to cope with pain and suffering and death, under the cool night shade of olive trees.' I think of Simon facing his future under the shade of the olive trees in Tuscany with Caroline. Perhaps there was an echo there for him too.

Simon had vowed to live long enough to see the vote on women priests and then to share the first ordinations and the first Eucharists. The first women priests were duly ordained on March 12, 1994 and Simon danced for glee (as he noted in his journal!). Both Sue Proctor and Alma asked him to preach at their first Eucharists, and the photographs of both occasions were prominently displayed thereafter; with Sue in her white robes, Simon gaunt but immaculate as ever in grey suit and white clerical collar, and standing proudly, formally robed, next to a beaming Alma. He was delighted to finally use the pronoun 'she' in talking about a priest. Dinnington organised a parish outing to Manchester to see Alma ordained, and Simon preached the sermon at her first Eucharist the next day. (She says she was absolutely determined to have him there even if he had to be brought on a stretcher.)

It began to seem as if Simon could go on like this forever. My husband called him the bionic man. The carers had committed themselves so willingly with no idea of how long it would last; who could have expected over two years? But there was always a waiting list of willing helpers. They were all very sensitive to Simon's sense of independence, and understood how crucial it was to his dignity. Margaret observed, 'I try not to be too motherly, we try not to intrude on his privacy too much.'

When we visited, family members too took their turn though I was always a bit concerned that we had not had any training. There was one occasion I was there when there were electricity cuts after a big storm. Simon's pump cut out, and I had to keep phoning the electricity board to see when they would fix the power lines. It was an anxious night. Always there was the possibility that things could go wrong, that he would suddenly need rushing to hospital. His temperature was the critical factor, if it rose it meant that an infection had set in and he would need antibiotics immediately.

But he struggled on, with regular hospital visits. Blood transfusions were now required about once a month, since the new blood was rapidly destroyed by a combination of the virus itself and the toxic drugs he was receiving to combat it. The hospital were incredibly accommodating about the timing of his treatment, always willing to fit it round Simon's work schedule, acutely conscious that this was why they were keeping him alive. If it was not convenient he could postpone a transfusion for several days and struggle on, or if necessary they would fix him up for a particularly strenuous commitment; the occasion when he had a double wedding to do for example. Kinghorn explained, 'He always found the time to do things that were important to him, instead of living from one treatment to the next.' Everyone seemed to be aware that Simon was on borrowed time, that many patients in his position would already have given up.

The question was always whether Simon himself wished to go on fighting, and further intervention was discussed with him in those terms. The doctors would explain the options, the disadvantages or side effects of new drugs, but it was always his decision whether to carry on. What is abundantly clear from reading his medical notes and talking to his doctors is how effectively the doctors and patient worked together for a common purpose; the level of trust and sympathy is salutory.

At the end of June one of the hospital sisters commented that she had never known anyone keep a Hickman line in so long, presumably a tribute at least in part to Simon's own scrupulous hygiene. He began hydrotherapy sessions, and it really helped to firm his muscles. He always loved swimming and the relief of an hour floating in warm water was palpable. His eyesight had not deteriorated further, but as a result of the drugs needed to control the virus affecting the eye, his liver was beginning to suffer. He was beginning to look oddly tanned but it was somehow flattering.

He began a Well book, detailing his daily medical condition. He listed the different drugs he needed for his various afflictions, from diarrhoea to thrush, and all the various side effects like nausea and heartburn. He tried to record everything he ate and drank; one ironical Sunday entry notes, along with the tinned pear, tea and apple juice he consumed, 'rather a lot of wine to finish off at communion...' The books are an invaluable record of his illness and the inexorable, boring detail makes reading as strangely compelling as Andy Warhol's diaries. It was another way of retaining control, to know in precise detail the problems and the effects of the drugs he was taking, and meant that the medical process was always a mutual affair between patient and doctor, and of benefit to both.

There were always anxieties; he notes one day in trepidation, 'I think there may be slight loss of memory, but I've never been good with names and numbers etc!' I remember one occasion when he forgot to read the wedding banns for a young couple and he was devastated, terrified that his brain was beginning to be affected. He was always worried that the deterioration in his sight meant he would have to give up driving. There was a period when Simon always seemed to have the television on, as if he really would watch anything, an easy way to block out reality, I suppose. I eventually found myself begging him to turn it off or at least turn down the volume. (In fact I think I said something terrible in my irritation like, 'Are you going deaf, as well?' But he forgave me.) Then suddenly a few months later he stopped, and hardly watched it, as if he didn't need it any more.

Simon continued to hold his parties and events at the Rectory and that June the parish had a very jolly Strawberry Sparkle party in the garden. As usual the ladies turned up laden with vast supplies, with home made cakes and great bowls of strawberries, cheerfully taking over the kitchen to supply endless pots of tea and ferry them out to the garden.

They began a series of spiritual development meetings at the Rectory called the Well Within, inviting people to come and share their own spiritual resources – what feeds and sustains you, what rock do you rest on, what stirs your soul. Simon started off the first session, describing friendship, religion and sense of tradition and roots, his beloved islands soaked in prayer, waterfalls, the Eucharist, music, poetry, Matisse, icons and calligraphy. Subsequent contributors included the Archdeacon Stephen Lowe, the Bishop, Margaret Selby and Janette Moon, one of the artists working on the Miners' Memorial. Many people have said how profound and moving these meetings were as individuals plumbed their souls. My mother also participated. Simon wrote in his journal at this time, 'I salute my mother especially. I'm deeply proud of the way she has not only accepted my sexuality and also AIDS but has become an advocate when she can be. Of course, there was a struggle for her, but she has moved so far for me and I admire her for it. Ironically though, it makes it all the more painful to hurt her as the illness progresses.'

My mother and I sat in the kitchen together one evening in the Rectory after Simon had gone upstairs and she recounted the turning point for her in coming to terms with Simon's illness. She reminded me that Simon had been very ill as a child, with something like diptheria at only two and a half. She and my father spent one night sitting each side of his bed, instructed by the doctor to watch for any change in his breathing. (I was irresistibly reminded of the scene in *Little Women* when Beth is dying.) They prayed over him, and Father begged God to spare him, vowing that if he was saved, he would dedicate his son to God's service. (It still seems to me to be a somewhat high-handed attitude to take to someone else's life, but that was my father.) Ever after Father would refer to Simon as a 'brand from the burning', a reference to the young John Wesley being saved by his father from a burning house. Now, for my mother, the experience made sense. She felt that he had been given back to her then, that she did not need to resent giving him up now; that every day he had lived since then was already a gift. Sometimes our discussions took a more mordant turn. Funerals became a frequent topic of conversation and it became almost a joke that mother kept changing her mind about where she wanted her ashes scattered. I wondered what Simon had planned for us, afterwards. Perhaps a pilgrimage to some windswept sacred island that we would never forget.

In August there was a parish holiday, again to Cumbrae. Simon with grim determination drove himself, mother, Alma and Kath Graham, the car stuffed with supplies, detailed at length in his Well book. Nevertheless he was so much better than he had been the year before in Iona and he astonished himself and everyone else by cycling several miles round the island one day. He was by then about eight stone in weight, over two stone heavier than he had been the previous summer.

Soon after his return, though, he had to be rushed to hospital on a Saturday night because his Hickman line was blocked, but he still managed to get back for the Sunday morning service. A week later he was back again, having developed a high temperature, and Walter had to drive him in. He needed urgent antibiotics and was clearly in need of rest, so he was warned this might be a long stay. And every time we wondered is this it, can he make it through again . . . Holidays were always difficult, you always wondered if you would have to rush back – would there be any point in rushing back?

Again the hospital stay was a retreat, a time for reading and reflection. He read several novels with AIDS as a theme, including *The Celibate* by Michael Arditti, and Carrie Fisher's *Delusions of Grandma*. How strange to be reading about other's deaths; I read them later and cannot imagine what pain it must have caused him. But perhaps it helped; to know others feel similarly can illuminate one's own experience. He notes from Carrie Fisher her observation, 'There's something called reverse labour when you come to die, a rhythm that rides you out, not in.'

His sight had begun to deteriorate again, which filled him with dread. In his Well book he meticulously sketches the stars and spots on his eyes, observing the deterioration with horror. His right eye was reduced to about half-vision and there was serious concern about how safe it was for him to continue driving. The doctors told him the photos of his eye looked beautiful. 'To whom?' he asks dryly. His journal notes philosophically, 'The photographs of the retina of my eye look just like a little planet, a moon – it's this inside and outside again, this interior mirrored in the universe . . .'

We had occasionally, tentatively, suggested that he think about making a Living Will, and he considered the possibility then as he wrote in his journal. 'It would have to include the degrees of pain I can tolerate; the quality of life below which I couldn't bear it – mobility, sensory awareness, pain, dependence on others, physical restriction, depression.' In the end he couldn't do it; he persuaded himself that there were no circumstances where he could definitely predict he would choose to die, and he concluded the only principle he could truly affirm was to 'preserve life at any cost'.

He wondered how long he could go on expecting the parish to support him, 'At what point of illness would I feel impelled to resign, unable any longer to be a priest? I want to die as a priest because life includes being hurt, ill, in pain, dying. It's not a secret, nothing to be guilty about or ashamed of, but a fact of life . . . is that enough justification for the demands I will make of the parish by doing this?' He longed to be back there in that little church with familiar faces, familiar cupped hands, 'I find myself preparing for communion here in my room listening to the most glorious church music in the world, Vivaldi's Gloria, Bach, Purcell . . . but I'd still rather be going to the altar at home.'

All this time he was grasping for a way to make his illness meaningful for himself and others, 'The wounded surgeon . . . me . . . the dying surgeon . . . but there's something significant isn't there, for prayer, for spirit, that I as a "victim" of AIDS preside at the Eucharist, offer the sacrifice.' Then one night he dreamed of a little boat, and wrote to my sister Jackie about it the next day. It became a recurring image and eventually a story; the boat in dock, being built, rocking unsteadily as the props are taken away. It was the nearest he could get to imagining what death would be like, 'The tide is swirling in and I shall discover that the props have to go if I'm going out into that great swelling ocean in my little boat – the ocean that I'm made for.' It was beginning to sound a seductive prospect. I wrote to him then about a dream I had of trying to rescue him, to hold him up in tumultuous buffeting waves, trying to carry him in my arms like a baby out of the sea. He said my letter made him cry.

It was a long hospital stay, three weeks in all, but finally by mid-September he was out again, another reprieve, like a condemned man sent back to his cell from the executioner. 'Every stay in hospital feels like another step down, another little defeat . . . Am I asking too much?' But he was so tenacious, 'I want to do something more, something else, creative and good before I die.' In a letter to me he wrote, 'I know I shouldn't take any of these things for granted; they could all have been taken away from me long ago and I feel I've been given them back as rather more precious, fragile and cherishable gifts . . . and if (when) the time comes and I have to "give them back" – reading, writing, even driving, and all the other things too – well, I think I can feel I've tried to make the most of them.' He was getting closer, it seems from his journal, 'I want to go to the sea, but it suddenly felt like the English Channel wasn't big enough and then I thought of the North Sea and that wasn't big enough either or even the Atlantic – they all come to an end: it's got to be endless, and I know what sea that is . . .'

His treatment had become more complicated, the drips and infusions took even longer, and the juggling act had become increasingly delicate. In October he needed a new Hickman line inserted, but was very pleased to have survived long enough for two. He spent a few days at the Sanctuary, a retreat for AIDS patients in Bournemouth, where he was able to reassure another sufferer with his own low CD4 count, now down to 4. He particularly relished meeting an ex-drag queen bemoaning the loss of his lovely long red hair.

Then in the journal there is a stark and all too familiar journal entry. 'T. died today. 22.10.94.' It echoed the meticulous and discreet entries Simon had made for so many he knew who died of AIDS over the years. 'T' was Terence Keeton, another person with AIDS in Dinnngton. He was Walter Hawley's nephew and Margaret Hawley was with Simon when Derek, who lived nearby and had been a great support to the family, called to say Terence had died, 'Simon was very upset, and I just sat and held his hand and put my arm round him and said, Simon I don't know what to say, there are no words.'

Terence, who was forty-two, had left Dinnington for the south of England where he was a successful chef, living with a partner and visiting his time-share on the Costa del Sol whenever he could. Everybody said he looked like Barry Manilow. He only came back to Dinnington, to his family, when he was very ill; on previous visits his family had noticed he had a bad cough, but then one day he arrived back so ill they had to help him out of the car; the blue Nissan with the personalised number plate of which he was so proud. He was taken straight to hospital with pneumonia and a collapsed lung. AIDS was diagnosed a few days later and he was told he had been probably been HIV-positive for about ten years. He died eighteen months later.

He was very anxious about the effect the diagnosis would have on his family; what people would think, 'He thought it would be a stigma for us,' his mother, Margery Keeton, said to me. Margaret recalled, 'We tried to persuade him to be more like Simon, but he was so afraid of people knowing. He wanted to shield his mum and dad.' Derek Norbury visited Terence and the family while he was ill. He understood well enough Terence's reluctance to be open about his illness. 'He just said he didn't want people in the street to have a go at his mother and dad, I couldn't say to him it won't be like that.'

Simon had tried to see Terence, and Terence had at one stage asked to see Simon, and wanted him to take his funeral. But one or other of them always seemed to be in hospital. On one occasion they were even on the same ward, and Simon tried to see Terence, but he was undergoing treatment. It is hard in any case to imagine the dialogue, even for Simon. PWA talking to Priest with AIDS . . .

It was very strange for Simon, as he described to me later, 'He was in the middle of some treatment, and when I finally did get to see him he was not conscious, and he died later that week. The oddest thing for me on the ward was when I went to the nurses' station and said which room is Terence in. When they asked why I said, "Well I'm his parish priest . . ." '

Setting aside his own distress the day Terence died, Simon went round to see the Keetons, switching in that moment from patient to priest. Perhaps no other experience exemplified for him so painfully the wounded healer he had become, as he wrote in his journal. 'I saw the family this afternoon. It's all so laden with ironies: on the ward the other day, with the nurse, I suddenly switched from patient to pastor wanting to see a parishioner. And they want me to take the funeral . . . talk about the "wounded surgeon". I don't think I can do it alone, but I will do it – who better, in one sense?' And then later that day after visiting the Keetons, Simon sat down alone in his study, clicked on a small video camera on a tripod facing him, and recorded his feelings for a BBC television documentary. 'I cried for him, for me, it makes me think is it me next, will I go the same way?'

there is nothing to be afraid of

'*At the heart of every living parish is a dying priest.*'

Archbishop Robert Runcie at the funeral of John Eastaugh, the
Bishop of Hereford

The sadness and secrecy of Terence's death contributed to
Simon's determination to be open himself about AIDS, to try
to ease the path a little for others. He wrote in his journal, 'I
have now grown towards wanting to say something about living
with AIDS – that you can live with it, that a diagnosis or
symptoms is not all-life-ending and utterly negative. Of course
it's life changing but it really doesn't have to mean secrecy,
shame, hiding – it can be lived with openly. I feel I can say that
with some conviction from an occupation which after all might
have been the *worst* place to be with such a diagnosis.'

Earlier that summer, the Archdeacon, Stephen Lowe, had
arrived at the Rectory for a meeting to find Simon settled on
the sofa in the sitting room, hooked up to his drip, with
everyone else comfortably clustered around him. Lowe had
previously suggested to Simon that he had an important story
to tell, and he was so impressed by the equanimity of all present
that he began to think about a television programme. He
approached Angela Tilby, a highly respected religious broad-
caster who was then acting editor of the BBC Everyman series,
and they discussed the possibility of a documentary in the
series. Lowe explained to me how difficult it was to find an
opening with Angela Tilby and then persuade Simon. 'I had to
talk hypothetically about this person I knew who was a priest –
if I can get his consent is this a story you would like to tell? I
saw no point in talking to Simon unless I was sure they were

interested. They showed considerable sensitivity and were very concerned to find the right producer.'

Stephen Lowe had seen something universal in the story of Simon and Dinnington, 'Maybe he actually holds something symbolic for a dying community which somehow keeps going despite it all. I think he has provided a voice for other peoples' pain, an articulation of their pain in the way he preaches, talks and writes and the way he is.' Simon was very unsure about the idea of a television programme at first, as was almost everyone else. Most people's first reaction was to say no, that it could only be painful and exhausting for him and the parish, and that the media could never really be trusted. Friends working in TV were unquestionably the most cynical, convinced Simon would be manipulated. My brother Martin who works as a television researcher and producer was vehement; nobody who knew the business would ever consider offering themselves as subjects.

It was a difficult decision, to come out openly about it, both nationally, and more important locally. By no means everyone in the village knew at that stage. Ultimately for Simon it was too good an opportunity to miss. 'I remain an "inward" kind of person and yet I find myself being increasingly public about a profoundly personal situation.' he observed. He wanted to show first that you can 'live with AIDS'. He wanted also to pay tribute to the support he had received in Dinnington. Most of all he wanted to try and say something about living in the face of dying. 'It is, of course, what we are all doing, but those who live with terminal illness are forced to have, are given perhaps, a special vantage point, maybe even a vocation to live directly in the face of dying and speak – if they can – from there.'[1]

In the end though the decision was sealed by his frustration at the continuing hypocrisy of the Church of England on the issue of gay clergy. 'It's too important, too central to suppress. Deliberately or not, the church induces so much prejudice and fear and guilt in this area. Deep-seated guilt in those who happen to be "different", a lurking guilt, destructive and deathly, in those who happen to be ill with this condition. Isn't there enough to carry without this too?'

He was, I suppose, well-prepared for the task. He had already gone through major emotional and spiritual crises in his life; the difficult process of rejecting his evangelical background to become an Anglican; then the slow reconciliation with his homosexuality. He had, as a priest, already spent a lot more time than most people thinking about death. While coping with AIDS and the prospect of premature death was another burden, he was well-used to difficult terrain. Indeed, in as much as most homosexuals have already had to struggle with a fundamental aspect of themselves, at odds with the rest of the world, they are in a strange way perhaps better equipped than many others might be to cope with AIDS.

Naturally there were protracted discussions. Simon said later, 'We agonised over it for months. What would the media do to us? What would the rest of the parish think?' Everyone lived in anticipation of the story coming out in the press at some point, and the local diocese had had a press release ready prepared for a long time, which stressed that Simon was continuing to work in the parish, with 'the full consultation and co-operation of the Parochial Church Council and with the support of the Bishop of Sheffield.'

The BBC assigned a researcher, Abigail Saxon, and a freelance producer, Charles Bruce. The BBC team began their research, meeting Simon and then the PCC. Suddenly there was a whole new dimension to life in Dinnington. The Television People. Charles, confident and sympathetic in his tortoiseshell glasses, a bit patronising about the 'punters' at first; Abigail, a very pretty young woman with a mane of long brown hair and smart jackets, who immediately seemed to be on intimate terms with everyone; and with them a team of camera and sound technicians.

For Charles the story had enormous potential, as he explained to me later, 'It was presented to me as a story with in-built elements of conflict, which is what an editor is always looking for – you can't make a film out of everybody agreeing with each other. The bottom line was, here is a gay vicar, not known to be gay, who comes out when he discovers he's HIV-positive, in a former Yorkshire pit village, not famously tolerant. I was expecting something fairly grimy, conflict generating. It was a cracking human story but also difficult, because it's not like everybody is going to be alive at the end of it.' But Charles did feel he had to challenge Simon, 'The thing he couldn't get away from was – you've broken the rules – you knew what they were when you joined – It's all very well to say I'm part of God's creation – but the outfit you're in doesn't think that – you shouldn't be in this club.'

Charles went to discuss his approach at one of the Monday morning meetings at the Rectory, 'There was relief when I said I wanted to understand the differences of opinion, the conscientious conflict within individuals.' But it was a difficult task, 'Telly likes things simple, telly never deals with ideas. It was difficult because there *weren't* two sides, most people encompassed both, and felt the conflict within themselves. So I had to pick out the elements in different people.'

It was crucial to discuss the matter with the PCC and congregation so in September an open meeting was held in church, with dozens of people crammed into the dusty little Sunday School room upstairs. Abigail Saxon made a persuasive presentation, several people including Simon said how they felt, and it seemed as if the decision was a fait accompli. That is, until Steve Kohut turned up about an hour late. He insisted that the decision could not be made there and then and should wait for the next PCC meeting, 'I could not believe that so many people were prepared to go with the flow and make such a monumental decision there and then, since so many had expressed reservations and quite rightly so.' To Steve it was very ironic that having kept the matter so quiet, suddenly there was support for a national TV programme. His main objection was that they would have no control and that the issue could be exploited by the gay lobby, 'It was potentially great gay propaganda. The main issue from a church point of view has been not to float support for homosexuality and gay clergy.'

It was very frustrating for Simon, as he told me, 'It became very difficult to know how to make the decision, who was making it. It wasn't strictly speaking a PCC decision since more people were affected than that, but also in a sense less, since the main person to be affected was me.' My mother was at the meeting; all she remembers is Simon sitting, looking completely exhausted, at one point with his head in his hands as the debate raged.

Abigail Saxon found it a difficult meeting, 'People were very protective of themselves and of Simon. They didn't want to be seen as "the church who likes queers." I did feel I'd nearly lost it when Steve Kohut arrived, obviously feeling it was being steam rollered through.' Although Steve says some people were hostile to him at the meeting, quite a number told him afterwards that they agreed with him. Mike commented wisely that he had an important role to play in articulating people's anxieties. Sam Robinson was certainly dubious, 'I didn't think we ought to have it. But Simon wanted it. It was his life, and we weren't doing any more than living with it anyway, and it might help someone else, other people who are HIV as well.'

It was decided to delay any decision until the next PCC meeting in October. This was held at the Rectory, with Simon hooked up to his drip. Steve Kohut again spoke against the programme as did Geoff Gillard. Simon, Derek and Sue Rafferty were in favour. Simon said he didn't really want there to be a vote (he usually managed to avoid votes at PCC meetings, hoping always to get a sort of consensus without polarisation). This time Simon made his own case. As Steve put it, 'Simon made an emotional little speech which he is prone to do like a card sharp pulling an ace.' Simon recalled, 'After that most people said if that's what you want to do, then go ahead.'

Interviewing and filming began, and Simon was asked to make his own video journal. So for the next few weeks he recorded his feelings and ideas alone in his study, in a series of video soliloquies. Sometimes they were prepared, sometimes they were emotional responses to events, like his reaction after Terence's death. It was an inspired idea, and produced the most memorable and poignant moments in the final programme. For Simon it provided a direct platform and he preferred to participate in this way, able to stay in control, and choose the subject he wanted to talk about. He was never an easy subject to interview as Charles discovered when he did a two hour interview with him, which exhausted everybody. 'He was not intimidated by a producer turning up. He certainly wasn't going to talk to an outsider. In the end I binned the interview.'

They filmed Simon at home, doing his infusions, visiting the hospital, his usual common round. They recorded jumble sales and services, and were particularly anxious to film him celebrating the Sunday morning parish communion. Most people did not seem to mind. The BBC team had very much wanted to feature my mother but in the end she decided not to appear, though she ran the gamut from what will the neighbours say if I'm in it to what will the neighbours say if I'm not. She felt that the programme should focus on Dinnington as the real story, and not on the family. Caroline did appear, representing the family as it were, in an elegiac sequence walking with Simon at Roche Abbey.

Some people were interviewed several times. Kath and Walter in particular willingly re-recorded segments, with Kath repeating a sequence of coming in the back door of the Rectory, and shouting her characteristic, 'It's only me.' (Mind you an awful lot of people came in the back door and shouted, 'It's only me!' so you could never be sure who it was.) A few were reluctant to talk on film, while others like Steve Kohut and Geoff Gillard bravely expressed their misgivings. Others were firm in their support. But it was difficult to convey quite why they valued Simon so much. It was frustrating for Charles, 'I kept asking people why they supported Simon, and most of them just said because they loved him, and why, because he had helped them so much spiritually, which is a tough one to get on film!'

For Charles, Sam and Joyce Robinson typified the way people in Dinnngton had responded to Simon. There is wonderful footage of them which reveals the closeness of their relationship, sitting on a sofa together, their heads getting closer and closer as they talk. Charles observed, 'These were good hearted people you would trust with your life, whose horizons you would not expect to be much wider than the context in which they lived, and Simon clearly showed to them that they had a capacity for something much wider than that. For them it was a complete transformation.'

The Bishop was perhaps the most difficult interviewee. He had said he was 'content' for Simon to make the programme, and it would have been difficult for him to say anything else since it was his own Archdeacon who had suggested it. The organisation of the Church of England is devolved in such a way that the Bishop has a very autonomous role, and he had no need technically to seek the approval of his peers. However, he needed to try and appear publicly to be observing the accepted doctrine of the church on homosexuality. He obviously realised this was not going to be easy. He agreed, reluctantly, to be interviewed, saying he knew he was bound to look a fool. But he told me, 'If I'd been asked I would have advised against the Everyman programme. It was a toss of the coin whether they made a programme about how wonderful that this man had been accepted by the community, or what a scandal it is that the church is condoning immorality and no wonder everybody is up in arms. I don't trust them – their criteria are viewability rather than accuracy and truth.'

Technically, of course, the diocese was flouting the rules since Simon himself had said he was not celibate, and had contracted AIDS through a sexual relationship. Fairly fancy footwork was required and not surprisingly both Bishop and Archdeacon stumbled. Equally unsurprisingly those were the key moments that the Everyman editors focused on, highlighting their ambivalence, and the precise point at which both tried to fudge the issue. One of the key quotes they used from a long and thoughtful interview with the Bishop was, ' . . . my knowledge of his present lifestyle that it was entirely in keeping with the faith of the church, and what may have happened ten, fifteen, twenty years ago didn't seem relevant to the situation we found ourselves in.' The Archdeacon was more ambivalent, 'Simon convinced me or at least I never enquired . . . I don't want to know what is going on behind bedroom doors.'

Sometimes the television people appeared less than sensitive. At one point Abigail called Simon and said they hoped they would be able to re-use the film material, eventually incorporating his funeral. Even Simon was a bit surprised by that but just said, rather drily, that he was sorry he couldn't give them a date for his funeral. Abigail, however, robustly defended the question later, 'We had to ask. We always thought mentally the project will end when Simon dies, and we had to ask what happens if he dies before the programme goes out. It was a difficult question and I had to rehearse it in my mind, but we needed to know how he would like it done.' She felt annoyed with him for being upset about it, 'He knew what we were doing, he had signed up to it, and he knew he might have died mid-programme.' Her experience was similar to that of the family, trying to get Simon to discuss terminal care. 'He was more comfortable with abstract philosophical things. He could talk about not being afraid of death but not about the practicalities of the funeral,' Abigail observed later.

The strangest aspect of it all for Charles Bruce and his team was that they were involved in the story, and their publicising of it made a material difference to the outcome, in that they presented the story from a positive angle. 'It is not usual to feel you are an instrumental part of the story when you're making television programmes,' he said afterwards. For once he had felt manipulated by his subject instead of the other way around. 'Simon was a man with things to do before his time was up and you'd got on to the list, and he was going to check you off while he had the capacity.' There was a personal resonance for Charles too, because his own mother was also dying, 'It was the final chapter of someone's life, and I was going through it at the same time. I didn't find it difficult to talk. He was a lot further down the line than me.'

Then I was recruited as well. Simon called and said it had been suggested I wrote an article to go with the programme. I suppose I had always thought this was a subject I might write about one day. I kept a journal anyway, but I assumed it would be years hence before I could deal with it. But Simon was living through it, surely I could simply write about it? I had already involved myself by that time anyway. There was a crucial moment when Charles first came to see Simon, and I arrived just as he was leaving. I wavered, wondering whether to declare myself a journalist too. In the end I asked him how he was intending to handle the story. He replied, 'You'll just have to trust me.' Once I began writing the article I was also experiencing everything through a reporter's as well as a sister's eyes. I was full of doubt about it, of course, and there were times when someone – usually a member of my family – would say they felt constrained by my role – was I going to write down what they had just said?

The Miners' Memorial service in November to dedicate the screen, finished at last, provided a key moment in the story of Simon and Dinnington, and accommodation had to be made for the film crew. Even then there were a lot of people at the service who probably did not realise that the filming was of their rector with AIDS and not the Memorial itself. It was a big event. The Bishop came. An awning was erected outside the

porch to accommodate the overflow of people and a videolink –
just as well, since it, inevitably, rained. The finished memorial
screen portrayed a tree of life etched in glass, its roots buried
in coal, its branches blossoming with hope, surrounded by the
coloured mosaics made by the people of Dinnington. Below are
inscribed the names of the seventy-four men who died digging
coal in the pit.

It was a moving service, packed with miners and their families. The church was in darkness and then candles were lit for
each of the miners who died, and every one of their names was
intoned in turn. People wept. The Bishop preached, taking as
his subject the Resurrection of the Body. (Simon commented
wryly afterwards that he supposed that had been for his benefit,
though the Bishop failed to enquire after his temporal health,
then or on any other occasion.)

Ninety-year-old ex-miner Alan Harvey came up to the
lectern to recall life down the pit, describing in unsparing detail
two accidents with which he was involved; one when a large
stone fell on a miner's back and forced the shaft of his adze
right through his body, and another when a miner was killed in
a roof fall. Alan was asked to take the body up to the top, but
not to tell the other miners in case they stopped work.

A flute played a slow Celtic lament. A forty-strong male
voice choir sang and local schoolchildren performed a mime of
the tree of life. Then everyone sang 'Jerusalem'. All had a role
in the ritual. After the service there was tea and biscuits served
by the ladies of the church. Then the Bishop in gold mitre and
vestments, crosier in hand, joined Simon to greet everyone
crowding the church porch. Simon looked tired, his face etched
with lines of weariness, but he was clearly very happy, and
resplendent in the brilliant yellow and green cope reserved for
ceremonial occasions. The memorial was beginning to look like
being a swan song for him as well as the miners of Dinnington.

Dinnington seemed to be whirl of social activity those weeks.
The following weekend we returned for one of Simon's parties.
'A Year Down the Line' said the invitations, to celebrate a year
of TPN. A lot of people didn't even get the reference, but they
came anyway; friends, family and parishioners. Theo helped
decorate the drip stand with coloured balloons. There was a
tricky moment that weekend, when Simon shared an apple with

Theo. I didn't know, don't know, if there was any possible risk, but it didn't seem like a very good idea, so I gritted my teeth and asked him not do it. I know he was offended. The virus does not survive in the air, but perhaps had he had any blood in his mouth . . .? (Families are warned about toothbrushes, after all.) Again it highlighted the tension of conflicting loyalties, and for me at least, my child was ultimately bound to take precedence over anyone else. He was a total responsibility I had freely chosen. Unlike the rest of my family.

There was quite a lot of discussion at this point about how best to promote the programme. I had discreetly approached a sympathetic editor at the *Independent on Sunday* and they had commissioned an article to coincide with the programme in January. It was a long article, and I put my heart and soul into it. It was sometimes difficult interviewing friends and carers; there was little point in trying to be objective about the story, and there were several occasions we had to get the tissues out. Simon submitted himself to my questioning with good grace, but it can't have been easy; I often wish I could have entertained him more instead of interviewing him about his own death.

In the end the careful preparations were pre-empted, and the local press finally got the story. News of the television crew in Dinnington got through to the *Sheffield Star*, the left-leaning local tabloid. John Spencer, the assistant editor, recalled discussing how they should handle the story at an 8 am news conference in the editorial offices. 'It was a good story, a very sad story, but a good story. We were conscious of the fact that there were two ways to do it, but we are a local newspaper and there's no point, unless it's necessary in upsetting people.' He also expressed great surprise at the *Sun* reporter not breaking the story over a year before.

Reporter David Clarke was put on the case. He works out of a tiny office in Rotherham surrounded by great piles of old newspapers, and was on the phone doing a story on Asian babes when, later on, I went round to see him. He is a young reporter, and was eager to stress that he always followed NUJ guidelines on stories about HIV and AIDS. 'But it was one of the biggest stories of the year for us.' They decided to treat it sensitively, he said, and Clarke smiled ruefully at the contradiction, 'So at

8.30 the next morning there were two reporters and a photographer round there.'

Simon was still in his pyjamas, but he received them graciously. Already he had worked out in his journal with typical thoroughness the questions he would need to address:

What is it like?
What am I afraid of?
What has it done to me?
How do you cope with pain?
What can people do?
Do I feel guilty?
How can I go on believing?
What can I do with it?
What am I going to miss?
Living with it, from it.
Affliction and all of us . . .

Having decided to go public there was clearly no point in being difficult about it. His openness made a difficult task much easier for Clarke and further increased his sympathy. The story ran later that same day, taking up the whole of the front page. There was a full page photo of Simon looking particularly ill, with 'Vicar Dying of AIDS' as the headline. It was criticised as sensational by the Terence Higgins Trust, but it was no more than anyone would really have expected.

Despite the dramatic headline, the story was not so much that a Vicar had AIDS but that he was being supported by his parish, and that was the angle the *Star* chose. They ran a very sympathetic editorial column, which perhaps set a pattern for the subsequent press. The *Star Opinion* said,

'Despite unemployment, economic decline and a range of other problems, the people of Dinnington deserve a pat on the back. Their support for their local vicar who is dying of AIDS shows us what Christianity should be, and often is, all about. Those who know Simon Bailey talk of a caring, compassionate man who has brought joy and warmth with his religious message. He retains their confidence, respect and compassion – all things he has given to them in his ministry over the years.'

It was a big local story – it had everything, after all; sex, religion, disease and death. The same day ITV North Calendar news came and interviewed Simon, filmed him in church, and interviewed folk in Dinnington. He was the lead item that evening and in a lengthy interview Simon explained that he was willing to be public about his illness because the issues of AIDS and homosexuality in the church could not be hidden any longer. He looked thin and the thrush in his mouth made it hard to talk, but he concealed it well, and appeared very calm and clear. Margaret Hawley was also interviewed, 'We just try to carry on as normal really,' she said, in her calm, matter-of-fact kind of way. 'Well, you're not going to catch AIDS from going to church, are you?' said one woman in the high street briskly. I think there was also a little bit of closing ranks in the community, too, very Yorkshire somehow.

The *Sheffield Star* followed up the next day with a longer interview and pictures, 'My Life by AIDS Vicar' was the front page strap, with a story on Dinnington, 'The hard town's soft centre.' The story was picked up by other local papers and the national press, including the *Guardian*, *The Times* and *Telegraph*. It was run alongside stories about the outing of gay Bishops by Peter Tatchell, an oblique contrast to Simon's decision in favour of voluntary exposure.

This time it was very different from the *Sun* reporter turning up on the doorstep. Simon was in control, and once having decided to go public, he willingly talked to reporters and did several radio and television appearances, including the Radio 4 Sunday programme. The worst aspect for Simon were the people who knew him but only found out from the press. An old friend from Norton, who had been chairman of the Tenant's Association, and played the priestess in the Chad miracle play, saw the headline when she was out shopping. She hadn't seen Simon for years, and was devastated. She went back to work and sobbed her heart out, she told him later. But then she offered to come and stay if he needed more carers. 'That was one of the nicest things that happened.' Simon said, a bit sadly.

There were a lot of supportive and sympathetic letters from friends and acquaintances who had not known, and several from local clergy who said he had already been in their prayers for a year or two, so they had at least suspected. Most understood very well why he had not come out before.

He carried on with his parochial duties for Christmas, and was still invited for the annual Christmas Day drinks with the British Legion, and to the Dinnington school concerts. He was, oddly, celebrated. 'I think people were amazed I was still there,' he told me. He also gave a talk for World AIDS day, the first time he had openly addressed AIDS from a personal viewpoint, 'Some people think I should have kept my head down, kept it as secret as possible, not disturb "the peace of the church" yet again. But I can't keep living and at the same time keep this a secret.' It was true – he had nothing to lose in a sense, without the central importance of his work he would not have wanted to live, to leave it would have meant death anyway. This way he had something really to live for. He ended, 'I don't want to die. I know we all do die, but I passionately don't want to die. So I'm determined to live – really live – until I do.'[2]

But the flesh was weakening. He was just over seven stone at this time, but it was winter and heavy sweaters and socks disguised his emaciated limbs. By now he could encircle his upper arms with his hand. Even as he talked to the press about his passion for life the vision in his right eye was worsening, and was now limited to the upper right quarter of the eye. More drugs meant he had to increase the drips from twelve hours to fifteen hours a day. It is totally amazing, looking at his daily record, the sickness, the diarrhoea, the thrush, the fatigue, the drug routine, to imagine how on earth he managed to do everything. I supppose he didn't have to waste time eating or cooking – or washing up, for that matter. He began to notice how much weaker his legs were, finding it more and more difficult to walk any distance. He would drive the two hundred yards to church now rather than walk, and found it difficult to stand for any length of time. He commented that even cleaning his teeth required every ounce of vigour he could muster. Taking out the dustbin one day he fell over in the snow. After one exhausting Sunday of morning service and afternoon christenings, he wrote, 'Not sure how much longer I can hold babies at baptism . . .'

The Everyman programme was broadcast on January 15,

1995 and my article published the same day. Simon did publicity for the programme, including several long radio interviews and an appearance on morning television with Anne Diamond, where he was slotted between items on hatmakers and cosmetic surgery. He looked well, in a carefully chosen red sweatshirt over his clerical collar, and he answered their gentle questioning patiently, even occasionally squeezing in a reference to the controversial issues brought up by his personal situation.

The Sunday of the broadcast was very busy and in his journal Simon observes that it was only adrenalin that kept him going. He cut himself shaving in the morning, an inconvenience to most men, rather more difficult if you have AIDS. He preached a sermon in the form of a letter to Jesus, a very personal plea for help, and the church was very quiet indeed when he finished. And then he slipped away, to drive to Sheffield for a live interview with Radio Sheffield. When he left the church that day in the middle of the service, it was almost theatrical, a presentiment of his eventual inevitable departure. Suddenly he was gone and everyone carried on just as before without him. I took communion for the first time that day since I was about fourteen. For me it was a gesture of solidarity, of entering more fully into this community.

The Radio Sheffield interview was long and very frank about his homosexuality, with Simon candidly admitting to having had several partners. When Simon returned another reporter was waiting at the Rectory, Malcolm Brown, the religious affairs reporter from the *Yorkshire Post*. He based his article on Simon's sermon that day, with the refrain, 'no self-pity' throughout. He asked Simon under what circumstances he might have left the parish. 'If there had been any pastoral breakdown, or threat of it, I would have gone. If people had said, "He's not baptising our baby" or "He's not conducting our so-and-so's funeral," or "I'm not drinking out of the chalice after him" then yes, I would have gone. But it hasn't happened.'

Mother, Kath and I watched the broadcast that evening with Simon. Simon and I had seen previews, but it was still somehow shocking to see the first images: the juxtaposition of his hands blessing the bread and wine at the altar, followed by pulling on his rubber gloves to set up the drips. It was titled Simon's Cross ('I'm not really,' Simon said). As much as was possible on television, they had succeeded in conveying the various issues and the ambivalence surrounding them, as well as arousing profound sympathy for Simon.

Before the broadcast had even ended the phone started to ring. A complete stranger had found out the Rectory number and rang to express their sympathy even before it was over. Over the next few days the phone rang constantly, and Simon tried to talk to everyone. A trickle of mail turned into a torrent. And it all came to Simon, rather than the BBC or the *Independent on Sunday*, in part because the programme struck such a personal note with the video journals. He wasn't hard to find. Some of the letters were addressed quite simply to the Rector, Dinnington.

Significantly, it was probably the element of the programme that Simon most disliked that produced the response. The footage of Simon at work, talking to pastoral workers, at church, the interviews with parishioners, the historical footage of miners and their families had been inter-cut with the video journals. The programme ended with Simon sounding very low, 'Take it away, take it away,' a note of sadness and depression, which Simon resented, since he said he rarely felt depressed, and the piece was cut from a longer sequence about how he did find courage despite the problems.

Charles explained, 'He didn't like it ending on a down. But it was important that the viewer wasn't left with a feeling of elevation – now we can all feel better. You don't want to let them off the hook.' He felt it would have over-simplified the story if it had been expressed simply as, 'one man's triumphant struggle against the odds'. He insisted, 'The last image was an image of trial not defeat, but trial.'

It was clear that the media presentation had defined the story, and how people initially heard about it to some degree affected their response. A negative tabloid story might have damaged him, but the Everyman programme inspired people instead. It seems safe to say now (finally – now he is dead, and only now!) that the way the press was handled turned out to be right. Make sure everybody that matters knows first, so there is no shock, no sense of scandal involved, and in effect no sleazy story to be had. There were reports of tabloid journalists making enquiries about Simon in gay clubs but they never got anywhere.

How to cope with media attention is a real issue for many

people in controversial situations, and Simon's experience indicates that, despite the odds, it is possible to have some control. While it was not easy watching my brother anticipating his own death on national television, in the end it was alright, because he was able to say what he wanted, to maintain his dignity. Just making the programme had already publicised the story, even before it appeared, changing the situation considerably.

Simon probably received about five hundred letters in the end, though after a while we stopped counting. It was a phenomenal response to such a programme, and he seemed to be permanently surrounded by a sea of letters and cards. He slowly and determinedly replied to them all, and then many were carefully filed in plastic folders. But it was not till a year later that I read through the more personal ones he had set aside; there were so many moving letters from friends, some he had not seen for many years. They all expressed their support and admiration, and many went further, finding it an opportunity to tell him how much they loved him. It was a bit like being around for your own funeral; receiving all the tributes and expressions of love before you go. One old school friend called after twenty years and remained in close touch thereafter.

So many letters! Mothers, sons, doctors, nurses, workers in HIV/AIDS, people with AIDS, lots of ordinary sympathetic folk from all over the country. Some like the seventy year-old retired headmaster said they wished they could take the illness on themselves. So many were sad personal stories from people who responded to him both as a fellow sufferer and a priest. The stories seemed wrenched out, feelings written down that sometimes had never been articulated before. It was perhaps precisely this combination that touched such a chord, the truth of the wounded healer that Simon had been trying to explore.

They would begin by expressing their sympathy and then pour out their own problems. People responded very emotionally; several started writing letters while the programme was still on air, sometimes tear-spattered as they explored the feelings that had been detonated. A lot were written immediately afterwards, applauding his courage and expressing such profound empathy. Some addressed him formally, some called him Father, but most wrote to Simon, questioning their presumption but feeling that they knew him.

Many wrote of their own pain, feeling he would understand; illness, bereavement, family tragedies, an extraordinary litany that fell through the letter box day after day after day. Many of the writers were homosexual, some of them openly so, but mostly not. Some were in the church, but most felt unwelcome. People wrote about their homosexuality or their homophobia, their confused feelings about their own sexuality or that of their children. There was the Anglican couple whose son had just told them he was homosexual, who said the programme would make them more sympathetic; the Anglican homosexual who did not dare use his name; the vicar whose son was gay; the potential gay ordinand who had decided to discuss his sexuality with his priest; perhaps saddest of all was the man of over sixty who said he had always concealed his homosexuality, 'my whole life I have lived a lie.' Religion was no comfort to him, 'I don't go to church because I feel gays aren't readily accepted and I wouldn't want to carry my lie into God's house.'

A significant number were gay priests. Some out, but most not. A few said it had given them courage to come out. One Presbyterian sent him a saucy picture to cheer him up. Several prominent clerics wrote in support, including Hugh Montefiore, Eric James and Derek Rawcliffe, the former Bishop of Glasgow and Galloway who was the first bishop to talk publicly about his homosexuality. Mark Santer, now Bishop of Birmingham, described the experience he had had with a priest with AIDS in London and said how glad he was that Simon's experience was proving so different. And of course, sadly, there were those with AIDS themselves, or supporting partners with AIDS, encouraged perhaps a little by Simon's fortitude. Most heart-breaking of all were those for whom AIDS had been a stigma they had to conceal, like the woman whose husband had died of AIDS and kept it a secret from everyone, even their three children till only a few weeks before he died. A 'buddy' wrote with the sad story of someone who had died recently of AIDS, whose family had felt they had to conceal the illness and pretend he died of a brain tumour.

People also sent gifts, an icon from an icon painter in Norwich; the Celtic cross which had belonged to a brother who had died of AIDS; book tokens and money; even a box of Newberry fruits from a lady who had noticed them on the dining room table in the film. People responded to such details; a potter enjoyed the camera lingering on the many pots and pebbles in the house. Someone who had not even seen the programme, but responded to the description of Simon's house in my article, sent him a glass prism. Another sent holy oil and Jordan water. An old age pensioner sent him a tape of his poems. Author Shirley Conran wrote a long letter, describing her own experience of nursing a friend with AIDS, and after Simon replied to her, she sent a donation for the church. Others offered hospitality; the Welsh harpist with a cottage in Wales; a gay couple, one of whom had AIDS, who invited him to their country place in Devon.

There were also endless earnestly offered alternative therapies, from Chinese herbs to acupuncture, photoluminescence to Argentinian cattle plasma supplement. The faith healers and evangelicals did not hold back either, urging him to repent before he met his maker; an evangelical preacher in Ipswich, whose gay son had committed suicide, sent a brochure about his counselling service which offered to free people from the burden of homosexuality; a seventeen-year-old girl from a Charismatic church stipulated chapter and verse from the Bible on homosexuality.

There was a handful of negative and cranky letters; anything truly unpleasant went in the bin. There was a nasty, bitter letter from a slater and tiler, who told Simon he was paying the price for his perversion, that he was 'leading silly people astray with your vile affections', and that he must 'repent and believe like the thief on the cross, just in time'. The programme was also shown on BBC World Service television, so another wave of letters came from Hong Kong, Australia, South Africa and Thailand, where a black American ex-ballet dancer, sixty-six years of age wrote of his own negative experiences of homosexuality in the USA in the 1950s.

Simon replied to them all, and then many wrote back again. In the end he developed a considerable on-going correspondence. There was a steady regular flow of cheerful, newsy letters from a Sheffield cleaning lady whose husband had died suddenly, whose daughter had committed suicide, and yet who simply wanted to show she cared. She constantly stressed he need not reply, though I think he always did. It must have been nice to have such letters drop onto the doormat, or brought up with the *Guardian* and the *Church Times* in the morning. And he may, perhaps, have found it easier to express himself sometimes to strangers, than to those close to him.

One real, deep friendship was formed, although the correspondents never met. Simon loved describing answering the phone one day to hear the wonderful rich Irish voice of Marie Joyce. Her brother, theatre director Michael Joyce, had died of AIDS only a few months previously. She called and wrote often, and Simon delighted in her soft voice and the warm sympathy and spiritual feeling she poured out on to the page.

People promised to say mass for Simon, to pray for him, light candles for him, always to remember him. No wonder he felt buoyed up by all those people out there. It was so sustaining to know people responded and cared so much. It was a mutual ministering, a true exchange of love. He reflected in his journal, 'There is a ministry in all these letters, too – their ministry to me – so often from their own brokenness. But also a reciprocation – people feel only someone like me can help them and hard as it is to take on what might seem an extra burden I can sometimes do something.' I am sure this knowledge helped keep him going even longer, knowing that he could still make a difference.

Attendance at church actually went up, and Simon observed that people made a special point of shaking his hand. Nobody balked at drinking from the shared chalice. More and more people in Dinnington began to sport red ribbons. Mike said wherever he went people would enquire about Simon. 'People are genuinely happy to share in this extraordinary journey,' he said. With such a spotlight on the parish, they had little choice but to carry on in their saintliness. Walter, for one, revelled in the impact they had produced. He sat down to write a report when he retired as fabric officer responsible for church maintenance, but typically got carried away far beyond the leaking church roof into a tribute to Dinnington. 'When we learned of Simon's illness we closed ranks, and as one, the majority pledged their support one hundred per cent. We talk about the pebble in the pond and the ripples – ripples! I think between us we chucked a ten ton boulder in the pond and the resulting waves came ashore and swamped the higher echelon people in the church, when they came back to the surface, spluttering and wiping the water from their eyes, they said "Where the 'firbeck hall' has that come from?" "Dinnington," they said, looking at the map to find where Dinnnington was.'

But for some members of the church the focus on Dinnington became too much, as did the discussion of homosexuality, and the parish magazine saw a terse exchange or two on the subject. In the eyes of some, Derek Norbury's articles in the parish magazine rather over-estimated the support for gay clergy, and finally Steve Kohut exploded about it, writing, 'There are still many in our congregation who feel uncomfortable with the subject of gay clergy . . . I continue to be dismayed by the barrage of views thrust down my throat by "gays" in the church as a whole.' Still Simon managed to slip in an appropriate joke someone had sent him, into the same issue of the magazine.

Child at bus stop: Mummy I know what men who love each other are called.
Mother (anxiously): Do you darling, what?
Child: Christians.

Reaction was very mixed in wider church circles. The LGCM (Lesbian and Gay Christian Movement) were delighted with the programme, although critical of some of the more negative reactions from parishioners, perhaps unaware quite how far some of them had actually come. Simon did receive many letters of support from other clergy, and only a few that were critical. Reaction from the local clergy also varied. The local Catholic church sent him a huge bouquet of flowers. Another vicar in a nearby parish wrote to say it had made him re-think his attitude to homosexuality, and applauded Simon for not resigning. However, he was attacked by another local vicar, Rev Colin Gibson, of Tinsley, in an article in the *Sheffield Star*, 'Fellow Vicar accuses gay AIDS victim of "hypocrisy" '. Gibson said Simon had no right to 'assert that Christian teaching about homosexual practices should be changed. The church's job is to call sinners to repent, and I believe we cannot do that job when we refuse to admit that we have offended God's standards.'

The Bishop and Archdeacon were in the firing line, and the Bishop did receive some negative letters. They were variously congratulated and maligned from both sides, but both had come across sounding ambivalent about the issue. Geoff Gillard, the Synod representative for St Leonard's, took a pretty conservative view of the effect the programme might be likely to have, arguing that the parish had supported Simon because of who he was, not because he was gay and that therefore what had happened in Dinnington was unlikely to have any effect on Anglican attitudes to homosexuality within its ranks. Perhaps he was right, though in reading all the letters to Simon there are a significant few who had acted differently as a result, either by talking to partners or priests, or declaring that it had helped them rethink their views on the matter, or indeed made them think about it at all.

Mother had been so worried about the reaction of her relatives, but when she finally told them they were immensely supportive and sympathetic. It is sad how we sometimes underestimate people. Even some of my father's deeply religious family were sympathetic and supportive although they were deeply shocked. The best way they could come to terms with it was to love the sinner but not the sin. Some of the more evangelical members of the family couldn't even manage that.

It was bitterly cold at the end of January and Simon was very low and very weak. He had to go back into hospital because his white cell count was so low (due, in one of the familiar ironies of the virus, to the drugs he was on for his eyesight) so he was especially vulnerable to infection, not to mention in need of a rest. He was finding it increasingly difficult to climb stairs, and sometimes now, reluctantly, used a stick to walk. He remained undaunted, however, and spent the time making plans to mark the aniversary of his ten years in Dinnington at the end of the year, analysing what he had achieved and what he had neglected. Mike commented to him that he was always planning ahead, but Simon said to me, 'I wasn't conscious of doing it, I just hadn't stopped.'

Feb 24, 95, journal, Dinnington
Theo and I arrived last night about 6.30 to find Simon has to stay in hospital. Poor Walter even went in to Sheffield to fetch him, and then the doctors changed their minds. We had planned a day in Whitby – perhaps there will be another

opportunity but it certainly makes me realise how precious time is.

Coming to the empty house was very foreboding. This is what it will be like. A rail has been attached next to the back door to help him climb the step – and it's such a small step really. But there are still so many affirmations of life here, in the kitchen a new yellow and blue striped curtain, and two new shelves filled with green glass, icons and a candle, all recent gifts. Such grace he has.

Mother and Theo and I went to see him in hospital the next day. It was the first time I had taken Theo to the hospital and I was warned when I arrived by one of the nurses that they did not recommend that children came to the ward, because it was for infectious diseases. I felt agonised over this – I couldn't visit without Theo, and anyway, it didn't seem right to exclude him or to deny Simon his jolly little presence. I knew Jackie had visited with her children, and she was a nurse, so I decided to risk it, another of those awful choices where there is no right answer. Simon told us he had just seen a new doctor. She asked how long he had had CMV retinitis in his eyes, and said, 'People are not supposed to survive this long.' Simon asked her what she meant by survive, 'Should I be blind or dead?' She said, 'Both.'

However, he rallied sufficiently to make several trips away over the next few months. He went to Wales with Alma for a few days, his car loaded up with all his kit as usual, and he notes the long exhausting process of getting bags, and pumps and all the medical paraphernalia down the stairs. They stayed with the rector of Aberdaron where R.S. Thomas was once rector. It was to be Simon's last sight of Bardsey. 'As always with the truly holy places it was difficult (for me) to get there, my legs so weak. I fell on the stile steps because my leg won't take my weight after a certain height.' He also went to Holy Island again but it was bitterly cold, so he stayed indoors, surrounded by hot water bottles, writing his stories. He was experimenting with style and rhythm and still striving to find ways to express his experience. But it was deeply frustrating not being able to walk on the beach or watch the waves, 'Then I find myself quietly thinking I'm ready to go now.'

Mostly his life was restricted to Rectory, church and hospital. But within this narrow compass he continued to find inspiration both for sermons and stories, even though sometimes Mike had to read his sermons for him. I remember one family weekend with several nieces and nephews visiting, noticing that he had not gone into his study as usual, but had chosen to stay on the sofa in the midst of bouncing, yelling children. He wrote a sermon about his life being in turmoil, 'My world turns upside down whenever my sisters arrive with their children: my house turns from being a haven of peace and quiet to a riot of games and fun and tears and Lego pieces to trip over, early morning little visitors, regular bright gifts of the latest drawing for Uncle Simon.'

Still the images flow, the metaphors rise. There was a picture on his bedroom wall, just by the door, a funny little drawing of umbrellas with, 'Everything is going to be alright,' written underneath. It became his mantra, and was often referred to in sermons and writings. It echoed the quotation from Mother Julian of Norwich, which was another favourite, 'All shall be well and all shall be well and all manner of things shall be well.'

Even so, I think everyone was sure this time would be Simon's last Easter, and people wanted to be there. Simon said he sometimes felt like a fraud, 'Someone said to me on Sunday well you've made another Easter as if they all live with a sense of imminent departure.' And of course we all did, we had to live like that, we had to be prepared for afterwards in a way he did not.

A healing service was held on the Monday before Easter and Simon preached about water, baptism, his own full immersion at age eleven. It echoed all the letters he had received, all the suffering he had somehow assimilated. He talks about plunging right under, before healing is possible. Then he described his hydrotherapy session at the hospital that afternoon, which ended with fifteen minutes of simply floating supported in warm water with gentle music playing 'That's part of my vision of heaven . . . to float in warm, deep water, to angelic music . . .'

On Maundy Thursday, there was the special service for the Washing of Feet, echoing Christ's washing of the disciples' feet. This year it was the turn of Simon's carers. Joyce and Sam Robinson were both there, and Kath Graham, Walter and

Margaret Hawley and Phyllis Marriott. My mother was also included. It was a simple ceremony. Simon held an earthenware jug and trickled water on to their feet while Mike Cameron washed and dried and kissed their feet in turn. It was a simple, direct tribute, easy to understand. Part of Simon's success in Dinnington had always been this revival of symbolism, providing people with everyday symbols as ways of articulating and interpreting their own experiences.

On Good Friday there was a service for children, an abbreviated Stations of the Cross, in which each child read one of the stages of the journey to the cross, remembering at each stage vulnerable and suffering people; the poor, the homeless, the dying. With some difficulty Simon knelt down on a cushion to talk to the children. I was so aware of how thin his legs were under the long black robe, and how painful it must have been for him to kneel. That Easter morning we rose again at 5 am, Theo and I, and joined Simon and his parish to light the Paschal candle as dawn broke and celebrate again the Easter Eucharist.

kingfisher days

There is an August within us, aeons of preparation for a few kingfisher days.

R.S. Thomas

It was already April but snow was swirling ominously past the windows of the rectory. Simon and I had decided to make a brief, nostalgic trip to the Lake District to revisit our childhood. Along with sturdy boots and a good thick cardigan, I packed my tape recorder and my camera. We only planned to go for one night so that Simon could go without his TPN supplies and pretend to be normal for once. But now the weather looked terrible, and the idea began to seem foolhardy as well as a bit morbid. I felt anxious, worried about what would happen if Simon became ill, developed an infection, what if we got stuck in the snow and he had no TPN supplies, as usual rehearsing all the things that might go wrong. I suggested tentatively we might consider postponing the trip. But postponement was not a word in Simon's vocabulary any more, if it ever was.

He sat on a chair lacing up his Doc Marten boots with profound determination. 'We can't not go now,' he said with such finality I abandoned myself to his power. It was my first direct taste of the strength of will that was keeping him alive. As we waited for the district nurse to visit and check his dressings, I contemplated the most recent picture Simon had hung in his bedroom. It was a huge black and white photograph of a lighthouse in a raging storm, a tiny figure at the doorway almost overwhelmed by waves as high as the tower itself. Somehow though the waves were not frightening, they looked almost as if they were embracing, sustaining the lighthouse. They are, I realised, the reason why the lighthouse is there at all.

We wound our way north-west through the grey granite suburbs of Leeds, across the Pennines, past fields of new lambs, tails in the air. By the time we stopped in Ilkley for tea there was a suggestion of sunshine. We passed a sign to the Hawes waterfall and Simon said almost casually, 'That's one of the places I've suggested scattering my ashes.' My skin prickled as it did when I was reading through a sheaf of his sermons and stories, and I came across the requiem mass he had written for his own funeral. He said I was welcome to look at his funeral arrangements too, 'But I do keep changing them,' he added wryly. I tentatively mentioned the issue of terminal care, but this was one thing he would never commit himself about. We never did really know what he would have wanted. Probably to die at home. But all he would ever say was, 'I don't think we need to talk about that yet.'

He took over the driving once we got to Keswick. He loved driving; I think it was a way of reassuring himself he was still in control. Before we got into Keswick we turned off to Castlerigg, near the Castlerigg stone circle. Here was the camp where we had always stayed, overlooking Derwentwater and surrounded by craggy peaks. Of course, it all looked smaller, but it was also now in a ruinous state and more closely resembled an army camp than a holiday venue. Perhaps it always did.

We drove further up the lane to the little beck at the foot of the steep footpath up Walla Crag, where we used to spend hours playing with stones and water. We took photos of each other on the little wooden bridge that spanned the stream. It was a struggle getting down there, but Simon resisted a supporting arm. But he observed he was not going to be climbing Walla Crag ever again.

We stopped at the lakeside tea gardens in Keswick but they were closed, and it was very cold. Simon reminded me how we used to sing in public on the steps of the cafe, 'We were a star turn,' he chuckled ruefully, and I winced at the flood of memory. I felt sad that Simon was too weak to walk up to Friars Crag and the lovely view of Lake Derwentwater. Ruskin called it one of the three or four most beautiful views in Europe, no less so for being one of the most popular these days. It is where my mother would like her ashes to be scattered. I found myself thinking that Mother would need a wheelchair if she is to get there before her ashes do. I contented myself with buying postcards so dated they must have been from the same batch we used to send over thirty years ago.

Our hotel was right on the lakeside, rather grand, chosen because it was somewhere we always said we would stay when we were grown up. We would look down from Surprise View on the hillside above, at the seductive sight – unimaginable luxury complete with azure blue swimming pool and tennis courts. I swam in the little indoor pool but Simon sadly declined. He was too thin and the Hickman line would have been too conspicuous, and the water was much too cold. It seemed unfair that he should not be able to swim because of his appearance – there is no other risk, as far as I know – I suppose I must admit I would be shocked to see an obviously ill person in a pool. But at least at that time Simon had hydrotherapy at the hospital every week which he adored, water making weary limbs light and pleasurable again.

Before dinner we sat by the fire in the lounge. A great wing chair seem to swallow Simon up. His brown eyes dominated his gaunt face. His skin looked quite a healthy colour, the combination of jaundice and drugs which made him appear oddly tanned. One cheek had a few bumpy mollusca, unsightly but no more, and occasionally his eyes appeared yellow because of the jaundice but it was really only his acute thinness which marked him. Indeed like so many men as they age his face had acquired more character, the features more firmly carved. His brown hair was cut very short but was wonderfully soft and in good condition, which I surmised was due to his excellent intravenous diet, exquisitely adjusted every week to suit his precise requirements. His nails, no longer bitten, looked better than they had ever done.

We talked about the family, our childhood, how we all seemed to have turned out so differently. Simon observed that he felt all the family tension had been creative, 'I have this visual image of electricity – all of us shooting off in different directions.' But at the core was so much shared experience, shared imagery; the books we read, the invented fantasies with which we regaled each other, all began to come back with greater resonance. So many iconic images: the great lion, the unicorn, the well, the magic kingdom, the last battle, began to surface again and again in the stories Simon wrote in the last year or two of his life. As they took on deeper meanings for him, as he followed the threads in his stories, for me too they began to reverberate, little powder trails that caught alight and began to detonate the past.

He told me about some of his dreams too, how he dreamt of himself as a small child but always attached to the drip like an umbilical cord, a part of him now. And of the small fair child, always playful, who kept re-appearing, joining the family for a meal, leading him along a path, beckoning. The child became the focus of another story.

The next morning I walked down to the lake and stood on the old wooden jetty jutting out into the water. The lake was smooth at first, then rippled by wind, cradled by mountains red with bracken, and the shadowy contrasts of clouds moving across the sky. Two determined ducks headed in a straight line across to the reeds. No wonder the poets loved it all so. It was all very Wordsworth, this whole enterprise, I thought.

It was a coldly beautiful day, hard azure sky and bright sunshine. Still Simon wrapped up carefully, layers of sweaters, scarf and woolly hat. He felt the cold acutely. Our itinerary for the day hardly needed discussing. Every year the camp used to make a favourite outing, taking a launch across Derwentwater, landing at a little jetty on the other side, and from there walking up the steep path to Ashness Bridge and about five miles on to the little hamlet of Watendlath at the head of Borrowdale. We stopped at Ashness Bridge, such an old familiar sight; great slabs of rocks to clamber over, fissured with little streams and waterfalls. Beyond was the favourite postcard view of Derwent-water and the great purple peak of Skiddaw. Ashness Bridge was traditionally the location for good clean Christian fun, which consisted mainly of throwing each other in the water. But the memory that came to me was of watching someone run away from it, up the steep incline behind until they were lost from sight.

Then quite suddenly the weather changed. It began to snow and hail, and once again I felt anxious, ready to turn back, worried we would get stuck, lost in the hills. I couldn't really remember how far it was to Watendlath, and it did seem a bit foolish to set off in a snowstorm. But Simon was as determined

as ever, 'We can't turn back now.' Even the sheep were covered
in snow, cowering on bleak hillsides, behind rough stone walls
lacy with pale green lichen. As we forged through the snow
flurries, I observed that Simon never seemed to worry very
much. He replied almost disdainfully, '*I'm* not a worrier.' I
found myself wondering how he could be like that. Was it his
faith which just unburdened everything on to God, or was it
his illness, which made everything else of such little consequence? He simply didn't waste time worrying, while I am the
kind of person, still, that thinks I have to keep the plane aloft,
thinking about it all the time.

In any case he was right. As we arrived the sun came out
again. Watendlath is Norse for 'the path at the end of a stream
or beck' and there is a lovely limpid tarn of water at the end of
the valley, and tracks over the tops of the hills which in the past
we would have climbed to reach the other side and a coach trip
back to camp. While Simon watched the endless flow of water
under the stone bridge, I climbed up the hill and remembered
our picnics, little groups sprawling in sheltered nooks, framed
by rocks and carpeted in soft turf. We were always ravenous,
content with the predictability of each individual paper bag
picnic; white rolls filled with meat paste, tomatoes, apples,
Smiths crisps with a twist of blue paper for the salt.

There were so many ghosts. Dad for one, bathing enthusiastically in the freezing water of the stream. We skimmed stones
on the surface of the tarn. It was deep and very dangerous, and
we had always been warned away from it. 'Didn't someone from
the camp drown here one year?' asked Simon, and the thought
sank as deep as one of the stones we were throwing.

Our trip to Keswick was odd, awkward. Simon didn't talk
much and we lacked the easy camaraderie of old friends. There
were some very long silences indeed. Nonetheless it was precious, a time to treasure. We had talked much of Father and
the many difficulties we had, so it was good to remember all the
happy times, the holidays and fun. It brought many good things
back for me.

I can't say I had got to know Simon very much better, but I
had no doubts this was a story I must write. It was the story
I was born with. Transcribing the tapes later I found, oddly,
that I had trouble sometimes distinguishing between the two

voices, despite the fact that we were man and woman, and despite my own acquired veneer of BBC English, and Simon's determined attachment to his northern accent. I'm convinced he must have had to work at keeping his accent, but my father was like that too. As if in the end Simon was as determined and self centred as my Dad was, undistracted by anyone else.

'Sometimes I just feel let's get on with it,' Simon said to me then. There was such a feeling in the last few months of this being extra time, and how best to use it. It had its down side, of course, the waiting that we were not as trained for as Simon had become. But there were many good things to remember, 'kingfisher days' to squirrel away in the memory for many people. Perhaps Simon may even have been conscious of doing that as he went on trips with different people, spent time with all the people he loved and who loved him.

He was very conscious of the idea of memory, and of memorials. A vast tome of a book he bought that year, a revisionist history of the English church before the Reformation, has a chapter on 'Last things'.[1] Perhaps it's the only one Simon read, it is certainly the only place he has marked; the importance of remembrance and memorials, 'What late medieval English men and women at the point of death seem most to have wanted was that their names should be kept constantly in the memory and thus in the prayers of the living.' Bequests for the vessels of the Eucharist were a favourite way of securing remembrance.

With the small fee Simon received from the BBC, he commissioned a ciborium to be made, a silver chalice with a lid in which is kept the reserved sacrament, ready blessed bread. The ciborium took a long time to make and wasn't finished before Simon died, but I am sure he intended it as his memorial anyway. It is now inscribed with his name and kept permanently in the aumbry next to the altar at St Leonard's, ready to be used to take communion to the sick. It seems an exquisitely appropriate memorial. In the commonplace book he gave to Margaret Selby, he ended the book with the words of St Monica, 'All I ask of you is that whoever you may be, you will always remember me at the altar of God.'

Simon was so tired when we got back from Keswick, and once he had organised his drips and medicines and settled himself in his bedroom, I gave him a foot massage with lovely fragrant aromatic oil, for once becoming Mary instead of Martha. It was the one time we read the Bible together since we were children; the story of the anointing at Bethany, a week before Jesus is crucified. Jesus and his disciples had arrived at the house of the sisters, and Martha bustled round and made supper. Mary, meanwhile took some costly ointment, anointed Jesus' feet and wiped them with her hair. The house was filled with the scent of the ointment. It was usually used only for anointing the dead and Jesus was criticised for allowing such indulgence. Jesus responded, 'Let her alone: against the day of my burying hath she kept this. For the poor always ye have with you; but me ye have not always.'[2]

What did it mean I asked, it had always puzzled me. Simon, the bibilical scholar, admitted it was a difficult text, but said he felt Jesus was saying there is a time for pleasure, there is no sin in pleasure for its own sake. Simon liked to argue that the very fact that sex could be pleasure without procreation, meant that human beings were meant for higher things, 'The fact that homosexuality serves no biological purpose is not a flaw or evidence that it should be eradicated, but a witness that humanity is here for more than a biological purpose, there is another kind of creativity than having children,' he noted in his journal.

After Easter, Simon went to lead a retreat at Alnmouth, on the coast of Northumbria. An old friend from college, Ian Paton, now vicar of a parish in Scotland, had been to see him, the first time they had seen each other since Cambridge. Ian read some of the material Simon was writing, both his stories and his writing about AIDS and death, and he later invited him to join one of his parish retreats with people who had seen the Everyman programme. Part of the time was spent in silent retreat, but they also read several of Simon's stories, and he explained how they were written within the consciousness of having AIDS. People responded in different ways; one woman continued a story for herself, another came to talk to him about becoming a priest using a story to articulate her feelings. It was, incidentally, a wonderful opportunity for a writer to have such direct response.

It was also another way for Simon to try and share what he was experiencing. Retreats had become increasingly important

to him, both personally and as part of his ministry, influenced
in part by his research into the monastic life of Gregory Dix.
He always stressed that the desire for meditation and retreats
was not escapist, 'As you go deeper in you get closer to other
people, not further away. What you achieve is something closer
to a common shared humanity. It is finding something you
share with everybody else. A vital ingredient in this is the
religious life, those who have apparently left society. At its best
what they are doing is going deeper into common humanity,
exploring what that means by writing and retreats and by
prayer.'

Then my mother was confirmed. The ceremony took place in
May in front of Sheffield Cathedral with a great crowd of
others from the diocese, and Simon presented her to the Bishop.
Neither Mother nor Simon could walk easily, but there is a
lovely picture of them together, Simon austere in his robes,
mother proudly next to him. Simon was greeted by many colleagues among the clergy, several of whom seemed distinctly
surprised to see he was still alive.

My mother had decided to convert from the Baptist church
of my father and all her years as a minister's wife to the more
accommodating arms of the Anglicans. Simon did not instruct
her, 'After all she taught me,' he said. Like Simon, years before
she acknowledged that it felt more comfortable for her, less
evangelical and prescriptive than the dogmatic creed of the
Baptists. My father dying gave her space to think and freedom
to choose her own way. Her son approaching death made it
more painful and more profound than anyone would ever have
chosen. But she was sustained by pride, both for herself and for
Simon.

Naturally there was a party for her at the Rectory. Among
the guests was the Abbot of Elmore who came to stay at the
Rectory that same weekend. I expected Father Abbot to be a
big enveloping figure, and was surprised by the small dark-
haired man with neatly trimmed beard, dressed in regular
trousers and shirt who arrived at the door. He seemed a lot
more comfortable once he had his robes back on, a long black
cassock encircled by a thick leather belt and a silver cross round
his neck.

Both my sisters were there and we had a family dinner, over which we bombarded him with questions about monastic life; rising at 5 am and bed at 9.30 pm with all the meals in silence, listening to one of the monks reading. The brothers did occasionally watch television together, programmes selected by the Abbot (his favourites were The Bill and Eastenders). The Abbot was equally intrigued by us, wanting to know details of the children's upbringing, and all the accompanying parapher-nalia of car seats and children's videos. We decided we ought to try a life swap since his calm, ordered existence struck me as very attractive at the time. Especially when we met up at some unearthly hour of the morning in the kitchen. He went off to say his daily offices while I poured Rice Crispies and put a Biker Mice video on for the children.

We discussed the Dix biography, which the Abbey had orig-inally commissioned and the prospects of publication. They had found a publisher who was proving to be rather slow. Simon of course was anxious to have it published as soon as possible. Meanwhile, he had also found a publisher, Darton Longman and Todd, for his stories, and was writing an introduction to them about the context in which they were written. He was delighted, since they were publishers he had always aspired to and had discussed several projects with over the years.

He began sending out invitations for a birthday party on June 16; he was almost forty and by some miracle looked as if he would actually make it. There was the usual extraordinary mixture of people at his party, family, parishioners, clergy and gay friends. So many friends came and brought presents, or wrote and sent cards. Alma insisted on making a speech. The nurses and doctors came from the hospital, bringing a great tub of flowers. One nurse, who was leaving, felt emboldened to tell him that usually people with CMV retinitis didn't survive more than a couple of months. Simon had already had 18 months and still retained (most of) his sight. It was, in an odd sort of way, encouraging.

Inevitably, as he went out less and less he lost touch with many of his friends, gay friends in particular, but a few continued to visit. Andrew in particular was very loyal, and sometimes came to stay overnight or would drive him to the hospital. But he himself had just been diagnosed with crytosporidiosis and was beginning to think about retiring from his job. Another of Simon's bleak RIPs in his journal in May was for a close friend of Andrew's.

A gay friend from Leeds still came sometimes; Simon delighted in his difference. He recalled their meeting, 'I met him when I accidentally gatecrashed a party at a pub in Leeds, after an LGCM meeting there. It was past closing time and people were still there, and sandwiches kept appearing, and this man kept offering me sandwiches. He was a skinhead, covered in tattoos, very rough, and worked on a construction site. But he'd written a book about skinheads and he liked to talk about books and writing. He was so different from me but we got on really well.' He didn't drive however so Simon always had to pick him up from the station when he came to visit, an option that was less and less viable.

Simon's close friends got used to living with AIDS, attempting to maintain as normal a relationship as possible. Sue Proctor told me she usually avoided asking him how he was, 'You know he'll say if it's very different. It's just an ordinary friendship – you can't talk about life and death all the time.' She added sombrely, 'I know there are times he feels like he's nailed on a cross and everybody has walked away. In his deepest darkest moments he must feel lonely and abandoned, but perhaps not quite as rejected as he used to feel, I hope not. He knows he isn't facing it on his own, he knows God is with him every moment.'

He still held the reins in the parish though Mike shouldered most of the burden of work. Mike always insisted that he could cope, that he didn't need help, and that he felt the whole situation was a great challenge, an unprecedented pastoral opportunity. 'I would not swap it. I felt when I came here I was cheating other people of a superb parish placement,' he declared. 'What we've gone through here is an extraordinary experience. Despite the pain this story is full of good things. I'm over the moon about it.'

Much of Simon's time was spent writing and working at home and holding meetings there. But he was still trying to make changes too; he had been trying for a long time to per-suade the PCC to try moving the traditional wooden pews from the North aisle of the church to create an open space for exhibitions, push-chairs, even performances and he actually succeeded for a brief period. However, even his most devoted acolytes were unconvinced and although the pews came out during May for one exhibition, and Simon even bought some new chairs himself as potential substitutes, the pews went back again. His radical initiative was doomed. 'Moving pews – what will the PCC think of next?' thundered the letters in the parish magazine.

He presided at communion as often as he was able and it was more and more the central focus of his life. He found in the Eucharist a way to come to terms with it, an almost Buddhist abnegation of self as opposed to the power of the priesthood. He noted, 'It is – of course – the losing of self that is so hard, truly to intercede at the Eucharist requires a loss of self; only that way do we truly bear the burden of a wounded world.' There seemed to me a certain irony in his growing focus on this symbolic meal, for someone who had effectively not eaten for two years.

He continued to write his sermons, which became less orthodox and increasingly powerful towards the end. They are however, sometimes annotated by Mike, who had to deliver them at the last minute. There were occasions when Simon could barely manage his physical duties, having to sit down to preach sometimes, taking a funeral when he could barely stand himself. On one occasion the server at the altar thought Simon looked as if he might be sick after finishing the communion wine. It was undoubtedly a strain for everyone, but somehow he stubbornly carried on. Perhaps it is true that his determination to carry on, and to continue his pastoral duties, was in some ways at the expense of his parishioners. He did consider resigning as he wrote in his journal, 'I'd be assured of a pension, housing, etc, the parish would be assured of a re-focussed ministry, a sense of permanence.' What would we lose, he asks? 'I'd lose purpose for myself still.' It was the only way, the only reason for him to carry on. But he also continued to believe that the experience was one that others could share and benefit from, 'I don't think we've explored far yet into "the wounded surgeon". *There is more to come.*' And as a fellow cleric, Sue Proctor was convinced he was still fulfilling his role as priest, 'I see him still being Jesus in the community, teaching, loving, healing; yes there will come a day when he can't do it, but I can't imagine his ministry coming to an end if he can't walk . . . or if he can't see . . . he knows the liturgy off by heart anyway. When he is too weak to celebrate communion . . . it'll be that. He'll decide.'

There were also special occasions when he felt really accepted, even honoured by the wider church. At a clergy conference in the spring he was warmly welcomed, and elaborate arrangements were made to accommodate him. He was invited to preach in Sheffield Cathedral on Trinity Sunday in June. This was both an honour and a burden, since the Trinity was one of the most difficult theological ideas to explore in a sermon. He asked the question head on – what on earth did these obscure points of doctrine mean to a place like Dinnington? And he avers that it is places like Dinnington, and in this instance the love they have offered him, that make sense of the doctrine and not the other way around.

Later in the summer he went to Westminster, invited to stay in the Deanery of Westminster Abbey. He had helped judge an essay competition to mark the 50th anniversary of the death of Gregory Dix, and the awards were held in St Margaret's Church, Westminster Abbey. It was difficult to see how he could manage to drive there and stay overnight until a mutual friend suggested the Dean, who graciously invited him and the friend who accompanied him, Jayne Cobham, to stay in the Deanery. It is a magnificent house with vast elegant drawing rooms and fine library, right next to the Abbey buildings. It even included a private box into the Abbey from which Simon heard a concert which included some of his favourite Bach cantata. His journal records his pleasure, 'It was entrancing – the evening light filters through the west windows, gold and deep reds, the arcade of pillars and arches framed the event and later they lit the crystal chandeliers.'

The next day I joined them for mass in St Margaret's and lunch in the college gardens. There were lots of friends there, the Abbot of course, and several people Simon had met while researching the book. We sat and ate lunch under a chestnut tree in the garden, it was a beautiful hot summer's day and we were all dressed in, well, Sunday best really. I even wore a hat, and Simon looked as immaculate as ever in a grey suit. But there must have been some who were puzzled, perhaps shocked, by his ravaged appearance.

I had begun to research my book, interviewing Simon, going through his diaries and journals, and talking to the parishioners. In July I spent a couple of weeks in Dinnington with Theo.

July 17, 1995
So lovely to be here. Always I dread it, plunging back in. But it's nice to get back to Gerard Manley Hopkins, 'Hurrahing in harvest,' above the stove, the oak table that used to be our family dining table, the quiet room with the icons upstairs. On the table is a bowlful of the lime-flowers I picked in France, still retaining some of the fragrance I tried to wrap up and send to Simon by post.

I always worry about seeing Simon again; how much worse will he look – he does look thinner but not really different. He seems more welcoming, somehow. He put out towels for us and he has even bought a paddling pool for the children. And he has been tidying up his files, sorting out some of his cupboards. It obviously makes sense.

He was worse of course. He was more jaundiced and was receiving more frequent blood tranfusions. He slept now for an hour or two early most evenings, and said it was difficult simply to fit in all the drugs. He was still attempting to eat occasionally though, a few strawberries, a slice of melon, but mostly he existed on hot water, cold water and Ribena. A further blow was that his hydrotherapy had been cancelled. He turned up for his regular session at the hospital one week and was told without warning that he could no longer have it. There had been a cryptosporidiosis scare in the district, because traces had been found in one of the hospital pools. Simon was angry about the way that it was handled, as was Dr Kinghorn, and enormous internal debate, both clinical and political followed. Simon knew he would miss it, both the sheer pleaure of the water and the soothing effect on his exhausted muscles.

Then there was the chicken-pox alert. My brother Martin and his family were on holiday nearby and we planned a family get-together, but it turned out that one of their children had chicken-pox. I decided it was fine for Theo to get it, but then

Simon said he couldn't risk the contact if he did, so in the end Mother and Caroline both went and I had to keep poor Theo at the Rectory.

Journal, July 20, 1995
What a strain this is becoming. Simon has kept going by sheer will power, faith or whatever it is, but it is exhausting for those who have waited over two years for him to die. He may insist he is living with AIDS but we have to come to terms with the fact that he is dying. It sometimes feels as if he is draining everybody else to keep himself going.

In an odd way, life for the person dying may be hard, but it is relatively simple, however, for those around it is very difficult, the waiting for death, not showing it, feeling guilty if you ever think let's just get on with it, as he sometimes does. And thinking about afterwards, how much there will be to do. You can hardly get started on it; we can't start sorting the house out as we know we will have to do eventually – asking him what to do with stuff . . . what do you want me to do with all your old copies of *Gay Times*, twenty years of postcards, the wok? Or am I just being Martha again, and losing sight of higher things?

Mother said she had been reading a novel in which a doctor observed that even when they are dying most women worry more about what will happen to their husbands than their own pain. Most men are concerned solely with themselves. And it is true that despite his concern for the community, for the idea of community Simon rarely seems to have made reference in any of his writing to the needs of specific individuals. (Though all were prayed for on a regular basis.) Perhaps he could only survive by focusing so much on himself, albeit as part of a community, but there was a price.

I wonder if he ever fully appreciated how much Mother suffered having to watch him die. She found it difficult to visit him in hospital, being either dependent on others for a lift or forced to take the bus or an expensive taxi. He took the attitude that there was no need for her to fuss, she didn't always have to come if he was only there for a few days, and sent a message to that effect, which upset her terribly. He didn't see that she needed to visit for herself.

It brought back to her so painfully the time when he was in hospital as a small child, when she wasn't even supposed to visit. She could only look through the door of the ward, so long as he wasn't aware she was there. What harm that must have done to them both. She so wanted him to let her share more, help him more. I kept suggesting she needed counselling, more support, but she argued that wasn't what she wanted. She wanted people who really cared, not professionals. Sometimes that too became a burden. I always felt as if I had failed her. I couldn't take it away, and I couldn't change it.

Then there was another crisis. He set off to go to Cornwall in August, via Manchester where he was going to pick up Alma, herself a very reluctant driver. He stayed the night, rigging up his drips as usual. However, he started feeling ill that evening, shivering at first and then his temperature soared. After several panicky attempts to get attention in Manchester he decided he needed to get back to Sheffield, but as it was a different health district an ambulance was not possible. Caroline, who also lives in Manchester was recruited to drive him back. He had taken Mother to stay with Caroline and she arrived at Alma's to see him before he left. She struggled up the stairs to see him, to hug him and try and reassure him. Yet again she wondered if she was saying a final goodbye as he left, so ill he had to lie on the back seat of the car. It was a hair-raising drive for Caroline, who had only recently passed her driving test and had to negotiate the hairpin bends of Snake Pass across the Pennines for the first time, convinced Simon was going to die on the way. But she said, like so many, that it was good to have the opportunity to do something for him – not that he accepted the role reversal very easily, even so ill he continued to issue her with directions.

So he returned to hospital, very ill, with all his holiday luggage. He had to be taken off all the other drugs and put on antibiotics again, and there was concern that there was internal bleeding too. He was there for two weeks, and Dr Kinghorn confirmed that this time it had really been touch and go. On the telephone he said to me, 'It is still possible to lose him through this current illness. But he is as tough as old boots, and if he doesn't want to go, he ain't going.' Simon by then had already survived almost two years longer than most AIDS patients with similar symptoms, 'His survival with CMV was exceptional at that time, particularly in someone whose CD4 count was virtually zero. But it wasn't remarkable for Simon,' said Kinghorn, 'As long as he had couple of hours it was worthwhile, for him, if he felt he could achieve nothing then the fight would no longer be worth it.'

When I went to see him that time, he looked so pale and sweet, propped up on pillows on the high white bed, big brown eyes in a thin face, yellow emaciated limbs, dressed in a white tennis shirt, pale bleached khakis loose around thin hips, and thick woolly socks. I wanted to ask him the obvious, most difficult question, how did AIDS fit into what he believed in, was there any point to all this suffering? He spoke in a quiet voice but with characteristic assurance, 'I don't think there is a point to it. That's just the bottom line I have to work from. It's a mystery, but there's no reason why I shouldn't experience it like anyone else. Why not me, after all? I can't escape from the overwhelming conviction that the good and the beautiful is always greater, though sometimes only by a fraction.' And he referred to a quotation from Jim Cotter, 'May the sum of evil balanced in this unreal world against the sum of good become diminished by my pain.'

Then he told me about another 'kingfisher day', for which in a way I was responsible. I had been to interview his friend Nancy, and she had said at the time she felt she should be saying all these things to him. So she did and wrote him a wonderful letter about how much he meant to her, how much he helped her spiritually and how she loved him. It made him so happy, and perhaps she wouldn't have written it otherwise.

That time was another reprieve, and Simon finally came home after two weeks, very tired and plagued by constant severe hiccups, and needing a stick for walking any distance. Emboldened, however, he decided he would have a stairlift installed. I remember him telling me on the phone it would cost about £2000, and I spent a night worrying about where the money would come from. Simon didn't worry about it of course and eventually half the money was lent by a church charity fund. It made an enormous difference to Simon, and to Mother who now could get upstairs and even stay with him overnight.

In September, Simon went on a coach trip with the parish to see the magnificent new oratory building at Elmore Abbey. No doubt there were sad farewells between Simon and the monks. Finally he made it to Cornwall in October, driving there with Sue Rafferty, to stay in the Bethany retreat at Bodmin. He went to see Martin's family in Devon. I am sure Simon was saying goodbye then. He and Martin drove round that lovely north Cornish coast, contemplating the seascapes and the water. I think for Martin especially that sea will always remind him of his lost brother.

At the beginning of November Simon was still planning ahead, quiet days and retreats, sermons, services, meetings, haircuts, the new vestry carpet, his Christmas present list, his book launch. He even had his name at the top of the list for the next year's parish holiday. I'm almost surprised not to see his funeral pencilled into his diary. He and Mike had one of their Quiet Days together, a memory Mike treasures, 'I never felt I got close to him before. I'm supposed to be a priest, but I usually feel more like a second hand car salesman around Simon. We searched for words, and he said he was just waiting now.' Alma came for a weekend and Simon asked her to preach and she assisted him at communion. It was the last time he celebrated the Eucharist.

I went to spend the weekend with him in November, conscious that I needed time with him on my own. The last tape we made is wonderful, we laughed so much (punctuated by Simon's constant hiccups), remembering his futile attempts to be a cox in Oxford. 'I was cox because I was too small to row, but I caused endless accidents. We got stuck in the trees, and once I managed to jam the rudder at 45 degrees so we kept crossing the river at right angles all the time. Finally the coach said, "I'll cox and you can follow along the bank and tell us how we're doing." Well, how was I supposed to know how they were doing?'

I sat in Simon's cosy study, curled up in an armchair, reading all his poems. Many of them were written for specific people and there was one about an old friend of Simon's which made me wonder if he too had been gay. I looked at Simon's photo albums, neatly lined up on the shelf. So many photos were of sea and sky and rocks and waves and clouds and Celtic crosses. But here was Simon and the Bishop on his Batemoor balcony; his ordination, laughing for joy on the steps of the church; receiving his masters' degree from Cambridge, a master of the universe in his black academic gown and white cravat; lots of pictures of Niagara falls, and sailing off Long Island looking so fit and well. Only one lover appears, sitting on a stone wall framed by trees and sky.

On a shelf in the study was a framed black and white photograph of Dad, not a posed smile for once but during a cricket match, all energy and long legs racing for the wicket. It had been a moment of triumph when Walter saved the day for his team. I began to think about him again. We had always said it was just as well Dad died without knowing Simon had AIDS, that he would be a burden rather than a help. I found myself wishing I could move on from that, find a more positive way of looking at it. I actually found myself wishing he was there, and glad that I did, that I didn't think of him entirely as a problem any more. Of course he would have been shocked, devastated, he would have blamed himself, as Mother said, but in the end he would have been there. I think he would have humbly learnt from the people of Dinnington, and he would have tried to understand. It would have given him the most unlikely campaign for an oppressed minority he could ever have had. Now I think he would have looked after Simon till the end. I dreamt of him being there, and Simon too dreamt of Father getting him ready to go to hospital. Perhaps even if I hadn't really found my brother, I had found a way back to my father again.

Journal, London. Nov 9
I read Simon's poem, 'The Icon', which has become a way through this for me, 'The night may yet be gentle, sad perhaps yet full of mercy,' and I look at the picture of him as I write. The tears come so regularly that it is like a constant sluice. I wonder how I will write afterwards. I think about the absence and then try to think about the actual process, what is to come and feel fear. Fear of what will happen, the

indignities, the mess, who will be there, all my images are of foetal bodies curled up in pain. Like becoming a baby again.

It is like waiting for a birth ... but you don't know when it will be – perhaps in primitive times they didn't know really either, just waited for the natural moment. But it is hard even to focus on the actual event, one thinks only of beyond ...

Dear god, whoever you are, help him. Help us all.

With great pride Simon gave me my signed copy of the Gregory Dix biography which had just been published. He was disappointed with the publishers; it was sloppily edited and they had left out all the photographs, and Simon wrote them a very stern letter, but it was still a considerable accomplishment. His commitment to the project and his determination to complete the book and to see it published undoubtedly was a significant factor in his survival. But now it was done. He began sending out invitations to his book party; for many people it was the last communication they received. And the invite was ambivalently worded; it simply said, 'Simon Bailey invites you ...' It didn't say he would be there.

He had, happily, already received an enthusiastic letter from the Bishop, commending his 'great achievement'. Simon had also just completed the introduction for his book of stories, *The Well Within*, an account of his experience with AIDS and how he had come to terms with it; how the act of writing and seeking metaphors had helped articulate it more fully. He signed the contract with Darton Longman and Todd with great satisfaction. There was little unfinished business (although there were plenty of potential projects earmarked for a conscientous literary executor).

The nights were drawing in, and it was beginning to get cold. Simon went and bought another heater for his bedroom, determinedly hauling it upstairs on the stairlift. This time he went too far, and strained his shoulders and back. By that Saturday night he was beginning to suffer severe pain. I could hear him tossing and turning all night, and by Sunday morning he said he would have to go back into hospital. When he called me into his bedroom early that morning he was already on the phone to Mike Cameron to tell him he would have to preach the sermon that morning. When Mike came round to collect it, I just fell apart. I was still in my nightdress and wrapped myself in the rough creamy blanket Simon always kept on the back of his study chair. 'Say a prayer for us Mike,' I begged, and he took a deep gulp, it didn't come pat, he struggled to find the right words, 'Make us calm, lord . . .' Then he ended with, 'All shall be well and all shall be well and all manner of things shall be well,' which was so familiar by now.

Poor Mike then had to go and preach Simon's (last) sermon. It was Remembrance Sunday, November 11, and it was all about peace, 'that peace we long for, that everybody longs for'. It was very personal and Mike said you could have heard a pin drop. Everyone understood it was Simon saying it. When everybody left at the end of the service they all said, give my love to Simon. Even the policeman who was supervising the Remembrance Day parade nipped back to say, send my love to Simon.

He was in such pain it was a real struggle getting ready for hospital. He asked me to wash his hair, as it required more strength than he had to lift his arms. Washing his hair reminded me of Theo, and that my own grieving is for a little brother, one I have failed to look after somehow. His last entry in the journal in the middle of November, recorded a dream. The writing is unbearably shaky. 'Once again the child appears. It actually began as a chimpanzee and we were heading for a Northern zoo in amongst rolling hills and fields and sunshine. It "metamorphosed" into a small blond boy sometimes definitely Theo, otherwise a shifting persona who spoke of "my sister" and her shared opinions. Wise and deep intimacies pass . . .'

He knew the end was near. He came out of hospital ten days later rather to everyone's surprise, since he really did not seem well enough, but he seemed to think that if they weren't pursuing active treatment he might as well be at home. His kidney function had deteriorated so much they had stopped the drugs to combat the CMV so his eyesight was further threatened. Hospice care had been suggested to him, which perhaps sounded warning bells. It certainly told him he didn't have to be in the hospital, so if at all possible, he wanted to be at home. There were, after all, still the Dix books to sign. Kinghorn continued to stress to the end that it was always Simon's decision when to go – so perhaps he did decide this was the time. He was very weak and very susceptible to infection, but there were still things he wanted to do.

Without really articulating it Mum seemed to have understood too. She had not as a rule stayed with him at the Rectory very often, but since the stairlift was installed she had been able to do a great deal more for him. Indeed, the installation of the stairlift probably did more than anything to bring their relationship to fruition. On this occasion she said, 'Don't ask anyone else to come, I'll come.' For the first time the issue of terminal care was mentioned. It was as close as he would get to admitting to her that he was dying.

So for the next two days mother looked after him, while he slept much of the time. She did his washing and even emptied the commode, a task I had always resisted. 'It's just like when you were young,' she reassured him. Finally she was essential. No-one else could have taken care of him so intimately, and certainly he could not have borne the indignity with anyone other than his mother. Somehow she seemed to be coping, she seemed like a different person to the needy, desperate mother I found it so hard to help a few months earlier. She conveyed such a sense of strength, not just brittle tension, but real fortitude. Perhaps because at last she could do something, something humble, but vital, that no one else could for him.

Even in those last days Simon struggled to maintain his usual routine. He did sign copies of his book, though he had to enlist Mother's help to open the boxes, because he was too weak to do it himself. Each day he would get up and bathe and dress, although it took longer and longer each time. Visitors helped as much as they could; Andrew helped him to bath, Sue Rafferty washed his hair one day and helped fix his line for him and do the medicines. People were glad to be allowed to help at last.

Although Simon didn't actually need twenty-four-hour nursing care at this stage, the tasks for the carers were onerous. The issue of care, that we had so often discussed, had finally become critical. It had finally reached the moment when Simon was no longer able to take responsibilty for his own basic needs. It was the point Simon dreaded so much himself. His last entry in his Well book, the writing so shaky but never illegible, details the accumulating problems: a cough, thrush infection which needed treatment dangerous to the liver, and an ear infection requiring antibiotics. He noted before he left hospital, 'To go home after final chest X-ray. To administer *morphine pain-killer myself* at home and find level to suit me . . .' This last was underlined – a note of exasperation indicating that he has finally had enough.

He remained the parish priest to the end. On Friday Sam and Joyce Robinson both came to the Rectory, and he insisted on getting dressed and coming downstairs. It took about two hours to go through his usual ritual of bathing, anointing and dressing before he appeared, immaculate if very shaky. The first thing he said to Sam when he saw him was to enquire about his shingles, something Sam says he will never forget. Indeed Sam (one of the traditionalists who much as he loved Simon was looking forward to a nice normal vicar with a wife and two kids) sat on the sofa later and said, 'What we need here is someone just like Simon.'

Charles Bruce, director of the Everyman film phoned that day. While Simon was in hospital, and obviously quite critical, the Archdeacon, Stephen Lowe, had been to see him and suggested he do more television. Simon insisted on talking to Charles. He said he would be willing to do more television but stressed that he didn't want to do more about AIDS, but wanted it to be about his new book of stories.

But there were serious problems including internal bleeding and it was clear to Simon it was time to return to the hospital. Mike Cameron arrived to take him, and Simon was aware, I feel sure, that he was leaving the Rectory for the last time. He remembered that he had not yet signed a copy of his book for Mike. Perhaps he was putting off the final moment. He insisted he did it before leaving, and went back into his study. He sat at his desk, fumbling slowly for the fat black calligraphy pen he always used. It took him about ten minutes to slowly and shakily inscribe the page, *To Mike Cameron. Love always, Simon*. It was the last copy he signed, the last thing he wrote. As they went out of the door he said goodbye to Mother, 'He kissed me on the lips,' she recalls, 'which was so unusual. Usually you kissed him. And he said thank you.'

That night Sue Rafferty came to stay with Mother at the rectory; it was like a vigil waiting for news. The next day we talked and it became clear that there was not much time left.

Again I found myself thinking of the death scene of Beth in
Little Women. And of my parents sitting all night by Simon's
bed when he was two, waiting, listening anxiously for a change
of breathing.

Journal, Nov 25

I sit by Simon's bedside in the Hallamshire. I've opened the
curtains to a view of Sheffield. It's wonderful seeing the lights
of the city from here. The nurses have turned him on his
side and I've put the lights down low so he is more settled.
It is midnight. His breathing is harsh and laboured but the
doctor assures us he is not in pain and is not as bad as his
breathing sounds. He is sitting up with a morphine drip
about to kick in and a saline drip. Jackie has gone to try and
sleep in the sofabed provided by the voluntary AIDS fund.
The support worker has given me a cup of tea in a china
cup.

No-one was here when I arrived – Simon had been asleep
and they had gone for tea. When I came into his room he
was sitting on the edge of the bed. I asked if he knew it was
me, and he said, of course, in that rather scathing tone, but
then when I told him Theo sent his love, he said, 'Has he
gone to proper art school now?' I asked him then if he wanted
to go home. In his characteristically ambivalent way he
replied, 'I would prefer to . . .' Why could I not bring myself
to say, do you want to die at home? But I didn't. When
Jackie came back we joked about him trying to escape. I
recalled women in labour changing their minds and walking
out of the delivery room. No I've changed my mind I don't
want to go through with this after all . . . But he has to. It
doesn't even register sitting here now that he will be gone.
That he has already gone.

They say the end is close but what does that mean. They
say it's up to him, but does he know that (and on morphine
anyway). I feel content – odd. I'm glad I'm here, it is the
right place, so right that the sadness is lessened. Because we
have already accepted the inevitability of it perhaps – we just
want it to be peaceful. He has suffered almost no indignity
at all. He kept going to the very end, kept his sight and his
mind, if little else . . .

Now, I just want there to be flowers, freesias, music, candles . . .

By Saturday evening quite a crowd had gathered, including Andrew who sat quietly by the window. Caroline arrived and Jackie had come with her husband, Pierce, and both the children. She has always involved them and told them what was happening, and for her, it seemed appropriate that they should come and say goodbye. Martha at four was very matter-of-fact. She had already asked if Uncle Simon would be dead by Christmas, voicing with children's clarity other's thoughts. 'Everything will be all right Simon,' she said to him, stroking his hand, her little blonde head not much higher than the bed.

Sometimes Simon struggled so hard to speak and then it would come out as nonsense – babbling about the three wise men, about gardens. Mostly it came out as grunts. 'Groaning also is one of the names of God . . .' he would have said, a quotation from Mohammed that he noted in his journal. At one stage Mother, my sisters and I went to sit out in the lobby together, and we just found ourselves laughing, somewhat hysterically, and repeating all the funny things he was saying, just like you would laugh over a child's funny remarks.

'Outlook very bleak,' says the hospital notes. All drugs and drip feeding had been withdrawn, and although we still spoke of taking him home, it became increasingly clear that it was not going to make much difference to him now. We were allowed by the hospital to do whatever we wanted to, even lighting candles, which must have been against the rules. We had little idea of how long it would be, days or even weeks, and no-one seemed able to tell us.

Alma came, both priest and friend, with her tiny silver jar of anointing oil. With great seriousness and dignity she donned her robes, draped her long white stole around her neck. Then she laid her hands on Simon's head and anointed him. After that she shared out her cheese and tomato sandwiches and a flask of orange juice, and sat down comfortably next to Simon to eat. It was such a reassuringly ordinary thing to do, the combination of the devout and the vulgar Simon had always so loved in her.

There was no shortage of priests. Sue Proctor arrived after
Sunday morning church in her black skirt and clerical collar.
Mike Cameron came, bringing with him the communion bread,
already blessed from St Leonard's. He said it had been a very
emotional service, and very hard for him. 'I told the congregation that it was Simon's last communion, and that I would
take it to him in hospital. Then when I came to give the
notices the tears flowed over, and I just said, "I'm sorry..."
But everybody in church was weeping.' The hospital room was
crowded by then, but the bread was shared between us all.
Simon was blessed and prayers were said,

> May the angels take your hand
> May the saints guard your way
> May the god of love take you in his arms and bless you
> So that now you may rest in his peace. Amen

Caroline read the lovely Celtic blessing,

> Deep peace of the running wave to you,
> Deep peace of the flowing air to you,
> Deep peace of the quiet earth to you ...

We played tapes of Taizé Gregorian chants over and over,
repetitive, incantatory and soothing; the refrain from the thief
on the cross, 'Jesus remember me when you come into your
kingdom...' It didn't matter whether you consciously prayed,
whether you believed in the Taizé chants, the words repeated
on the tape, Oh Lord hear my prayer, Ubi caritas. The Latin
was even more effective as a chant, the words themselves didn't
need to mean anything, they touched another part of you,
beyond language. It was all a long shared meditation for
everyone. Simon had finally had to abandon his beloved words,
had reached some kernel state beyond words, but was communi-
cating in animal grunts and groans. Again I was reminded of a
woman in labour, there was something so essential, so primal,
about the sounds. He seemed to be trying to sing the hallelujah
chanting on the tape.

We gathered up treasures from the Rectory to take to Simon;
a little wooden Celtic cross, candles, stones and an alabaster
egg, an icon, lavender water and perfumed oils. It was good to
be back in that little hospital room, the universe had narrowed

to this point for all the people there, sitting quietly, totally focused on Simon. Nancy was kneeling by the bedside, holding an icon and a candle up to him, her tears overflowing. I gave Simon the green veined alabaster egg I had brought from the Rectory. His fingers enfolded it and held it most of the night. Nancy said that it was the egg she had given him for his birthday. His hand soon warmed it, almost his last warmth went into that chilly little egg.

I had volunteered to stay at the hospital again on Sunday night, unwilling to miss anything I suppose, but eventually I retreated gratefully to the sofabed, leaving the vigil to Mum and Sue Proctor who had volunteered to stay with us. Early in the morning Sue came in and suggested it was time. With a bizarre sense of occasion I sprayed on the very last of my favourite perfume. Simon was sleeping. Mother and Sue had sat with him all night. It was right he had a friend there as well as family. 'He wouldn't close his eyes, he was always like that as a baby. He would never go to sleep,' said Mother softly. So she had sat and stroked him and sung lullabies to him, till he slept. 'I don't think I will ever be able to sing lula-lula-bye-bye, again,' she said.

They had been stroking his head with a cloth soaked in lavender water and they gave it me to stroke his forehead as he slept. The egg was still loosely clasped in his hand. As he breathed his last breath, the life just fluttered away, the merest zephyr. He was gone. Absolutely released. It was *so* gentle, *so* full of mercy.

They say it is the hardest thing to have your child die before you. But afterwards Mother said it was an easy birth as well. He had an easy death, just slipped out. And there was the most wonderful completeness about her seeing him in and out of the world. After the nurses laid him out, I hesitated for only a minute – was it the right thing to do – before placing a handful of freesias on his body. Really I think I would have liked to have strewn them gaily all over him. Later we placed the Celtic cross on his body, and lit a candle at the end of the bed, and played the Taizé chants again. My sisters returned and we stayed and stayed. We sat with him together, we all sat with him alone, time to cry, to mourn, to say goodbye.

As she took her final farewell Mother leaned across and kissed him and said the old favourite blessing, 'May the Lord make his face to shine upon you and give you peace.' Then she said, in a tone so distant, as if she really was transported back forty years, 'He looks as if he's smiling – people always say that, apparently. It's like they say babies aren't really smiling, they just have wind.' Simon had become her baby again, totally.

you only die when you fail to take root in others

The days after Simon died were strange – as I'm sure they are for everyone. When we finally, reluctantly bade farewell, and left his body in the hospital it was late in the day. By the time we got back to the Rectory, he was on the 6 o'clock news. It was so odd to see him alive again so soon. That first night I read his little book of Celtic blessings till I finally fell asleep. The letters and tributes poured in as they had done after the TV programme appeared. I was glad Simon had already received them all then. The *Guardian* and the *Church Times* published obituaries; appropriately they were the papers that had always been delivered to the Rectory.

Simon had gone to town on the funeral arrangements. He had plenty of time to plan it after all, and considerable experience of taking them for others. He did not discuss it with anyone else though. (Now I remember him suggesting casually that I could look at the arrangements if I wished. I didn't do so.) I wonder if we would have benefited from sharing it more, as some families and partners do. Shall we have Mozart or Bach? What kind of flowers would you like? But he insisted to the end that he was living with AIDS not dying from it so I suppose discussing his funeral would not have helped.

Anyway it was all clearly spelled out, typically only as 'suggestions', but he must have known we would go to great lengths to fulfill his requests. So we were plunged into planning a major spectacle. We sat in the sitting room with Mike Cameron the curate and read the neatly typed sheets labelled 'funeral arrangements.' (Mike was shocked that he had asked for black vestments. These days the tendency is to opt for white, to symbolise the resurrection. Black is more traditional, more sombre, more humble, less presumptious of eternal glory and for Simon, the theatre director, perhaps more dramatic too.)

He asked for his coffin be kept in church overnight after a
service of Taizé chants. Only a few friends and family were
there, we lit candles round the coffin and it was very beautiful.
Afterwards my mother stayed a while with the coffin, to make
her farewell vigil alone.

Alma seemed the obvious person to preside at his requiem
mass, his final Eucharist. She said later what a powerful experience it had been for her, presiding at his altar with his body in
a coffin before her. My brother, sisters and I read from the
eclectic selection he had suggested – from Shakespeare to Derek
Jarman. We read Simon's own poem, 'If I go', which he had
written shortly after his HIV diagnosis, spelling out all the
ways he would want to be remembered. Afterwards sheaves and
sheaves of copies were printed up as it was constantly requested.
Now it is true, every lovely bowl, every candle, every rainbow
reminds me of him. He chose the hymns and suggested the
Bach cello solo, Cello Suite No 1 in G. We tried so zealously
to find a cellist that we ended up with two.

The question of filming the funeral came up again. Most
people were vehemently against the idea. Abigail Saxon, the
BBC researcher, who came to the funeral, was later rather
regretful. She spoke wistfully of the cello playing to an empty
church, the coffin draped at the altar, the drama of the vestments. As usual I felt in two minds; after all why shouldn't we
film funerals, we film weddings and christenings. Mike had been
very concerned that the church would not hold all the mourners,
and we had realised he was right when a steady stream of local
people came to the door to ask when the rector's funeral was.
In the end it was decided to hold a memorial service in the
cathedral a week later as well. It was the day Simon had invited
people to the launch of his Gregory Dix biography so we went
ahead with that too. Both the Bishop and the Abbot came. It
was a fitting tribute. There was a final chaotic and tearful party
at the Rectory afterwards. Then a grey fog descended over
Dinnington like a shroud.

When one of the parishioners said in a radio interview that it
was a relief when Simon finally died I was shocked. I had to
think about it, but it was true. It is only afterwards you realise
what a strain the waiting has been. For the family at least there

was of course still plenty to do; an entire house to sort out (and Simon had kept everything, even his schoolbooks); a burgeoning literary estate, his book of stories to be edited and published. My mother did more than her fair share of paperwork including writing to the many people who sent cards and letters of condolence. Up to a point perhaps it is good to be occupied, but there is also a need to stop. Eventually she cracked. It was the anniversary of my father's death in January and finally a combination of stress and arthritis reduced her to a state where she could hardly move. But Mother coped as she had always done, and continues to cope remarkably with what has happened, with the drama and trauma, with losing a much loved son. She astonished me on one occasion not long after Simon died. I had been to see the Bishop and mentioned to her my surprise that he had agreed that perhaps many of the saints may have been homosexual. Mother said she thought it quite possible that Jesus himself may have been homosexual, citing the Biblical references to John, 'the disciple Jesus loved.' I confess I was shocked. For my mother to say this, just blew my mind. She said quite tartly, 'Well of course I've thought about it, my son is gay, so I have to think about it . . .' I realised that through all this my mother and I had reached a new point in the path of understanding, that we could perhaps now talk more openly than ever before.

There were many sad moments as we emptied Simon's house, took down the pictures, the icons, distributed and packed his belongings and all the gifts he had bequeathed. I remember one occasion towards the end when I was alone, the house was almost bare, the doors were open and the birds were singing and I thought this is how it must have been when he moved in. A house to fill with life and as he already then knew, perhaps too with death. But there was nevertheless something reassuring for me about the sense of continuity, the sense of connection. It helped a lot for me to have begun my work on this book, to be able to try and understand what had happened here.

I didn't know the end of this book when I started. I suppose I assumed it would end with Simon's death. Now I realise that of course that was not the end. I am a different person now from when I started. I did learn a lot, from the pain and sadness as

well as from Simon himself. Part of me regrets that I didn't get
to know him better sooner. But it would not have happened that
way. Of those who read this book in manuscript, my mother, my
husband, my sisters and Alma, some said the person I portrayed
was not the person they knew, or this was not their reading of
events. So be it. The man I got to know, the brother I found
again, was in some ways a different person. It seems important
to acknowledge that was part of what attracted me.

On my desk as I write I have two photographs of Simon.
One is the newly frocked priest, so happy and full of joy. The
other was taken almost ten years later in his little quiet room
upstairs in the Rectory; the face is thinner, more mature, lines
of pain and weariness etched in, but it has a reflective quality,
his big brown eyes somehow distant. That is the person I got
to know and the person I cherish. Mother has been asked
sometimes for photos of Simon as he was 'before'. He used to
hate us taking pictures of him when he was ill. 'Just remember
me as I was before,' he too would say. But for me the sick man
was who he was. He succeeded in integrating his illness with
his life, with his whole self, in a way that at least for me made
it an inescapable part of him. So the photo I will always keep
is the sick man, the man who somehow, miraculously made a
precious gift of his death. The Catholic priest in Dinnington
wrote afterwards that he had seemed to die not with a bang or
whimper, but in a golden glow.

But death can acquire a strange glamour. I remember being
struck by a report of Princess Diana in Chicago, after a great
ball in her honour, saying she wanted to go and visit a hospital,
to visit dying people. Someone commented it was almost as if
she needed to do it, as if she needed that fix of intense reality,
of connection with humanity, to give her fantasy life some
meaning. There is a sense in which someone near to death is
approaching mysteries that are closed to most of us who
presume we will live a normal span. Much as Simon tried to
avoid it there was a way in which his dying made him special.
It is entirely true that life is enhanced in the face of death, and
it has become almost a cliché that people facing death find
themselves valuing life as they have never been able to do
before. When I had a child I believed that birth was the most
dramatic, life changing event you could go through. But it's not

true, it is death. Death does change your life. It is death finally that makes you grow up.

In her funeral address for Simon, his friend, Margaret Selby, the diocesan lay worker who pioneered the pastoral workers' scheme, described his effort to come to terms with his death, 'It was a struggle to arrive at the place in himself where he knew for certain life and death were seamless, that having experienced life to the full, death had become his friend, death had become the only way he could finally find what had been searching for him all his life.' Simon himself wrote in his introduction to *The Well Within*, the book of his stories that was published six months after he died, 'It is obvious, really. We acknowledge that so many things we polarise are not really opposite at all: black and white, subjective and objective, male and female. But surely it is true of life and death. Not opposites but part of a single whole, for which in a sense we have no name.'

I used to wonder how anybody could embark on a relationship with a person with AIDS, as so many do, knowing the pain to come. Now I see how much there is of value in such a relationship, and not just in support for the person who is ill, but also, very much, for the person on the journey with them; the shared love, the sense of being needed, yes, but also a profound appreciation of life that perhaps can only be fully learned in the face of death. But getting to this point, this heightened perception, this intensity, can present new and subtle dangers. In this context, Andrew Sullivan, author of *Virtually Normal: An Argument About Homosexuality*[1] has written with great perception and candour about the strange feeling of let down with the prospect of a cure for AIDS, the impact that the prospect of recovery can have on the psychology of those who had prepared themselves for death. 'When you have spent several years girding yourself for the possibility of death, it is not so easy to gird yourself instead for the possibility of life,' he writes.[2] He acknowledges the value of the experience of being HIV-positive, venturing that he would not wish it had never happened, 'It allowed me to see things that I had never been able to see before . . . an awareness of death is always the surest way to an awareness of the tangibility of life.' He concludes, echoing Simon, 'In order to survive mentally I had to find a place within myself where plague couldn't get me, where success or failure in such a battle were of equal consequence . . . Only once or twice did I find that place, but now I live in the knowledge of its existence. So will an entire generation.'

There is, of course, deep irony in contemplating a possible cure for AIDS now Simon has gone. But the possibility does not diminish what he did with his own death. And perhaps ten intensely fulfilled years is a fair exchange for forty years of normal life. Who can say? If, at least for a privileged percentage, AIDS does not necessarily any longer mean death, the truth remains that a lot has been learned from so much pain. It has created a profound level of solidarity among homosexuals and seedlings of deeper sympathy and understanding in the hetero-sexual community. It has played its part in the current change in attitudes to death. Even the sometimes irreverent attitude to funerals among the gay community has contributed to a fundamental questioning of the conventional processes of death and funerals.

Like Simon with Gregory Dix, I put off writing the final chapter of this book. And I think like him it was not because I wanted to put off writing about his death, but because I didn't want to end the project. I didn't want to let go of it. My younger brother chided me gently at one stage for 'dwelling on it' and that is what I have done, dwelt within it, and contentedly so. It is in many ways where I have most wanted to be for a while. Indeed, I have felt privileged to be able to take so much time to work through the sadness. People have asked if it has been hard to write, and of course it has. I have written through a veil of tears sometimes. But it has been enormously therapeutic and cathartic too.

The process of writing, the effort to articulate one's feelings, to find the right words has helped greatly. It has been sad but inspiring to read Simon's journals and sermons. I have inherited many of his books, and reading them has been like a conver-sation, especially where he has marked passages he particularly liked. My son and I now read his copies of the C.S. Lewis Narnia stories, noting Simon's underlinings as we go. I feel I have got to know him better than I ever would have done had he lived. And if I try to analyse my motives for writing I have to acknowledge that Simon became interesting to me as a dying man in a way that he wasn't before. It *was* a good story. Maybe that sounds terrible but it is the truth.

When I first began to write again, a month or two after Simon died, I listened to the the Taizé tapes we had played in the hospital and plunged myself back into the memory of his dying. I wrote in great detail and it felt right to do so. I wanted to remember every detail of the experience. It had been very sad, but it was also very important. I even took a picture of his body strewn with freesias. I know to some this seemed macabre, but in fact it reflects a common process of dealing with death; the death mask, the death bed portrait. Talking through the experience is cathartic and important and something Simon himself found people needed to do. My mother and I have often talked of it. The Victorians used to make deathbed books; each member of the deathbed party would contribute to a memorial book to record their memories of the deceased, their physical symptoms, last words and spiritual state.[3]

I carried on interviewing, never sure how difficult it would be. In fact, talking about the experience and the issues it raised, often proved enormously helpful both for me and the friends and family I talked to. Among Simon's papers I found a description of a Sheffield funeral, in which he describes people's need to talk about the death, 'This shaping of the material into a story is a recurrent ritual of grief rendering the events more endurable, graspable, controllable.' For me, reading this a few weeks after Simon died was like a gift, providing such a positive affirmation of my own desire to recreate the story of his death.

As I talked to more people in the church I began to appreciate that a great deal more was being done quietly, behind the scenes, than I had understood while Simon was alive. Sadly, at least in part because the media response was so potentially negative and hurtful for individuals, it is not work that is widely known. One of my most precious encounters was meeting someone else on the same path as Simon. David Randall was the Anglican priest who started CARA, a programme providing education and pastoral care for those with HIV/AIDS, who had talked publicly about being HIV-positive on television. He was blind and close to death when I went see him at the London Lighthouse a few weeks after Simon died, and I expected it to be a difficult and painful experience. Instead it reinforced for me the value of learning from those who have prepared themselves for death.

Like Simon, David had discovered that it was in his suffering that his priesthood had the greatest meaning, progressing beyond his ministering to others, realising his own need. 'Nothing is invalid as a result of this virus, let alone your priesthood,' David said. He described to me a visit he had received from the Bishop of London, who said Jesus' major ministry was not when he was teaching or healing – it was in his passion and death. 'Being a priest with AIDS is a bit like that – how can you have true sympathy unless you are in there with them.' (David died about six months later in August 1996.)

I began to see that this was the key to Simon's death, that by sharing his suffering he had found a way through his illness and dying, and thus had most profoundly fulfilled his vocation. A priest's role is not simply to teach, heal and soothe, but to enable a constant exchange both of suffering and of love, the eternal mystical exchange Simon had tried to explain to me so long before.

What was also clear was that Simon did it, at least in part because he was homosexual. Perhaps he did have a natural vocation, a natural gentleness, spirituality and empathy with others, but it was also out of his very oppression that he could find a way to make something meaningful of AIDS. He was already in the crucible when AIDS came along. He had already suffered in secret simply for being homosexual. In an odd way it prepared him. And it began a process into which he drew many people, not least me.

The grief does not diminish, I realise, it merely becomes more familiar. The burden becomes easier to bear; the new-born baby you thought you could not carry in your arms for more than a few minutes can be carried throughout a sleepless night if necessary. When we went to scatter Simon's ashes, I dreaded collecting the casket from the church where it had been waiting. When I picked it up and cradled it in my arms I realised it was about the weight of a new baby. Not hard to carry really.

It was a beautiful sunny, windy day in May as the family gathered at a small village on the Yorkshire Moors. Simon had suggested several waterfalls for his ashes and we had chosen one near Whitby, one of his favourite places. There was something

wonderfully solemn as our cortege of cars wound its way across
the wild moorland one bright early Sunday morning. Martin
poured his ashes gently into the flowing water, we scattered
forget-me-nots and read poems. The children made a cairn of
little stones and we tied prayer flags with poems and messages
to the trees above the stream. Now I want to say with Graham
Greene, 'I no longer believe my unbelief.' I want to guard this
separate space, somewhere special to keep Simon and grow a
new shoot of my own stunted spirit, a shy quiet place, unex-
plained, a need, not a belief, a gesture, a ritual. Like him I can
feel profounder pleasure in mountains and rainbows, sea and
flowers.

Life in Dinnington goes on, too. Perhaps, after all, what they
did for someone they loved was not so unusual, not really so
surprising, once Simon allowed himself to be the conduit he
saw as his priestly task. They still miss him. The red ribbons
are still firmly pinned to Sunday best coats and anoraks alike.
Margaret Hawley made sure there were white freesias in church
for his birthday. Sam Robinson went and bought a tree to plant
as a memorial to him in the churchyard and it was dedicated
with prayers and poems and some tears in November 1996, on
the first anniversary of Simon's death. Perhaps most surprising
of all, the Bishop, that fierce opponent of women's ordination,
appointed Sue Proctor as the next Rector of Dinnington, their
first woman priest, and one they were willing and happy to
have. So there is a continuity still. Sue has moved into the
Rectory now, and put her goldfish in the pond. Sue now cele-
brates the Eucharist at the altar of St Leonard's in place of her
old friend. She doesn't do everything Simon's way. She is more
involved in the local community. There are more children in
church now.

Sue Proctor once said to me that I could not come out of
this story not believing. I have tried to open myself to it all.
But in the end such a story, this story of South Yorkshire does
not increase my faith in God. It does increase my faith in
humanity.

all shall be well

from *The Well Within* by Simon Bailey

On my bedroom wall is a framed postcard. The caption says: 'Everything is going to be all right'. Perhaps it sounds like a cliché, but for me, seeing it there every day, it has become something of a motto, a feeling I carry around with me, a more deeply-seated conviction. How, you may say, can that be in any sense meaningful since you're living with AIDS? A good question.

I made a programme with the BBC in the *Everyman* series about living with AIDS and at the same time continuing to be a parish priest. The programme inevitably approached all the issues raised in this situation. The issue of coping in the parish and in the wider Church (and personally) with this feared condition. The issue of homosexuality and the Church, homosexuality and the priesthood. The issue of trying to continue to minister out of infirmity. And many other issues. Why, you may ask, so deliberately raise all these issues? Why disturb the peace of the Church yet again over sex and sexuality? Why risk the peace of your family and friends – your own peace?

For a long time living with an HIV Positive diagnosis was for me a brick wall, a desert, a wilderness that seemed spiritually unapproachable. I didn't know what to do with it. It stayed in me as an unexplored, uncomfortable secret. But secrecy is tiring, concealment – and what amounted sometimes to deception – is a huge extra burden alongside the virus itself. As symptoms began to develop I began to divulge my 'secret' and at the same time I seemed to be able also to face the brick wall, to enter the desert and begin tentatively to explore the wilderness. I don't quite understand the connection between opening up to others and something opening up within, but it was – is – real for me. I remain an 'inward' kind of person and yet I find myself being increasingly public about a profoundly personal situation.

You may be asking why. Why make a film? Why talk to the press?

There are of course so many reasons, including those I can't articulate, but here are some: I wanted to say that you *can* live with AIDS. I wanted to say this both to others who are HIV Positive but also to the rest of the world that assumes it's HIV Negative. My immunity is seriously compromised. I am vulnerable to infections. I live with an inability to take nutrition from food so I'm 'fed' intravenously through the night. I live with a virus affecting my eyesight which also requires daily intravenous drug treatment. I live with other limitations and minor infections as well as the side effects of drugs but I am still living and working too. More than anything else, in the media attention I've resented the description of me as a 'dying man'. Of course I know that I'm very vulnerable to new infections that could change everything, but in this moment – the one in which I live – I am living, awake, aware and alive.

So I wanted to say that it need not take over your life. It's there always of course, the shadow at your shoulder, but that somehow just invites defiance, as so many others have demonstrated. We are not victims, we can keep it in its place. There are other things I want to do while I can – other things in which AIDS is irrelevant. It can be kept in its place while living and creating and growing goes on. The shadow is real enough in the parish, for instance, but our ordinary life goes on. We are living with it not under it, still less dying from it. There are those of course who want to make me a victim – because of their own fears or even because they can only care for others by making them into victims – but I, along with many others in this condition and with similar life-threatening illnesses – I intend to hold my head up, to stand upright and live.

And I also wanted to speak out openly in celebration of the support of the local church: our own parish and other local Christians too. So much support, so much practical help, so much prayer. I live with the irony, as so many do, of an openness of love and affection stirred in me, in others, by the prospect of dying.

But I did want also – less consciously perhaps, less clearly – to press the issues in the wider Church too. AIDS, sexuality, homosexuality . . . at heart I'm only ever a reluctant campaigner and yet there is something too important, too central, here to suppress. Deliberately or not, the Church induces so much prejudice and fear and guilt in this area. Deep-seated guilt in those who happen to be 'different', a lurking guilt, destructive and deathly, in those who happen to be ill with this condition. Isn't there enough to carry without this too? People with AIDS – and also gay people generally – need so much extra courage and defiance and dignity and integrity to throw off this demeaning guilt in the face of the Church. But they do it – and that needs celebrating too.

And maybe most of all, but somehow hardest to find words for, I wanted to say something about living in the face of dying. It is of course what we are all doing but those who live with terminal illness are forced to have, are given perhaps, a special vantage point, maybe even a vocation to live directly in the face of dying and speak – if they can – from there. Of course I am afraid. I'm afraid of pain, of weakness and disability. I'm afraid especially of dementia – I live so much in my mind, how could I live without it? I'm afraid of all the little failures and indignities that go with this condition, the lack of agility, the inability to run, to dance . . . I'm afraid, hate the idea, of being dependent, a burden. So I'm afraid of being mortal – a fragile 'living feature'. W. H. Auden's words go round in my head:

> . . . in my arms till break of day
> Let the living creature lie
> Mortal, guilty, but to me
> The entirely beautiful.

It's the last line that keeps me alive. Yes, I'm afraid. I'm mortal, I share in the guilt of the world, but living in the face of dying has transformed the world as well. I see that it is – we are – 'entirely beautiful', however fragile. Colours are more intensely real (yellow has simply come alive for me). The simplest things are so beautiful. People are beautiful.

And God doesn't go away – not for me – but draws closer and closer. In Passiontide this year I found myself accompanying Jesus in his pilgrimage towards dying more intensely, more personally, than I have ever done and he was – is – accompanying me. At the time I was in hospital for a blood transfusion . . . the resonances and ironies only grow stronger.

And at the heart of this intensity of living for me is the Eucharist, receiving it, presiding at it. 'The body of Christ', 'the blood of Christ' – the words reverberate in me ever deeper and deeper down. All the implications of being part – organically integrated into – the body of Christ become more and more powerfully significant. In that body, in all its manifestations, with my virus, is where I am alive.

Before I was instituted as rector in Dinnington, I made a retreat which included a visit to what, for me, is one of the holiest places in England: the shrine of St Cuthbert in Durham Cathedral. As I sat there in the silence I heard, felt, a message that there was nothing to be afraid of. It was a deep reassurance. I applied it then of course to the institution and my first living. It did apply to that. But when I got home I found waiting for me the letter which urged me to contact the hospital which led to my positive diagnosis. And now of course I hear the message in this situation too. 'There is nothing to be afraid of.'

I don't know where courage comes from, I don't know why some seem to have it (like Dennis Potter in his extraordinary last interview who said he hadn't had a moment's terror in his illness) and others don't. It is what I pray for. The Breton fisherman's prayer has become one of my favourites, not least for its brevity: 'Help me God, the sea is so vast, my boat is so small.'

I feel like a boat in dock, being built, repaired. The tide is slowly coming in . . . One by one the props are knocked away, sometimes more than one at once . . . I rock, uncertain, unsteady. It feels destructive, deeply threatening, unstable, unbalancing . . . But the tide is swirling in and I shall discover that the props have to go if I'm going into that great swelling ocean in my little boat, into the ocean that I'm made for . . .

'Everything is going to be all right'. One of the modern versions uses that phrase to translate Mother Julian's 'All shall be well . . .' in her *Revelations*. I am praying for the courage to believe it and to live it.

'Sin is behovely but all shall be well and all shall be well and all manner of thing shall be well.'

references

Many of the following references are to texts written by Simon Bailey. They often began as addresses, lectures or sermons and were subsequently published. I have tried to indicate wherever possible where they were first heard.

Prologue
1. Introductory lecture of a course for worship leaders. April 24, 1993.
2. 'The Body of Christ', *The Well Within: Parables for Living and Dying*, Simon Bailey, Darton Longman & Todd, 1997.
3. BBC Everyman, Simon's Cross, 1995.
4. *Independent on Sunday*, Jan 15, 1995.

1. From Whom No Secrets Are Hidden
1. The Transforming of Wounds, Published in *God Talk*, Westminster College Student Theological Journal, 1995.
2. 'My Story', 1993. A piece about coming to terms with his own homosexuality written by Simon for a parish meeting to discuss homosexuality, shortly after the parish learned he had AIDS.
3. Gloucester Report on Homosexual Relationships, 1979.
4. British Council of Churches, *'God's Yes to Sexuality'*, 1980.
5. Address on contemplative prayer, 1991.
6. Aelred of Rievaulx, *Spiritual Friendship*, Cistercian Publications, 1974.
7. Simone Weil, *Waiting on God*, Routledge, 1951.
8. Simon Bailey, *St Chad: A Miracle Play for Norton.* July 1985.

2. This Is My Body
1. Simon Bailey, *The Well Within: Parables for Living and Dying*, Darton Longman & Todd, 1997.

3. 'Great Things in Small Parishes'
1. Simon Bailey article for American magazine, *Good Tidings*, June 1987.
2. Pastoral workers AGM, March 23, 1991.
3. BBC Everyman, Simon's Cross, 1995.

4. 'The Meaning Is in the Waiting'

1. Simon Garfield, *The End of Innocence: Britain in the Time of AIDS*, Faber & Faber, 1994.
2. Ibid and see also Simon Watney, *Practices of Freedom: Selected Writings on HIV/AIDS*, Rivers Oram Press, 1994. ('The government acted about four years too late, and many lives were lost, but what did you expect?' Peter Scott, former education group leader at The Terrence Higgins Trust)
3. LGCM meeting in Leeds, 'Do gay people pray differently?' 1988.
4. *Church Times* article, 'Coming down from the Pulpit', 1988.
5. 'In St Cuthbert's Shrine. Durham', published *New Christian Poetry*. Collins, 1990 and 'Late Afternoon' in *Beyond Paradise: Poetry by Lesbians and Gay Men*. Crocus, 1990.
6. Simon Bailey, *A Tactful God: Gregory Dix, Priest, Monk and Scholar*. Gracewing, 1995.
7. *Church Times* article, 'Letter to artists', April 27, 1990.
8. House of Bishops statement, 'Issues in Human Sexuality,' 1991.

5. Love Comes Quietly

1. Originally, Quiet Day talks for St Leonard's. Published in *Affirming Catholicism*, summer and autumn 1992.
2. Carl Jung, Introduction to *The Religious and Psychological Problems of Alchemy*, Vol. 12, *Collected Works*, RKP, 1953.

6. The Wounded Healer

1. Steven Kohut has kindly allowed me to quote from his journal of the period, which he read aloud to me during our interview. Some of his quoted comments, therefore, were in fact read from his journal.

8. There Is Nothing to Be Afraid Of

1. World Aids Day service, *Living with AIDS*, December 3, 1994.
2. Ibid

9. Kingfisher Days

1. Eamon Duffy, *Stripping of the Altars*, Yale University Press, 1992.
2. John 12. 1–7.

Epilogue

1. Andrew Sullivan, *Virtually Normal: An Argument About Homosexuality*. Picador, 1996.
2. 'When Plagues End, Notes on the Twilight of an Epidemic', *Independent on Sunday*, February 16, 1997.
3. Pat Jalland, *Death in the Victorian Family*, OUP, 1996.

bibliography

Bailey, Simon, *A Tactful God: Gregory Dix, Priest, Monk and Scholar*, Gracewing, 1995.

Bailey, Simon, *The Well Within: Parables for Living and Dying*, Darton Longman & Todd, 1996.

Cotter, Jim, *Prayer at Night*, Cairns Publications, 1983.

Cotter, Jim, *Pleasure, Pain and Passion*, Cairns Publications, 1988.

Robinson, John A.T., *Honest to God*, SCM Press, 1963.

Aelred of Rievaulx, *Spiritual Friendship*, Cistercian Publications, 1974.

Weil, Simone, *Waiting on God*, Routledge and Kegan Paul, 1951.

Duffy, Eamon, *The Stripping of the Altars. Traditional Religion in England. 1400–1580*, Yale University Press, 1992.

Blythe, Ronald, *Divine Landscape*, Viking, 1986.

Fletcher, Dr Ben, *Clergy under Stress. A Study of Homosexual and Heterosexual Clergy*, Mowbray, 1990.

Babuscio, Jack, *We Speak for Ourselves: The Experiences of Gay Men and Lesbians*, SPCK, 1988 edition.

Loudon, Mary, *Revelations. The Clergy Questioned*, Hamish Hamilton, 1994.

'Issues in Human Sexuality', Statement by the House of Bishops, 1991.

'Sexuality and the Church response to Issues in Human Sexuality', Anglican Association for Social Responsibility, Feb 1993.

'Reconsider', Response to Issues in Human Sexuality, LGCM, Nov 1995.

Garfield, Simon, *The End of Innocence. Britain in the Time of AIDS*, Faber and Faber, 1994.

Sullivan, Andrew, *Virtually Normal: An Argument About Homosexuality*, Picardor, 1996.

Watney, Simon, *Practices of Freedom. Selected Writings on HIV/AIDS*, Rivers Oram Press, 1994.

Kirkpatrick, Bill, *Cry love, Cry hope Responding to AIDS*, Darton Longman & Todd, 1994.

Jalland, Pat, *Death in the Victorian Family*, OUP, 1996.

Sontag, Susan, *Illness as Metaphor; Aids and Its Metaphors*, Penguin Books, 1991.

Moffat, Mary Jane, *In the Midst of Winter: Selections from the Literature of Mourning*, Vintage, 1992.

Rose, Gillian, *Love's Work*, Chatto & Windus, 1995.

Dillard, Annie, *Pilgrim at Tinker Creek*, Jonathan Cape, 1975.
Hammarskjold, Dag, *Markings*, Faber and Faber, 1964.
Lewis, C.S., *The Narnia Stories*, Puffin Books, 1959.
Arditti, Michael, *The Celibate*, Sinclair-Stevenson, 1993.
Fisher, Carrie, *Delusions of Grandma*, Simon & Schuster, 1994.
Malouf, David, *Remembering Babylon*, Chatto & Windus, 1993.
Chatwin, Bruce, *The Songlines*, Jonathan Cape, 1985.
Creeley, Robert, *The Collected Poems 1945–1975*, University of California Press, 1982.
The works of R.S. Thomas, published by Macmillan, Bloodaxe and others.